The Hive

The Hive

The Story of the Honeybee and Us

Bee Wilson

Thomas Dunne Books
St. Martin's Press
NEW YORK

THOMAS DUNNE BOOKS.
An imprint of St. Martin's Press.

www.stmartins.com

Library of Congress Cataloging-in-Publication Data

Wilson, Bee.
    The hive : the story of the honeybee and us / Bee Wilson.—1st
U.S. ed.
        p. cm.
    Originally published: London : John Murray, c2004.
    ISBN-13: 978-0-312-34261-6
    ISBN-10: 0-312-34261-6
    1. Honeybee. 2. Bee culture. 3. Animals and civilization. I. Title.

SF523.3.W54 2006
638'.1—dc22

                                                        2006040416

First published in Great Britain by John Murray (Publishers)
A division of Hodder Headline

First U.S. Edition: June 2006

10 9 8 7 6 5 4 3 2 1

For Anthea Morrison

Contents

Acknowledgements

For help, advice and information of various kinds, I must thank the Cambridgeshire Beekeeper's Association, Julian Barnes, Catherine Blyth, Caroline Boileau, the British Library, Jeremy Burbidge, Stephen Butterfill, Cambridge University Library, Lauren Carleton Paget, Geoffrey Chepiga, Helen Cloughley, Laurie Croft, Santanu Das, Bob Davenport, Alan Davidson, Jane Davidson, Tamasin Day-Lewis, Katherine Duncan-Jones, Richard Duncan-Jones, Fuchsia Dunlop, Sam Evans, Robin Glasscock, Nico Green, Rob Green, Christopher Hawtree, Rose Hilder, Tristram Hunt, the International Bee Research Association (IBRA), Jacqueline de Jong, Andy Joyce, Thomas King at DC Comics, Dominic Lawson, Peter Linehan, Angus MacKinnon, Anne Malcolm, Laura Mason, the Maison du Miel, Anthea Morrison, The National Honey Show, Mark Nichols, Northern Bee Books, Cristina Odone, Charles Perry, Roland Philipps, Bonnie Pierson, Elfreda Pownall, Rory Rapple, Martha Repp, Matt Richell, Miri Rubin, Garry Runciman, Ruth Runciman, Magnus Ryan, Ruth Scurr, Rebecca Small at L'Occitane, Gareth Stedman Jones, Simon Szreter, Selfridge's Food Hall, Marlena Spieler, Tate & Lyle, Sylvana Tomaselli, Robert Tombs, Georgie Widdrington, A. N. Wilson, Emily Wilson, Stephen Wilson.

I am also particularly grateful to the fellows of St John's College Cambridge for their generosity in awarding me a research fellowship and for allowing me to use some of my time to write this book; also to the History Society of St John's, to whom I presented some of the material in this book.

ACKNOWLEDGEMENTS

This book has been constructed in large part from secondary sources, and owes a special debt to the work of the scholars Bodog F. Beck, Eva Crane, Austin Fife, Juan Ramírez and Hilda Ransome. I have been grateful on several occasions to a delightful short work called *Curiosities of Beekeeping* by L. R. Croft.

Caroline Westmore has worked heroically to turn my text into a book. Special thanks must go to my editor, Caroline Knox, and to my literary agents, Sam Edenborough, Christy Fletcher, Pat Kavanagh and Emma Parry. This book would never have been written at all were it not for Pat, and might not have been finished were it not for Emma.

Tom and Natasha Runciman helped me to taste honey.

My greatest debt by far, in every possible way, is to David Runciman.

The author and publishers would like to acknowledge Faber and Faber Ltd for permission to quote from 'The Arrival of the Bee Box' and 'The Bee Meeting' from *Collected Poems* by Sylvia Plath. Extracts from Constance Garnett's translations of *War and Peace* (Heinemann, 1971) and *Anna Karenina* (Heinemann, 1972) by Leo Tolstoy are printed with the permission of A. P. Watt Ltd, on behalf of the Executor of the Estate of Constance Garnett. Lines from C. Day-Lewis's translation of Virgil's Fourth *Georgic* are reprinted by permission of PFD on behalf of the Estate of C. Day-Lewis © C. Day-Lewis 1940.

'The Bee, therefore excelling in many qualities,
it is fitly said in the proverb

As { *Profitable*
Laborious
Loyal
Swift
Nimble
Quick of scent
Bold
Cunning
Chaste
Neat
Brown
Chilly } as a Bee'

Charles Butler, *The Feminine Monarchy or the
History of the Bees*, 1609

Introduction

Thou seemst – a little deity!
Anacreon, Ode 34,
To the bee (fifth century BC)

IMAGINE A WORLD in which the lights went off until daybreak as soon as the sun went down; a world in which, year in and year out, you could never taste anything sweeter than a piece of fruit; a world in which there was no satisfactory way of getting drunk. Imagine huddling in the dark on a cold winter's night with neither sweets nor alcohol for comfort. If you got wounded in this world, your wound might well fester, untreated. If you got a sore throat, there would be no syrup to soothe it. It would not be unlivable, this life, but it would not contain much of the sweetness that helps us to swallow the bitter pill of existence.

This is what life would have been like for our distant ancestors had it not been for the presence of honeybees, those marvellous insects the *Apis mellifera*, which supplied them, if they could afford it, with artificial light from wax, with intoxication from mead, and, above all, with energy from golden, dripping honey, a medicine as well as a food, whose sweetness in a culture without sugar must have seemed simply wondrous. If the bees had never made honey and wax, human civilization would still have survived – just. If you chanced to live in the right part of the world, you might get some artificial light from oil, or from tallow candles, and sweetness from dates (the only things in nature sweeter than

I

A classic medieval image of a wholly benevolent beehive, from
the fourteenth-century Luttrell Psalter

honey), and, eventually, alcohol from grain or grapes, and you
could treat your wounds with various soothing leaves, which
might or might not stop you from dying. But something would
be missing. A little poetry would be missing. From the earliest
times, bee colonies supplied humans not just with some of life's
luxuries, but also with food for the imagination. High on honey,
our ancestors decided that bees – despite their stings – were the
'most mysterious and therefore magical creatures'.[1]

Peering into the glowing hexagonal rows of the bees' home,
men thought they should look and learn. Here was not just something delicious to eat, but a little society in miniature. Here were
architects, and here was a ruler. Were the bees, who worked so
ceaselessly and produced such goodies, a kind of message from
God (or Nature) to humankind? The ancients returned obsessively
to the idea that the bees were the only creatures to rival men in
their social gifts. 'The bee is wiser and more ingenious than all
other animals,' insisted one ancient authority, before adding that
this insect 'almost reaches the intelligence of man'.[2]

Others went further, and wondered if the bees didn't have some

advantages which men lacked. Pliny the Elder, the Roman ency-
clopedist, felt that bees surpassed humans in various ways. He suggested, wishfully but understandably, that bees were the 'only
insects to have been created for the benefit of men'. The praise that

This superhero bee on the label of Capilano Honey from
Australia shows how the love of bees has endured

Pliny heaped on the bees would be repeated countless times over
the course of human history; it was already a bit of a cliché by the
time his book was completed, in AD 77. 'Among all insect species,'
he wrote, 'the pride of place is reserved for bees'. Why? Because:

Bees collect honey: the sweetest, finest, most health-promoting
liquid. They make wax and combs for a thousand purposes, put up
with hard toil and construct building works. Bees have a government; they pursue individual schemes but have collective leaders.
What is especially astonishing, they have manners more advanced
than those of other animals, whether wild or tame. Nature is so
great that from a tiny, ghost-like creature she has made something
incomparable. What sinews or muscles can we compare with the
enormous efficiency and industry shown by bees? What men, in
heaven's name, can we set alongside these insects which are superior to men when it comes to reasoning? For they recognize only
what is in the common interest.[3]

It is not surprising that the bees have tended to make us feel a little inadequate. The oldest bee society is far older than the earliest human society.

Studying bees is a way of studying ourselves. I have always felt fond of bees – or at least fond of the idea of them – on account of honey, which I consume, greedily, almost every day: most often Manuka honey dissolved in hot water instead of early-morning tea, but also liquid honey poured over yoghurt or bread or porridge in rivulets, and sometimes, at tired moments in the afternoon, crunchy mouthfuls of energy-giving comb. For the past six years I have been lucky enough to be a food writer for various British publications. While researching articles on certain ingredients, I have found that many foods pall the more you eat of them. A week of cooking squid or tasting Camembert can be enough to put you off food altogether, however delicious both squid and Camembert are in small doses. Honey is different – to my palate, anyhow. The more honey I consume, the more it seems to be one of the greatest natural foods – as varied and splendid as olive oil, as consoling as chocolate, as flavoursome as garlic, as health-giving as fruit, as wholesome as bread. If one admires honey, it is logical to take an interest in the insects who made it. But my passion for bees is more than culinary. It is historical. My hobby is food-writing, but by profession I am an academic: a historian of ideas. While reading books of political theory from centuries past, I kept being struck by how often the community of honeybees was used as a model for human society. This image occurs in Aristotle and Plato; in Virgil and Seneca; in Erasmus and Shakespeare; in Marx and Tolstoy. You find it in ancient times and in modern times. This struck me as interesting, and odd. My desire to find out more resulted in this book.

Bees were with us from the very beginning. Before man had discovered how to produce bread or milk, before he had domesticated any animals or planted any wheat, when his diet was still entirely hunted and gathered, man had 'found in the wild bee's nests the sweet food which must have been such a welcome add-

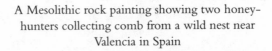

A Mesolithic rock painting showing two honey-
hunters collecting comb from a wild nest near
Valencia in Spain

ition to his simple fare'.[4] Man had begun hunting for
honey in palaeolithic times, at least 10,000 years ago,
searching for it in hollow trees and rocks. We know this
because some very early rock paintings, in a Spanish
cave in Valencia, depict two naked men climbing up a
tall ladder, basket in hand, stealing a bee's nest. It looks
a perilous undertaking. The ladder, which appears to
be made out of some kind of grass, is long and wobbly,
and the bees are flying angrily near the hunter at the
top. Clearly, honey was so precious that men would
risk death to get it.

This book is about the strange and wonderful story
of man's relationship with the honeybees, his attempts to master
them, his attempts to understand them, his attempts to copy them.
Bees are nothing like men, and yet human beings have always seen

their own hopes and fears played out in the life of the beehive. Bees and their honey constitute one of the miracles of nature, but the way in which the honey is produced is almost mechanical in its regularity and efficiency. We have never been sure of how to think of bees: whether as God-given wonder-workers, or as little factory workers, just like us. The beehive is a place where the world of nature and the world of artifice collapse into each other, which is why it is so mysterious. Whom are they working for, these tireless little creatures: God, us, or themselves? This book will try to provide a kind of answer.

There are two more immediate questions that a reader might want the author of this book to answer. The first is: Are you a bee-keeper? To which the answer, despite many apiary visits and a few stings, is no. Cowardice, a small city garden and two young children are my excuses – mainly cowardice, because small city gardens and young children are no deterrent to those who are truly infected with bee fever. I am a member of my local beekeeper's association, and have spent summer days in buzzing apiaries, coming home with my clothes reeking of honey and smoke. I have attended lectures at the National Honey Show and have talked to numerous beekeepers. I have acquired my own veil and boots and protective gloves. But mostly I read about bees in books. Sometimes I daydream, idly, of taking up beekeeping seriously in some far-off retirement, like Sherlock Holmes – of planting a thyme-scented garden and ordering a queen through the post and harvesting my own honey. But I cannot claim to have wax under my fingernails, or propolis (bee glue) on my shoes, as beekeepers say of each other. If the truth be told, I am still sometimes rather frightened of bees close up – frightened of squashing them when I pick up a frame of brood to examine it, or of putting them in a temper – though I find them and their works beautiful. This is not a beekeeping manual, or a work of entomology. It is a history of ideas, of human ideas. It is more about beekeepers than about about bees. And perhaps – this is my defence – my inexperience might enable me to see some aspects of this noble occupation which its full-time practitioners are too close to make out. The second question you might like answered is: How can someone named 'Bee' have the nerve to write a book about bees? It is a fair point. I was christened Beatrice, but have always been Bee, not Bea. I can only think that my parents must have been suffering a little from the very mania this book describes. They would never have called me Wasp.

Who's Who
in the Beehive

> The first time that we open a hive there comes over us an
> emotion akin to that we might feel at profaning some
> unknown object, charged perhaps with dreadful surprise.
>
> Maurice Maeterlinck, *The Life of the Bee* (1901)

THE AVERAGE HEALTHY bee colony should contain, at the
height of summer:

One *queen* – the only fully female bee, who lays the eggs from
which all the rest are born.[1] She is much longer than the other
bees, as a result of being fed royal jelly while growing, instead of
the usual diet of pollen mixed with honey. This royal jelly is a 'yel-
lowish, milky, viscous liquid', secreted from glands in the worker
bees' heads.[2] She develops in a queen cell much larger than any
other cell in the hive, shaped like a thimble. She gives off around
thirty different pheromones – sometimes referred to as 'queen
substance' – which keep the other bees calm and productive and
send them chemical instructions about what to do. She cannot
make wax or honey, and depends on the worker bees to feed her
and clean her. She has a sting, but uses it only against other queens.

This queen bee lays two different kinds of egg: drone eggs,
which she lays parthenogenetically – i.e. without sexual intercourse – and worker eggs, which are the result of her mating with
male drone bees. A few of these worker eggs will be nurtured with
royal jelly into more queen bees. The most significant event in the
queen's life is the so-called mating flight, which happens, over the

course of one or two days, when she flies out of the hive to copulate with several drones – as many as fifteen of them – sometimes from another colony. The drones die in the encounter. On her mating flights, she stores up enough sperm inside her body to last her for life, which may be up to five or six years long. After a mating flight, she returns to the hive with a distended abdomen and sets to work laying thousands and thousands of eggs in open cells, attended to all the while by a small group of worker bees, who surround her in an oval shape, licking her thorax to get her scent and feeding her now and then with more royal jelly. The queen may never leave the hive again, unless she quits the colony with a swarm to found a new colony.

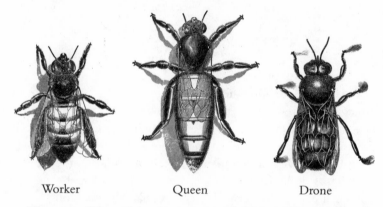

Worker   Queen   Drone

The rest of the colony is made up of the queen's offspring:

Six thousand *eggs*, as yet unhatched – a stage which lasts for only three days;

Nine thousand *hatched eggs* or *brood larvae* in the open cells, who need to be fed by the workers on a rich diet of honey, pollen and brood food (see below) for about five days, until they can join the ranks of the –

Twenty thousand *older larvae* or *pupae*, kept warm in cells sealed with wax, and each encased in its own cocoon of silk;

Three hundred to a thousand *drones*, the males whose life of a few months veers from happy leisure to certain and brutal death.

Their function is simply to compete for the task of mating with the queen. A dozen or so will succeed. Otherwise, they can laze around eating honey, while the workers clean up their mess. They have no sting. They are fatter than the queen, but shorter, with huge eyes, which help them to spot the queen on her mating flight. The drones' life changes suddenly after the summer mating season ends, when they are no longer useful. In autumn, the workers stop feeding them. If they resist starvation, they may be pushed out of the hive and even have their wings bitten off;

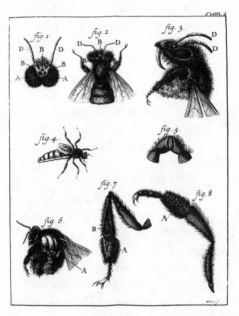

Bee anatomy as depicted in Gilles Bazin's *The Natural History of Bees*, 1744

Forty to fifty thousand *workers*, non-reproductive females, who keep the colony going in every possible way except reproductively, and work until they die, aged about six weeks. Workers do many different jobs, which are mainly determined by age.

Workers are born when a pupa uses its mandibles to chew its

way through a cocoon inside a waxen cell, and then through the wax ceiling, to emerge as a supple young bee. Straight away, they get to work. Already they are fully formed – except that their glands have not yet developed to the point where they can make wax and honey. Very young bees keep the cells clean and patrol the hive looking for interlopers. They also eat some pollen, a protein food which stimulates their hypopharyngeal glands, which begin to secrete brood food, nourishment for the hatched eggs. At six days old, workers will be capable of feeding the baby larvae, as well as tending the queen, capping the brood larvae with wax to keep them warm, and grooming and feeding younger bees. At a week old, the worker bees start to secrete wax from glands on their abdomens. They take this wax from their own bellies, chew it to soften it, then work together, using their legs, to manipulate this softened wax into regular hexagonal cells: the honeycomb. Hundreds of comb-building workers must coordinate their activities to build up this intricate structure. At twelve days old the worker moves into food storage. She packs pollen into the cells she has helped to make.

The next stage in her relentless working life is to make the honey which will feed the colony during the winter. Older bees arrive at the hive with nectar which they have sucked out of flowers and carried in their honey sacs, pouches inside their bodies. The older bees pass this nectar into the mouths of the younger bees – it looks as though they are kissing – and the young bees spit it into the wax cells, where enzymes from the salivary glands help to thicken it into honey. But still it isn't ready. More worker bees must now ripen the honey by energetically flapping their wings until the unwanted water in the honey is driven off and they have a concentrated syrup which will keep through the cold months. Then they cap the honey-filled cells with beeswax.

There are yet more jobs to do. The workers in a healthy colony are meticulous about hygiene, and there will always be some slaving away to clean cells and to remove debris and dead brood, pushing them out of the hive. When a worker feels dirty, she stamps her legs, and a nearby bee will recognize the signal and clean her, especially on that hard-to-reach spot between the thorax and abdomen. Others work as guard bees, standing near the entrance to the colony and barring entry to any enemies – such as wasps, or foreign bees.

Now comes the moment of a worker's life that we think of when we visualize what bees do. The last part of a worker bee's existence is spent foraging. A few bees go in search of gleaming brown loads of resin from trees – called propolis or bee glue – which is used to plug any cracks and holes in the architecture of the honeycomb. But most of the foragers are looking for pollen and nectar, the essential foods of the colony. A single worker may visit up to 10,000 flowers in a day before returning to the colony bearing pollen on her back legs or nectar in her mouth for honey. While gathering the nectar she will have pollinated countless plants. When she returns to her colony she does a dance to show her fellow bees where the best sources of nectar are. If the nectar is nearby, she does a round dance, and other workers smell the flower scent on her body and know at once which flowers to look for. If the nectar is further off she does a waggle dance, which tells the other bees which direction to fly in, based on the angle between the flower source and the sun. The workers crowd round to see the dance, before flying off themselves, knowing, with uncanny accuracy, exactly where to go.

After this life of productive toil, the worker bee will probably have produced only about a teaspoonful of honey.

In winter, the colony will look very different, reduced to perhaps 5,000 workers and a queen, with no drones, surviving on honey supplies until flowers blossom again in spring. In nature, this bee colony will live inside a hollow tree or log, or in a rock crevice far up off the ground. This is a wild bee colony. When it decides to leave its habitation in search of a new one, it is called a *swarm*.

A hive is something different.

In a *beehive* – a man-made habitat for bees and their honey – a colony will also require at least one *beekeeper*, a human being who attempts to control activities in the colony, contriving whenever possible to maximize honey production. Hives are much newer than colonies. There have been social honeybee colonies for perhaps 20 million years, whereas hives have been in existence for only about 10,000 years. At first, the beekeeper would catch a wild colony when it swarmed and put it in a suitable container. (Some still do.) Many of the early hives were hollowed-out logs, mimicking the bees' natural habitat. But man's interaction with bee colonies has also created numerous changes.

Now, most beekeepers order their bees as a package that comes through the post, complete with the requisite balance of drones, workers and queen. They will choose a variety of honeybee that has been bred by other beekeepers to be disease-free, docile and hard-working, in contrast to the more unpredictable wild or 'feral' colonies. Because the personality of a colony depends to a large

A mail-order queen bee from A. I. Root's American classic,
The ABC and XYZ of Bee Culture

extent on its queen, the beekeeper will often re-queen a hive long before the old queen's natural lifespan is up, because younger queens lay more eggs. When the new queen that has been ordered is introduced the old one is discarded and killed. Humans breed queens on bars containing nothing but queen cells and cups, like a row of thimbles. The queens are put in tiny wooden boxes the size of a matchbox, called queen cages, and are fed with queen candy – a mixture of icing sugar and sterilized honey: something they would never taste in a wild colony.

Modern beekeepers supplement many of the tasks in the bee colony. Beekeepers reinforce the job of the guard bees, by protecting the hives from wasps, toads and ants. They help keep the hive hyper-clean, to minimize infection. They destroy diseased hives. They also try to make the bees' work more labour-efficient, by cutting down on the burden of comb-building, and separate the brood comb – where the eggs are laid and hatched – from the honeycomb, to make harvesting the honey easier. After the colony arrives, the beekeeper will put the bees in a structure of wooden boxes or 'supers' filled with frames of ready-made comb or wax foundation – sheets of wax which the workers can use instead of their own secretions to build a comb. At the bottom of this structure, below the lowest box, there will be a board with a small hole, so that the bees can come and go. At the very top of the top box there will be a ventilator, to assist the bees in keeping their air clean. The bottom box forms a brood chamber for the queen to lay eggs in. On top of this is another box, called the 'honey super'. The queen is kept out of this latter box by a piece of mesh called a queen-excluder, which allows only workers to pass through, so that she cannot lay eggs there. This encourages the bees to fill this box with nothing but honey. In very successful hives, receiving a lot of nectar, there will be more than one honey super, stacked one on top of another. Commercial beekeepers move their hives around to keep pace with the best flowers, and to pollinate different crops.

Twice a year or more, depending on how rich the nectar sources are, the beekeeper will harvest honey from the hive. While removing the cover of the top super, he or she will first smoke the bees to calm them down, using a few puffs from a bellows device filled with smouldering leaves, straw or wood. The smoke probably works by preventing the bees from detecting alarm odour from the guard bees. The frames of honeycomb are then lifted out to check that they are full of ripe honey. Any bees clinging to the frame get swept off with a bee brush. A machine will scrape off the wax cappings from the honeycomb, and another machine will spin the comb round so fast that the liquid honey flies out, into strainers which remove dead bees and froth. The honey is then bottled and sold or eaten, instead of fulfilling its natural role as bee food.

The empty honeycomb is put back in the hive, ready for the bees to make more honey for more human beings to eat. If the workers get hungry over the winter, after honey production has ceased, they will be fed with man-made sugar syrup.

I

Work

Behold the School of Sobriety, Industry and Oeconomy!

John Keys, *The Practical Bee-Master* (1780)

IN THE SUMMER of 2003, IBM ran a lavish advertisement in the British press, citing the honeybee as a model of good business practice. 'The waggly bee dance and the responsive enterprise,' ran

A logo from an industrial assurance policy

the headline, next to a picture of Ming Tsai, an enigmatic-looking IBM business strategist sitting casually yet formally on a green wooden chair.[1] Bees, the ad revealed, might hold the key to transforming your retail business, assuming you own one. Bees communicate by doing 'waggle dances' to show each other where to fly to find the best nectar and pollen.

> Upon arriving back at the hive, a bee with pollen-coated legs does a waggly dance for her fellow bees. The thorax motions are actually a map drawn in the air, entomologists have suggested, indicating both the direction and the distance of the pollen source.

What on earth does this have to do with IBM? Apparently, this:

> Most corporations only dream about this kind of behaviour: instant, automatic, cross-enterprise communication that enables you to take advantage of any opportunity that presents itself. This is the kind of sense-and-respond behaviour that defines on demand business.

There follows a lot of stuff about responding quickly to customer needs and creating a 'sense-and-respond' retail environment, before the advert reaches its punchline:

> The bees know. Make your business waggle, and it will show you where the money is.

'*Make your business waggle.*' It's a classic piece of modern management-speak, with all the usual tics of that genre: the appeal to folk wisdom, the incomprehensible jargon, the attempt to flatter the reader's intelligence, the sheer cutesiness of it all. '*Make your business waggle.*' It's as of-the-moment as smoke-free offices, Starbucks and text messaging.

But there is also something deeper going on here. Humans have long believed that they could learn about how to work by looking at the busy bees. Well before they had any inkling of the bee's waggle dance,[2] they felt that the bees – more than any other creature – had something to teach them about industry. From ancient times, it was a commonplace that bees were wise, ingenious, social, architectural, pious and, above all, industrious beings. The difference between this and the IBM ad is that the industrious bee was not usually offered as a model for selling things. On the contrary, the bee colony, which worked so hard to store so much honey while eating so little of it itself, seemed a reproach to human avarice. Unlike the IBM waggly retail bees, the bees of traditional Western mythology were indifferent to money. Work, for them, was an end in itself, not a means to corporate profit.

Selfless Industry

'Non nobis' reads the inscription on many old pictures of beehives, meaning '[We work, but] not for ourselves': we work, but not for our own greed. The beehive is an unusually benign piece of iconography. When it appears in classical Western art, almost always in the form of a domed straw 'skep', it stands for some aspect of the goodness of work. Sometimes it denotes eloquence, because the sweetness of honey was meant to be like the sweetness of beautiful words. (The root of the word 'mellifluous' is '*mel*', or honey, and '*fluus*', or flowing.) Sometimes the beehive symbolizes the

The selfless industry of bees: a seventeenth-century woodcut praises bees for making honey 'not for ourselves'. The man writing at his desk shows the symbolic link between bees and eloquence; the cleric is eating honeycomb

golden age of the past, when work was simpler and slower. But from the Renaissance onward it almost always means selfless industry.

It is not very hard to imagine how this idea may have started. Human beings become most aware of honeybees on hot summer days – days when we feel too drowsy to move, when the only sound is from the ceaseless bustle of bees, popping in and out of blossoms like frantic couriers. We particularly notice that bees are busy because of the contrast between our own afternoon indolence and their energy, as their workaholic humming disturbs our nap. They are a hive of activity, while we are a gardenful of inactivity.

> How skilfully she builds her Cell!
> How neat she spreads the Wax!
> And labours hard to store it well
> With the sweet Food she makes.

So goes the hymn by Isaac Watts (1674–1748) whose title is 'Against Idleness and Mischief'. The hymn famously begins:

> How doth the little busy bee
> Improve each shining hour
> And gather honey all the day
> From every opening flower!

These irritatingly buzzy words are now so familiar that we can't think of the bee as anything other than busy.

But why? It was not as if bees were the only insects praised in the ancient world for being hard-working. The spider was often commended for its web-making skills. Termites and ants were revered for the way they worked together to accomplish great things. 'Go to the ant, thou sluggard', orders the Book of Proverbs; 'consider her ways, and be wise: which having no guide, overseer, or ruler, provideth her meat in the summer, and gathereth her food in the harvest.'[3] Yet, compared to the cult of the bee, the cult of the ant was nothing. The ants might work hard, but, at the end of it all, what do they produce? An anthill. The industry of the bee, by contrast, results in wonders as great as any produced by human civilization: the geometrical marvel of the honeycomb, and the gastronomic marvel of the honey inside. Unlike the ant's labours, the bee's industry directly increases man's happiness, so no wonder it was ranked in a class of its own. Man's adoration of the selfless labours of the bee has not itself been particularly altruistic. In fact you might call it downright self-interested. We want the bees to be 'selfless' so that they won't mind us eating their honey.

Bees, wrote the apiarist Samuel Purchas in 1657, are 'indefatigably [but] not covetously laborious, always working, but never satisfied, always toiling, but never coming to a period of their endeavours, still progressive, never at their journey's end'.[4] Anyone who has ever stared at the swirling mass of bees in a healthy colony must agree. In the bee's world, there are no holidays, no early release for good behaviour (though some scientists have referred jokingly to the bees' 'lunchbreak', a slight lull in the activity of the colony which tends to occur around noon, probably due to a dip in the nectar levels in flowers[5]). As a bee, you are born, you work and you die, with no interlude even for schooling. Generation after generation of worker bees learn their tasks not from moral teaching, but largely from gland development in their bodies and from hormonal signals of various kinds. Another Renaissance bee-lover, John Levett, marvelled in 1634 that the bee 'never giveth over his dayes labour from the midst of Aprill till the beginning of November, neither would he then cease, were it not for his two mortall enemies, Snow and Frost'.[6] In fact this is not quite true. The bees may be busy from April to November, but it is not the same bees who are busy. Each worker lives for only a few weeks, but during one lifetime she will have flown afield many times.

Man is a purposeful animal, and no sooner had he admired the industriousness of the bees than he felt that he – or even better, his wife – must emulate it in some way. The ancient Greek

historian and huntsman Xenophon (*c.* 430–*c.* 355 BC) was sometimes called the Athenian Bee on account of his eloquence. (Bees
were associated with special powers of prophecy, poetry and
speech.) Xenophon argued that Greek housewives could take a
lesson or two in modesty and industry from the queen bee. He
offered this dominant insect as a template from which blushing
teenage brides could learn their duties:

> She stays in the hive and does not suffer the bees to be idle; but
> those whose duty it is to work outside she sends forth to their
> work; and whatever each of them brings in, she knows and receives
> it, and keeps it till it is wanted. And when the time is come to use
> it, she portions out the just share to each. She likewise presides over
> the weaving of the combs in the hive, that they may be well and
> quickly woven, and cares for the brood of the little ones, that it be
> duly reared up. And when the young bees have been duly reared
> and are fit to work, she sends them forth to found a colony, with
> a leader to guide the young adventurers.[7]

Most of this is pure fantasy, bearing no resemblance to the life
of the real queen bee. In actual bee life, the queen does not over-
see the nectar-gathering, as Xenophon says she does, nor the
comb-building; nor does she care for the brood after she has laid
it. Except on the infrequent occasions when she leaves the hive to
copulate – a lifestyle not quite so seemly for Greek matrons – she
actually spends her days doing little but laying thousands of eggs.
But even if most of what Xenophon said about bee life was wrong,
his reference to the hive is still telling. It is an early example of the
way that bees have persistently given men licence to moralize about
themselves. The beehive seems to lend a kind of natural authority
to exhortations to work which might otherwise sound unfair.
Working like a dog suggests the burden of hard labour; but working like a bee suggests the joy and dignity of being productive.

More than 2,000 years after Xenophon, the poet William
Cowper (1731–1800) was also using honeybees as a medium for
moralizing about work, though in his case it was manual labourers rather than housewives who were meant to follow the ex-

ample of the hive. In his poem 'The Bee and the Pineapple', Cowper tries to show how futile it is for human beings to go lusting after exotic greenhouse-raised fruit that they cannot afford. (At that time, pineapples were the luxury fruit par excellence: their spiky looks were adored by the aristocracy and barely seen by the poor.) Instead of pursuing unattainable pineapples, we should be happy with our lot, and work, if not like dogs, then like bees. Cowper has a gardener turn to the hive and say:

> Poor restless bee!
> I learn philosophy from thee,
> I learn how just it is and wise,
> To use what Providence supplies,
> To leave fine titles, lordships, graces,
> Rich pensions, dignities and places,
> Those gifts of a superior kind,
> To those for whom they were designed.
> I learn that comfort dwells alone
> In that which Heaven has made her own,
> That fools incur no greater pain,
> Than pleasures coveted in vain.[8]

Bees were particularly useful for drumming home the message that social order came from harmonious, uncomplaining labour. Referring to the busy bees was a way of prettifying even the grimiest of human activities. London's Great Exhibition of 1851, at which Britain's status as 'the workshop of the world' was paraded for all to see, was reported in the *Illustrated London News* as 'The Great Gathering of the Industrious Bees':

How beautifully is the Palace of Industry represented . . . where more than two hundred thousand little labourers are diligently engaged in their various daily duties, while their reigning sovereign reposes quietly in her regal apartment, attended to by her subjects with the utmost regard to her comfort and convenience.[9]

To describe these 'little labourers' as bees was to praise them, but also to deny them individual personalities. The hive as it was imagined by Victorians could be a deeply conservative society: to paraphrase Mrs Beeton, there was a place for everyone and everyone in their place. The beehive was not just a symbol of industry in general. It also stood for industry in particular: a world in which different people were allotted different tasks and no one envied the position of anyone else.

The Division of Labour

The Roman poet Virgil (70–19 BC) was the main source for more or less everything written about bees until Renaissance times. In his pastoral poem the *Georgics* he idealized the charm of beekeeping and bees. Virgil noticed that, on a blossom-scented spring day, different bees spent their days in different ways – some 'busy in the fields' and others 'indoors' gluing up combs.[10] His theme was taken up again in the Middle Ages, when bee writers really developed the theme of how bees divide up their labour. If we were to attach a reason to this we might say that the hive echoed the feudal structure of medieval Europe, in which there were those who worked, those who fought, and those who prayed – all of them sinners with an allotted role in God's order which must not be questioned. In addition, medieval writers about animals were more unselfconsciously fanciful than their ancient counterparts. They were apt to see animals as hieroglyphs sent by God with moral lessons inside them for men. The whole world was composed of hidden messages, and everything held together as part of a single Creation. In this system of hieroglyphs, real animals and imaginary animals could easily get muddled up. Medieval bestiaries, or books of beasts, included winged horses alongside ordinary ones, manticores and mermaids and monoceroses as well as sea urchins and partridges. Everything *meant* something. Indeed, St Augustine had earlier gone so far as to state that it did not matter whether certain animals even existed, because what really mattered was what the animals *signified*.[11] That seems peculiar to us now, and rather anthropocentric. On the other hand, we continue to cling unthinkingly to many of the medieval animal symbols without recognizing that this is what we are doing. The wily fox, the newly wed turtle-doves, the stubborn mule and the industrious bee are all still with us. Moreover, if the IBM 'waggly dance' advertisement is anything to go by, we are still pretty fanciful about the way that bees organize their working roles. It is just that, as our own working lives have changed, so too has our vision of work in the hive.

The leading British entomologist of honeybees, Professor Francis Ratnieks, compares the partitioning of roles in the hive to the efficiency of a modern supermarket.[12] The shoppers, Ratnieks suggests, are the forager bees. The cashiers are the nectar-receiving bees, who hold out their tongues ready to suck up the nectar as it is regurgitated by the returning foragers. For an efficient hive, you need a good balance of foragers and receivers, just as a profitable supermarket needs a good balance of shoppers and cashiers. All too often the human supermarket gets this wrong, resulting in either rows of bored cashiers with no one to serve or, more often, great snaking queues of harassed customers all waiting for a single checkout. Yet in the hive, astonishingly, such imbalance is almost unknown. Ratnieks argues that honeybees are superior to humans in the way they partition tasks because, whereas a supermarket depends on centralized management, the honeybee colony works in a decentralized way, each forager making her own decision about which receiver will get her nectar. If there is a delay in a forager being served by one receiver bee, she will simply go to another; she will not wait, fuming and silently cursing, in a line, as the hapless human shopper does. If there are too few bee receivers, more workers will switch to this task straight away; the problem does not have to be identified by the supermarket manager and blared out over a tannoy. The way that the bees partition their work is 'simpler' than that of humans, concludes Ratnieks. 'And it works.'

The admiration which Ratnieks clearly feels for the honeybee division of labour is almost medieval in its fervour. Yet the message he takes from the hive is very unmedieval. Ratnieks's supermarket model is all about expanding individual consumer choice. Medieval writers about bees admired the 'hive of activity' just as much as Ratnieks does, but for very different reasons. Then, the bees' division of labour seemed to promote a society freed from individual greed, where everyone was happy with what he or she had. Here is how the working structure of the hive was seen by one anonymous writer of the twelfth century:

> You can see bees all vying with each other in their tasks. You can see some watchful in the search for food, other showing an anxious guardianship over the hive, others on the lookout for coming showers and studying the way the clouds run together, others making wax from flowers and others collecting in their mouths the honey-water which has been intruded on the blossoms. Yet none of them is encroaching on the work of his neighbours, and none is getting his living by robberies. Would indeed that they had not themselves to fear the tricks of robbers![13]

What seemed so extraordinary was the obedience with which the bees slotted into their different roles. They seemed to have learned the art of competing with each other in their work, without ever becoming so dangerously competitive that envy set in. Another medieval animal writer, Bartholomew the Englishman, who produced an encyclopedia of natural history in the thirteenth century, saw the work of the bees as a way of meekly and patriotically supporting the 'king bee', who needed soldiers, cooks and bodyguards to support his own life, which consisted of not working:

> And of a swarm of bees none is idle. Some fight, as it were in battle, in the field against other bees, some are busy about meat, and some watch the coming of showers . . . and only he [the king] is not bound to travail. And all about him are certain bees with stings, as it were champions, and continued wardens of the king's body. And he passeth seldom out, but when all the swarm shall go out.[14]

Needless to say, such accounts were simply a projection of human values on to the bees. Not least, it was always assumed that the different bees were equivalent to different groups of grown men. In real bee colonies, on the other hand, worker tasks are divided mainly by age, and are determined not by virtue but by gland development. From the time of Aristotle onward, men believed that bees could live for as long as five or six years. Actually, during the height of summer, a worker bee will probably live for only five or six weeks, but during that time she will have performed numerous different jobs. From the moment she first wriggles out of her cell, all golden and wet, she will set to work keeping brood larvae warm and cleaning the cells of the young. When she is three days old she will switch to feeding older grubs, and then at six days she is promoted to feeding younger grubs, and the queen. At one to two weeks old her glands have developed to the point where she can make wax, so her job switches to that of comb-building and maintenance of the hive, fetching propolis to fill in cracks. Soon after that, she may decide to guard the entrance of the hive; or ripen nectar into honey; or store pollen in cells, or keep the colony clean. Finally, at three weeks old, her honey-making glands have developed and she will spend the rest of her days flying off in search of nectar, dancing, receiving nectar, putting it into cells, and flapping her wings to evaporate the nectar into honey, until one day she dies.

In truth, the real story of division of labour in the hive has little to teach human beings. If we really tried to follow the bees, we would set our babies to work the minute they are born; switch jobs as our hormones dictated; train as a builder only to change our minds and become a chef; and never, ever retire. The bee model of labour begins to make sense only if we assume – wrongly – that the different bee groups each stick with their tasks for life, or at least longer than a few days. The hive seems to be saying to us that, if work is to go well, we mustn't all do the same thing. This message seemed all the more pertinent as the Middle Ages gave way to the Renaissance and human trades diversified. Shakespeare

Some beekeeping tools from the great Enlightenment
Encyclopédie, 1751–72

reflects this in *Henry V*, where he gives the Archbishop of Canterbury a speech praising the bees for teaching men how to partition their work. Like the medieval bestiary-writers, Shakespeare still treats bees as a social hieroglyph. But the society at stake is no longer feudal but mercantile – a society of jobs rather than estates. Men, explains Canterbury, are divided by heaven into 'divers functions'; and the proof of this is found in the bees, who teach men about 'order'. The details of Canterbury's interpretation of the hive are almost all inaccurate; and yet the tone of what he says immediately summons up the busy activity of the hive in a way which is perfectly plausible:

> . . . so work the honey-bees,
> Creatures that by a rule in nature teach
> The act of order to a peopled kingdom.
> They have a king, and officers of sorts,
> Where some like magistrates correct at home;
> Others like merchants venture trade abroad,
> Others like soldiers, armèd in their stings,
> Make boot upon the summer's velvet buds,
> Which pillage they with merry march bring home
> To the tent royal of their emperor,
> Who busied in his majesty surveys
> The singing masons building roofs of gold,
> The civil citizens kneading up the honey,
> The poor mechanic porters crowding in
> Their heavy burdens at his narrow gate,
> The sad-eyed justice with his surly hum
> Delivering o'er to executors pale
> The lazy yawning drone.[15]

What makes this speech so brilliant – so Shakespearian – is the final inclusion of the drone, the bee who does not work. Bartholomew the Englishman had been wrong to say that none of the bees was idle. He had forgotten 'the lazy yawning drone'. What makes the hive an exceptional image of activity, rather than merely a good one, is that it contains ready-made within itself a symbol of its opposite. How would we recognize the quality of industry if we didn't also know of the existence of slothfulness?

Drones

The ancient Greeks spotted that in the colony of bees there were some who were bigger than the rest, with bigger eyes, and bigger waxen cells to live in, who, in marked contrast to the others, didn't seem to do much, even though they ate a lot of honey. Like almost everyone since, the Greeks disapproved of these lazybones. For example, the ancient poet Hesiod, who lived not long after Homer, wrote that 'Both Gods and men are angry with a man who lives idle, for in nature he is like the stingless drones who waste the labour of the bees, eating without working.'[16] It seemed outrageous that these lumbering creatures should get the benefit of honey without doing any work for it. In *The Republic*, the philosopher Plato (*c.* 427–347 BC) compared drones to greedy men, and to tyrants.[17] The comic playwright Aristophanes (*c.* 448–*c.* 388 BC) thought that drones were good-for-nothing parasites.[18]

No one knew at this point that the drones have a reproductive purpose: that they are male bees who inseminate the queen; that without the drones there would be no colony at all. People just looked at the drones and saw morally abject beings. The only thing that they liked about drones was that they all got killed off every winter, which seemed to offer a morality tale for the sluggards in human society. Virgil wrote of the bees driving forth the 'lazy tribe' of drones.[19] Aristotle (384–322 BC) – the ultimate Greek expert on just about everything – observed that 'When honey runs short they expel the drones.' Others wrote of the 'massacre of the drones' being a 'punishment' for devouring the food which was due to others – a just retribution for not working. In some books of 'husbandry' it was suggested that humans should do the bees' job for them: that a beekeeper's job was to kill off drones.[20] In some early Christian legends it is said that God created the bees and the Devil created the drones.[21]

Whenever people wish to speak of an idler, a parasite, a do-nothing, the first image to spring to mind is often that of the drone. Even insect biologists, who are supposed to remain dispassionate about such things, have been known to call the drones 'a little stupid and lazy'.[22] The drones have provided an irresistible metaphor for all kinds of idlers, but especially for members of the aristocracy. As the clergyman and social critic Robert Burton put it in *The Anatomy of Melancholy* (1621), the drones of society spent their days without any employment, in 'hawking, hunting etc.'; 'Amongst us the badge of gentry is idleness: to be of no calling, not to labour, for that's derogatory to their birth, to be a meer spectator, a drone.'[23] Such drones, both human and bee, seemed an affront to the workers. The poet Shelley (1792–1822) asked why the working classes should slave while the aristocracy lived from their labour:

> Wherefore, Bees of England, forge
> Many a weapon, chain, and scourge,
> That these stingless drones may spoil
> The forced produce of your toil?[24]

Needless to say, there are those to whom a drone's life sounds rather appealing. Being a busy bee is all too much hard work. The most splendid example of this attitude is surely the character of Harold Skimpole in *Bleak House* (1852–3) by Charles Dickens. Skimpole is a childlike man, forever scrounging, but so innocently and benignly that people hardly begrudge him the money he cadges. Skimpole is a drone if ever there was one: he 'never kept an appointment, never could transact any business and never knew the value of anything'. But, true to his childlike merriness, Skimpole is quite happy to be a drone not a worker:

Mr Skimpole was as agreeable at breakfast, as he had been over-night. There was honey on the table, and it led him into a discourse about Bees. He had no objection to honey, he said (and I should think he had not, for he seemed to like it), but he protested against the overweening assumptions of Bees. He didn't at all see why the busy Bee should be proposed as a model to him; he supposed the Bee liked to make honey, or he wouldn't do it. It was not necessary for the Bee to make such a merit of his tastes. If every confectioner went buzzing about the world, banging against everything that came in his way and egotistically calling upon everybody to take notice that he was going to his work and must not be interrupted, the world would be quite an insupportable place . . .

He must say he thought a Drone the embodiment of a pleasanter and wiser idea. The Drone said, unaffectedly, 'You will excuse me; I really cannot attend to the shop! I find myself in a world in which there is so much to see, and so short a time to see it in, that I must take the liberty of looking about me, and begging to be provided for by somebody who doesn't want to look about him.' This appeared to Mr Skimpole to be the Drone philosophy, and he thought it a very good philosophy – always supposing the Drone to be on good terms with the Bee – which, so far as he knew, the easy fellow always was, if the consequential creature would only let him, and not be so conceited about his honey![25]

The Skimpole mentality finds its apogee in the books of P. G. Wodehouse (especially those of the 1920s), where foppish young men with such names as Oofy Prosser and Pongo Twistleton-Twistleton waste their days at the Drones Club, a Mayfair establishment where bread fights and hangovers and 'inhaling' over snifters are the order of the day. The absurd patrons of the Drones Club are true parasites, whose feckless existences entirely depend on the wealth of their relatives and the labour of their servants. They are deliciously funny to read about, but not everyone finds self-indulgence of this kind amusing when encountered in the flesh. Certainly the Americans have always found this form of British parasitism to be distasteful. In American self-mythologizing, the Wars of Independence were fought so that America could be a country of equal and industrious workers, with no place for arrogant drones.

American Workers

Honeybees, like white men, were not native to the lands that would later become the United States of America, but they settled there so easily that they soon seemed quite natural citizens. The exact date when honeybees arrived on American soil is unknown, but they must have come over on the earliest ships of German and English colonists, because bees had settled in Virginia by 1622.[26] As early as 1640, the town of Newbury, Massachusetts, had established a municipal apiary. As with the colonists, it took the bees much longer to settle in the West. Bees did not reach California, that honeyed paradise where there were such rich nectars – the light basswood, the suave blueberry, the perfumed sage – until 1853. For the native American Indians, bees were soon synonymous with the baneful effects of European civilization. They called the bee the 'white man's fly', and saw it as the harbinger of misfortune. In *The Song of Hiawatha* (1858) the poet Henry Wadsworth Longfellow imagines how the Indians saw the invasion of bees and men:

> Where so'er they move, before them,
> Swarms the stinging fly, the Almo,
> Swarms the Bee, the honey-maker;
> Whereso'er they tread, beneath them
> Springs a flower unknown among us,
> Springs the White Man's Foot in blossom.

Washington Irving, author of 'The Legend of Sleepy Hollow' (1820), said much the same thing: wherever the bees advanced, the Indians and buffaloes retreated.

As it happened, the white men were more than happy to be identified with bees. Especially after the American Revolution of 1776, the beehive seemed the perfect symbol of the new, hard-working, virtuous, commercial republic. Gone were the British drones, who did not bear arms and did not work. Every true

American was a worker bee. An allegorical painting done soon after the Declaration of Independence – Joseph Strutt's *To Those Who Wish to Sheathe the Desolating Sword of War* (1778) – depicted America as a woman kneeling to honour the war heroes who had died to free her. Joining her are other classical figures: Peace, with an olive branch; Liberty, with a bell-shaped cap; Plenty, with rich fruits; and Industry, with a beehive.

America, as Alexis de Tocqueville observed in his book *Democracy in America* (1835–40), was a nation in which 'The notion of labour [is] presented to the mind, on every side, as the necessary, natural and honest condition of human existence.'[27] The Americans took on board the idea of the virtue of industry more than any other people. In the process, as Tocqueville also observed, they made themselves very rich. How were they to square the tremendous wealth they accrued with their image of themselves as frugal and virtuous? Easy: just argue that commerce was itself virtuous. To be rich in corrupt old Europe might be a sign of droneishness; but to be rich in fresh young America was the fruit of hard work. The beehive provided Americans with the ideal image for their religion of work.

Beehives were adopted as motifs by all different kinds of American worker in the new republic. Most obviously, the humble straw skep fitted easily with the mood of American pastoral: the dream of the independent yeoman farmer, as espoused by the third president, Thomas Jefferson (1743–1826). Bees were a pleasant image of the down-home American farmer, whose daily life was a bustle of different activities, all taking advantage of the raw materials of this land of plenty, where meat was almost as plentiful as corn and 'the kitchen flows with milk and honey'.[28] A farmer's monthly called *The Cultivator* advertised itself with a beehive emblem; it sought to 'improve the soil and the mind'. Bees went along with the American attachment to small-scale, small-town community spirit. But pictures of beehives were also adopted by big business, to lend a little of this frugal charm to enterprises otherwise lacking in it. In Salem,

Massachusetts, jewellers and mechanics, cabinet-makers and lawyers all chose the beehive for their logo to symbolize the goodness of commerce.

These beehive business logos show how eagerly the industrious bee was embraced in the USA. (From the collection of the late Frank Alston)

The more that America industrialized, the more important it seemed to be to sanctify the virtue of labour through bees. In 1826 a popular playwright called George Baker, whose countless didactic works have now, justly, sunk into obscurity, brought out a characteristically one-dimensional play called *The Revolt of the Bees*. *Animal Farm* it isn't. But, like much bad literature, it summons up the spirit of its age rather potently. Baker imagines what happens when a group of worker bees get influenced by some butterflies and start to question the value of work. The butterflies encourage the bees 'to sport and flutter in the breeze', to lead a 'free and roving life', which leads to a rebellion in the hive. But the queen soon comes in to show the rebellious workers that the butterflies' existence is fool's gold:

> Their life they picture as so bright and gay
> Is short and vapid, lasts but for a day.
> While we by labour energy and worth
> Long live and prosper; o'er all the earth.

The moral of the story is that industry is the only 'germ of joy and peace', and 'love of labour is the richest treasure'.[29] Social conformity and hard work will lead to riches.

You might argue that this in itself – the American dream of prospering through work – is the real delusion. For those at the very bottom of the pay scale, labour brings not 'treasure' but poor health, lack of respect and misery. The successful worker bees of the original American republic gave rise to wealthy dynasties of American aristocrats as droneish as any in Europe (think Dickie Greenleaf in Patricia Highsmith's *The Talented Mr Ripley*), while the real workers still scrub floors for the leisured classes. This, at any rate, is the theme of the American poet Harry McClintock's stirring 'Hymn of Hate' (1916):

> And the Day shall come with a red, red dawn, and you in your
>   gilded halls
> Shall taste the wrath and the vengeance of the men in overalls
> .   .   .   .
> For ours are the hands that govern in factory, mine and mill.
> And we need only to fold our arms, and the whole wide world
>   stands still!
> So go ye, and study the beehive, and do not quite forget,
> That we are the workers of the world, and we have not spoken –
>   yet.[30]

The workers still have not spoken, and McClintock's is still a minority view. Meanwhile, the beehive as a symbol sanctifying the supposedly virtuous industry of the USA goes from strength to strength. No fewer than sixteen of the fifty states have adopted the honeybee as state insect. It was adopted by Arkansas and North

Carolina in 1973, by New Jersey in 1974, by Georgia, Nebraska and Maine in 1975, by Kansas in 1976, by Louisiana and Wisconsin in 1977, by South Dakota and Vermont in 1978, by Mississippi in 1980, by Missouri in 1985, and by Oklahoma and Tennessee in 1992, the latter with the support of Al Gore. In each and every case, the bee was chosen for its industry. This makes it officially America's favourite insect.

The original 'beehive state', however, is one which many still consider to be the least 'American' in the whole of the union, namely Utah, which was named The Beehive State in 1959, but whose honeybee connections go as far back as 1848. The industrious beehive can be put to as many different symbolic uses as there are different kinds of human work. It is a sign of how flexible a motif it is that it could be adopted both by America at large and by the Utah Mormons, whose values – *against* property, *for* polygamy, and *for* the mixing of Church and State – threatened for many the very existence of the United States.

Mormons and Masons

If you visit Salt Lake City today, you can still see Beehive House, an adobe building gilded with bees and reminiscent of a hive, where Brigham Young (1801–1877), leader of the Mormons, once lived with thirteen of his twenty-seven wives, whey-faced and sad-mouthed the lot of them. I don't mean to be offensive. Who wouldn't be sad, married to such a despotic loon as Young? Look at their picture if you think I'm exaggerating. The streets of Salt Lake City are still paved – some of them, anyway – with a honeycomb motif. You can no longer stay at the old luxury Hotel Utah, since it was turned into a heritage centre in the early 1990s, but you can still see its distinctive 'beehive tower', decorated with eagles. When you spot the state flag flying, you will notice that its only heraldic device is a straw beehive, and that the state motto is 'Industry'. Highways, universities, cleaning companies

Brigham Young, the Mormon leader, alongside twenty-one of
his wives

and clothing mills all use beehive signs, which are so ubiquitous
that you barely notice the meaning of them any more. Should you
venture to visit the main Mormon temple of Salt Lake City, you
will notice that it is inscribed with various symbols, including the
sun, moon, stars, an all-seeing eye, some clasped hands – and a
beehive. The Beehive State takes its name very seriously.

Right from the beginning, the Mormons under their prophet Joseph Smith revered the honeybee for the way it seemed to work its way through adversity, extracting honey from weeds. Joseph Smith, a troubled boy from Vermont, took it upon himself to found the Mormon Church on 6 April 1830, aged just twenty-five, after he had rejected conventional Christianity. The 1820s and 1830s were a time of great religious revivalism in America, but Smith's spiritual vision was weird even by the standards of his day. His disordered mind splurged out a strange stream of revelation called *The Book of Mormon*, which offered alarmingly definite answers to all the great problems which had ever vexed mankind. Smith claimed that these revelations came from an angel in heaven called Moroni, who had written them down on gold plates in a strange Egyptian tongue. Smith's task, as prophet, was to translate these truths for the rest of humanity. In his Mormon language, the bee had the name of 'deseret', which meant 'virtue', 'thrift' and 'industry'.

Mormonism's great claim, which soon won it many followers, was that it could help the faithful in every aspect of their lives, through continuous revelation. With this in mind, the Mormons under Joseph Smith tried to build their Zion, their heaven on earth, in the unlikely setting of Illinois, naming their new city Nauvoo. This strange place prospered for a while under its despotic rulers, becoming a boom town for temple-building and Mormon baptisms, but soon success bred resentment and in 1844 Smith was murdered. The Church needed new leadership, and a zealous entrepreneur called Brigham Young quickly stepped into the breach. The Mormons, he decided, needed a new promised land, where they could be free from persecution. In 1847 they found it, 1,600 km to the west. Young decided to name this place after the deseret or honeybee, reflecting his commitment to the gospel of work. 'Deseret' was the name of the new government, as well as of the place it occupied, 'The Provisional State of Deseret'.

Bees offered the Mormons the hope that, through working together in common, anything was possible. At first their new

UTAH.

Utah: 'The Beehive State'

land, with its great salt basin, seemed almost uninhabitable. But remarkably quickly they achieved their goal of economic self-sufficiency. As part of this they brought buzzing hives with them on wagons on the long journey west, to make honey for the faithful. Both the bees and the Mormons prospered. As early as 1850 the Mormons in Deseret included eighty-five different occupations, ranging from architects to woollen-manufacturers, butchers and bakers and candlestick-makers. Young insisted that profit was not incompatible with virtue – that it was 'no sin to gull a gentile'. Bees made the honey – the honeybee had settled in Utah by 1851 – and Mormons made the money.

Mormons, like bees, were a community apart, in which the usual rules of property-holding and marriage did not apply. (Mormon polygamists ignored the fact that in the bee colony there was one 'wife' to several husbands, rather than the other way round.) It was precisely this Mormon separateness which offended the federal government. Before Utah was admitted to official statehood in 1895, it was forced to abandon its name of Deseret, along with religious schooling and polygamy. From henceforth it would be called Utah, after the Indian tribe of Utes.

Of all the Mormons' peculiarities, their attachment to the beehive as image of work was probably the most mainstream. Their mistake seems to have been taking this attachment a little too far, thereby making the mainstream values of America appear weird by association. However, they weren't the only guilty ones in this respect. In the nineteenth century the beehive had a symbolic affinity with many secret societies, including many that the US federal government wanted to suppress. In particular, the beehive was associated with the Masons, whose supposed malign influence caused ructions in US politics and bred anxiety even overseas. (It is striking how many of the villains in Sherlock Holmes stories turn out to have been mixed up with American Masonry.) Indeed, this beehive connection may well have provided the source of Joseph Smith's original revelation about the 'deseret', since his father, like many disillusioned working men of the 1820s, was a Freemason.

For the Freemasons, the beehive is a 'hieroglyphic emblem', meaning a mythical symbol containing some kind of truth. Masons have always held a number of different emblems dear – the all-seeing eye, the pentagram – but the hive has a special significance for them, because it has always seemed to reflect so well their own lives as cathedral-builders – it contains, as Shakespeare put it, 'singing masons building roofs of gold'. An eighteenth-century book of Masonic catechisms notes that Masonic lodges were referred to as 'hives', and that the meetings there were known as 'swarms'. Why was this so? Because 'A bee has in all Ages and Nations been the Grand Hieroglyphick of Masonry because it excels all other living Creatures in the Contrivance and Commodiousness of its Habitation or Combe . . . nay Masonry and Building seems to be of the very Essence or Nature of the Bee.'[31] Like the cathedral-builders, the bees worked for the group rather than selfishly for themselves. Like the Masons, they seemed to respect the rule of law in their own community, and wanted to keep out enemies.

Even now that they are no longer builders of cathedrals, the Masons still respect bees. A modern Masonic textbook praises the hive for teaching that we are born 'rational, intelligent and industrious' and that we must not sit by 'while our fellow creatures around us are in want'. Another Mason observes, ecstatic, that the genealogical pattern of bees follows the Fibonacci sequence – a number sequence supposed to show the extraordinary chain of unity in nature, visible in everything from sunflowers to artichokes.[32] To a Masonic mind, the bees confirm the wonderful order of the universe. But you do not have to be a mason to think there is something pretty wonderful about the architecture of the hive.

Beeswax

Honeycomb is one of those natural phenomena, like a peacock's tail, so marvellous it is hard for us to believe they weren't made by human hands. An anonymous twelfth-century bee-fancier expressed the bewilderment that most of us still feel on contemplating a frame of comb:

> What four-walled houses can show so much skill and beauty as the frame-work of their combs shows, in which small round apartments are supported by sticking one to the other? What architect taught them to fit together six-sided chambers with their sides indistinguishably equal? To suspend thin wax cells inside the walls of their tenements?[33]

The ancient *Geoponica*, a collection of agricultural lore, thought that 'the ingenuity of this animal seems to approach human intelligence in that they make cells with six sides'.[34] But what human architect ever made anything as timelessly perfect as a honeycomb? Maurice Maeterlinck, the celebrated bee-lover and early-twentieth-century playwright, who reawakened bee love among modernists, was awed that: 'For thousands of years they have constructed their marvellous combs, to which we can add nothing, from which we can take nothing; combs that unite in equal perfection the science of the chemist, the geometrician, the architect and the engineer.'[35] If you set out to construct a waxen casing for liquid honey in a given

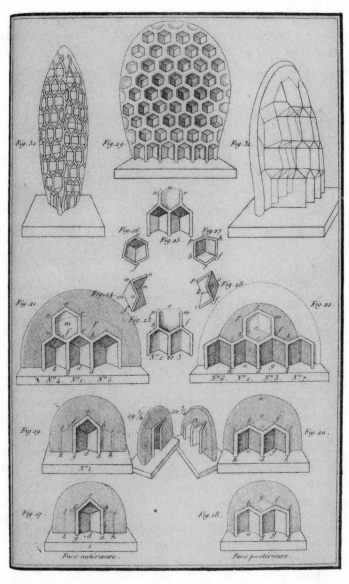

The wonderful architecture of bees, taken from François Huber's
Nouvelles observations sur les abeilles, 1814

space, which extracts the maximum capacity from the minimum wax, you cannot do better than the hexagonal honeycomb. It has been described as 'a geometric fact' that when regular hexagons are used to fill a circular figure the largest possible part of the space is thus utilized.[36]

Karl Marx (1818–1883), the foremost theorist of modern socialism, liked to blow a hole in anything too reverential. He argued that the architectural power of the bee was very limited compared to that of man, because, whereas man could build anything he liked, the bee could make only honeycomb. Men should therefore stop emulating bees and recognize their own potential.[37] But Marx had reasons of his own to talk up human industrial capacity. Most people, when they looked at the construction of the hive, were deeply impressed and not a little envious. In the seventeenth century, the bee expert Samuel Purchas decided that the building abilities of bees had been sent as a message by God to show man what to strive for in his own buildings. The beehive was a product of the 'great Artifex of nature'. Honeycomb was natural, yet it showed men what they should aspire to in their artificial constructions. Men should try to copy the beehive and the spider's web, and thereby recognize the greatness of God's works. Purchas looked at the hive and decided, 'Here is *magnum in parvo*, a little in quantity but much in worth and quality. What is wiser or better instructed than the Bee? What Artificer is so Various, what Painter, what Geometrician can imitate her works?'[38]

By the eighteenth century, bee writers were comparing wax comb to human architecture in a more prosaic way, treating bees not so much as wonders set above themselves but as colleagues and rivals, worthy of professional respect:

> In constructing habitations within a limited compass, an architect would have three objects in view: first, to use the smallest quantity that can be of materials; next, to give to the edifice the greatest capacity on a determined space; and thirdly, to employ the spot in such a manner that none of it may be lost. On examination it will be found that the bees have obtained all these advantages in

the hexagonal form of their cells; the economy of wax; and of space; and the greatest capacity.[39]

A hundred years later, in his book *L'Insecte* (1858), the zealous French historian Jules Michelet took this view of bees-as-architects still further by commending the bees for their flying buttresses, counterforts, pillars and beams, as if the little bugs had been trained at the Parisian academy of architecture.

But Marx was right about one thing: however clever bees are at building their little homes, humans are better at exploiting them. People have always found it hard to admire the structure of the hive without wanting to take some of it for themselves. They have taken the bees' wax and turned it into something new and entirely human. Men have used beeswax for lip salves and ear-plugs, for lubricants and sealants, for polishes and preservatives, for writing tablets and as a modelling material.[40] Beeswax has also always been credited with a strange and often macabre affinity with human skin. Once it had been realized that wax could be separated from honey, artists soon found that it could be tooled and coloured and had an uncanny resemblance to the texture of skin and human tissue. Wax was used in ancient 'encaustic' paintings, whose subjects seem much more vivid to us now than painted portraits of the same time. One Egyptian lady of AD 250 painted with encaustic wax looks as vibrant and present as Frieda Kahlo does in her paintings from seventeen centuries later, with the same eyebrows and slight moustache shining waxily out at us. Wax was used in casting models too. Giorgio Vasari, Renaissance author of *Lives of the Artists*, described waxen statues of Lorenzo de' Medici as so 'lifelike and well wrought, that they seemed no mere images of wax, but actual living men'.[41] By extension, if you wanted to place a curse on one of your enemies by fashioning his image and torturing it by sticking it with pins, you would use wax, because it would be more realistic than any other medium. Often these sinister dolls would include a lock of the enemy's hair and a torn shred from his clothes. To inflict agony on your enemy you would melt him on the fire, the wax and the human hair burning horribly together. Even the law seemed to believe in the malign power of wax dolls. Numerous cases of wax-doll curses cropped up in British courts during the Middle Ages. In the late fifteenth century a certain Marjorie Jourdemayne was burned at Smithfield for attempting to kill Richard III by murdering a waxen version of him. The fact that her method was so ineffectual, compared to what they were going to do to her, does not seem to have bothered her accusers.

Instead of killing the living through wax, the galleries of Madame Tussaud served the opposite purpose: the dead would be immortalized in a state of waxy vitality beyond the grave. Madame Tussaud, née Marie Grosholtz (1761–1850), first showed an aptitude for waxen art – or ceroplasty – when she was commissioned to make death masks from the severed heads of victims of the guillotine, during the French Revolution. Among her masterpieces are masks of the king and queen themselves, Louis XVI and Marie Antoinette, who look so peaceful and doll-like that it is almost impossible to remember the mess of bleeding heads accumulating in the prison cell that Madame Tussaud called her 'workshop'. Even today, the waxworks of Madame Tussauds in London are made predominantly of beeswax, because nothing else makes the texture of head and hands look human enough, though it is also what gives the models their pasty, bloodless, unconvincing hue.[42]

Waxwork models are frequently hideous, and not particularly useful. The same could not be said of another device which the beehive made available to human beings – the beeswax candle. These candles were being made at least as early as the New Kingdom of Egypt, 3,500 years ago. A few hundred years later they were made by the Romans, who coated threads of flax with pitch and wax to make sticks that they could burn for light. The main components of beeswax are wax esters, hydrocarbons and wax acids. The ancients did not know this, but they did know that when beeswax was melted down, strained and bleached it made candles much better than any others. Beeswax candles did not gutter and spit in the way that tallow candles – made from meat fat – did. (The nineteenth-century novelist William Makepeace Thackeray wrote of how 'Horrible guttering tallow smoked and stunk in passages.')[43] They gave off not a smell of burned meat, but the heavenly honeyed scent of the hive. Beeswax candles were always seen as special. At first they would be made on an ad hoc basis, at home, by servants and monks; later, in the twelfth century, they came to be made by professionals – the wax chandlers, practitioners of a respectable occupation. Chandlers set themselves up as independent craftsmen, and invented numerous categories of candle: slender 'tapers', long coils of 'trindles', square 'quarerres' for funerals, and tall 'perchers' for altar displays.

As is clear from this list, the major consumer of candles was the Church. Wherever Christianity spread in Europe, so did beekeeping and candlemaking. As candles were used more and more in church services, so Christians revered the bee and its works, with a kind of circular reasoning. The bee was a sacred being because it made sacred wax; and wax was holy because the bee was holy. The early Christians sometimes baptized themselves with honey and made crosses out of wax.[44] In Christian worship, the flame of the candle represented Christ, the light of the world; the wick represented his soul; and the wax was his spotless body. Wax was treated by Christians as more pure than any other substance. Bees were chaste (or so it was believed), like Mary; as Christ was born of Mary, so wax was born of virgin bees. (There was much vagueness about how wax was really made, right up until the eighteenth century.) On every Candlemas (2 February) the year's supply of candles would be blessed, on the day when Simeon had supposedly declared Jesus 'a light to lighten the Gentiles'.[45]

The Reformation was a great blow for the wax chandlers. Suddenly candles were forbidden in churches, and the monasteries that had supplied much of the wax were closed down. When Catholic Queen Mary was crowned, there was a brief flicker of hope for the industry. In 1559 a ceremonial paschal or Easter candle weighing 140 kg was set up under Mary's aegis in

Westminster Abbey. It was a short respite. When the Protestants got the Crown back, the candles went out again. In Elizabeth's reign (1558–1603), use of beeswax candles declined to the point where there was a large wax surplus, much of which was adulterated and then exported.[46] The sacred bee became a Catholic phenomenon rather than a generally Christian one. (Only since 1900 has there been any papal sanction for the use of candles that are not made out of beeswax.)[47] There is still a Worshipful Company of Wax Chandlers in the City of London. They still dine at least once a year by beeswax candlelight in a great hall. They drink mead from a giant silver loving cup decorated with scenes of merry beekeeping. Before dinner is served, they still say a grace for 'Thy Creature, the bee'. But the world that would make sense of all this is gone. We get the light we live by from sockets, and only our fancy light from candles, which, in any case, are usually made from paraffin and perfume. Beeswax candles are now just one more kind of exotic scented flame.

Hive Architecture

Even after candles had begun to lose some of their sacred connotations, there were other ways for men to express their respect for the works of bees. Sometimes they changed the bees' home to look more human; at other times they changed their own homes to look more like the architecture of the hive.

The earliest hives in Poland were all of the upright-log variety. Poland is a heavily forested country, and so its honey-hunters naturally associated bees with the hollowed-out trunks where the bees usually made their homes. When Poles graduated to hive beekeeping, they hollowed out their own tree trunks and set them, upright, in rows to make an apiary. Usually this was all that they did. But Polish beekeepers grew very fond of bees, and sometimes wanted to express this fondness. So occasionally, before settling their swarm, they would carve the hive log into the shape of a giant human being. In this way, bees would live in a human body, flying in at the chest or navel, and out at the back. These human hives were made elsewhere in Europe too, and sometimes took the form of the body of the Virgin Mary.

There were many other, more low-key ways in which men tried to make bees feel at home. They might hang hives under the eaves of their own house, to show how much the bees were part of the family. They made holes in stone walls for hives, so that the bees would feel more protected and permanent. As hive design developed, men added all kinds of nice flourishes, some homely and some grand. One of the first architectural drawings made by Sir Christopher Wren (1632–1723) was of an octagonal hive composed of three elegant wooden boxes, to be placed in a case of stone. It was a very practical design by the standards of the day – each of the three boxes opens at the bottom, and each is equipped with small flight entrances. A few years after Wren, the bee-master John Geddes designed a very similar hive, remarking that the bees needed to be saved from 'inconveniencies'; what they needed was a 'commodious' hive.[48] On a less grandiose scale, many beekeepers tried to make their bees' lives more commodious by fitting their skeps with cute little straw roofs as if they were thatched cottages, and festooning them with ribbons in times of celebration.

The original rustic skep beehive, made from wicker or straw, is very similar in shape to the huts that savage man built for himself. As human standards of living changed, so did those of the hive. Nineteenth-century hives were often absurdly ornate. In the 1820s a certain Thomas Nutt designed a hive which looks rather like an Aga oven, fiddly with multiple compartments, and complete with an internal thermometer and a tower with an acorn on top. In the twentieth century, by which point humans had finally managed to make box hives that fulfilled all the main practical requirements of bee management, the only way for hive design to go was up, and the skyscraper hive was born – an invention in the 1940s of a French Trappist monk called Pierre Dugat, who suggested that it would be an improvement to build multiple hives on top of one another, just like the many families in an apartment block. In the skyscraper hive there might be as many as seven queens, each in a separate colony jammed on top of another one.

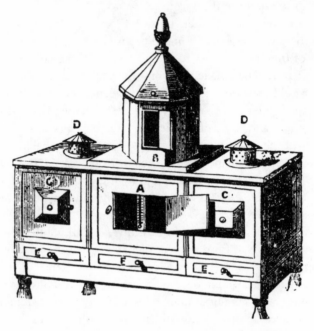

Thomas Nutt's elaborate Victorian hive, which included a thermometer to predict swarming

Just as men imposed their own architectural ideas on the hive, so the look of bees' own architecture has exerted a huge influence on human constructions. Throughout history, architects have emulated the building powers of bees by using honeycomb motifs in their designs. This has continued into modern times, and has led architects in wildly different directions as they have tried again and again to transpose the spirit of the beehive on to human living space. For example, both Antoni Gaudí (1852–1926), arguably the greatest architect of the late nineteenth century, and Le Corbusier (1887–1965), arguably the greatest of the first half of the twentieth, drew inspiration from the lives of bees, but with starkly diverging results.[49]

Gaudí was an eccentric but pious man, who died aged seventy-five when he was hit by a trolleybus on the way to vespers. He never married. For him, the beehive provided a way of fusing his Catholic faith with an almost Moorish love of organic natural forms. Gaudí's designs, often for Catalan chapels, were florid, symbolic and somewhat mind-boggling, with bizarre mixtures of reptilian metalwork and geometric forms so intricate and alive that you can barely look at them. Gaudí's most famous architectural invention was the parabolic arch, whose haunting shape was exactly the same as that made by the bees when they build a natural honeycomb, unaided by the hives imposed by men. From the 1880s onwards, these parabolas became Gaudí's trademark. He used them in entrances, in attics, in windows. Gaudí loved bees for all the reasons you might expect a frugal working-class Catalan vegetarian to love them. Honey was the only luxury food he allowed himself in a diet which otherwise consisted of green vegetables, wholemeal bread and yoghurt. Gaudí revered the bees as workers like himself, who knew the necessity and pain of sacrifice. He was a champion of the Catalan co-operative movement, and drew worker bees on posters to promote the cause. Meanwhile, in one of his most famous buildings, the Palacio Güell in Barcelona, he designed a vast honeycombed cupola, with some of the cells cut out so that light shines through – forming a kind of symbolic hive in which anyone entering can feel that they belong, like a bee.

It was a very different vision of bees that informed the work of Le Corbusier. Where Gaudí was anarchic, Le Corbusier was formal. Where Gaudí was traditional, Le Corbusier was a modernist through and through, the author of books called *Urbanism* (1925) and *The City of Tomorrow* (1929). It was he who declared, 'The house is a machine for living in.'[50] Where Gaudí borrowed from the exuberance of natural honeycomb, Le Corbusier used the box-shaped forms of the modern apiary. He read *The Dancing*

Bees by the scientist Karl von Frisch several times, making extensive notes in the margin. What excited him about the beehive was the cleanliness and efficiency, the dream of collective action. He stole from modern apiculture the idea of 'precise breathing' or

The honeycomb cupola of Gaudí's Palacio Güell

temperature control. Humans, he believed, would live best if they could accommodate themselves in 'individual living cells', self-sufficient housing complexes in which all needs could be met under a single roof. After the Second World War, he oversaw the reconstruction of Marseille, where he built vast, concrete vertical communities, each of which could house 1,600 people. Like the beehives of his native Switzerland, these human hives were raised off the ground on stilts. He hoped that the people living there could forget the troubles of war and learn to lead a perfect life, motivated by 'the desire to live efficiently and in harmony'.[51]

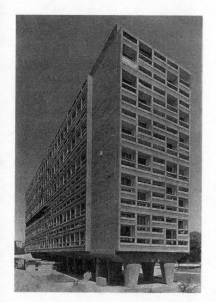 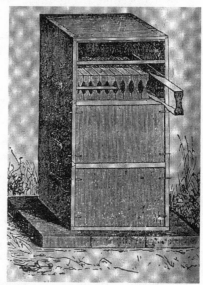

Le Corbusier's architecture compared with a 'progressive' beehive of the nineteenth century

But efficiency is not everyone's idea of harmony. When we look now at Le Corbusier's concrete blocks on stilts, it is easy to get the creeps. For many people, they have a sinister, totalitarian feel. Sometimes when people wish to disparage concrete apartment blocks in the style of Le Corbusier they refer to them as 'anthills' or 'beehives', implying that the collective has taken precedence over the individual. Little do they consider that this may have been precisely the architect's intention in the first place.[52]

Bees and the Human World

Bees have not only been a symbol of work for human beings, and a model for the industrious to emulate: they have also helped to determine the kind of work we do. Even now, human industry has not become so big that it can do without bees. Where bees are scarce, plants fail to pollinate, fruits fail to grow, species die out, and the air is less oxygen-rich for us to breathe. Even in these days of agribusiness, bees remain a more efficient way to pollinate an orchard than any other, and farmers will pay beekeepers to set up apiaries on their land. The bee-rental business began in a New Jersey apple orchard in 1909. Now, truckloads of honeybee colonies are heaved all over the United States. These hired bees will pollinate blueberries in Maine, cranberries in Cape Cod, cucumbers in Michigan, melons in Florida, and almonds in California, where 900,000 colonies are used for the purposes of pollination. It has been estimated that 'If no bees were available to rent, the California almond industry (which produces more than half the world's total) would disappear'.[53]

Evidently, the busy bee still helps us in tangible ways. But bees have also been important catalysts for change in the way in which we work. Some of the building blocks of civil society – property rights, law, taxation – were partly shaped in response to problems posed by the honeybee. Thus, while men have presumed to cultivate bees, the bees in turn have helped to develop some of the rules that regulate the workings of human life.

In all pre-capitalist societies where beekeeping has been prevalent, honey has been used in the payment of taxes and tithes. In a sense, honey *was* money. For example, in ancient India a king might expect to take a sixth of all honey production as his due. When the Aztec emperor Montezuma conquered nearby tribes, he added insult to injury by demanding 700 jars of honey as tribute from the poor people whose lives he had just overturned. Similarly, according to the ancient laws of Wales, the king was to receive a vat of mead from every village. This all sounds very archaic, but such practice is not entirely obsolete. As recently as the 1980s, when the vicious mujahidin ruled in Afghanistan, they would take one-tenth of the honey harvest from beekeepers.[54] We might look on such customs as primitive. But in other ways bees and honey have laid the foundations of the way in which we still organize our societies.

For example, bees were instrumental in establishing the foundations of property law. This was in part because they were such tricky little beasts. As one legal expert of the 1930s put it, 'Few animals are more prone than bees to furnish lawyers with attractive problems.'[55] Put another way, few animals have been simultaneously such a liability and such an asset.

In so far as bees have been an asset – as makers of honey – men have wanted to own them, for as long as there has been any concept of ownership. Initially disputes arose over wild honey nests. Who owned the honey in a tree? This was a problem which vexed Roman lawyers. Some said that the honey was owned by whoever owned the tree. Others disagreed, arguing that bees in a trunk were just like birds on a branch – not owned by anyone. The implication of this was that the honeycomb belonged to whoever was cunning enough to find it first – a kind of 'finders keepers' system. But, as with all such systems, this provoked as many complications as it resolved. For example, what were you to do if you found a bee tree where the honey was not yet ready to harvest? Were you to relinquish all claim on it? In Germanic and Slavic lands, honey-hunters would often mark bee trees with a special personal sign of ownership so that others would know to stay away. From the Ukraine there are records of hundreds of subtly different bark etchings. But this was a rather fragile solution, to say the least, and was rendered useless as soon as the bees decided to swarm off in search of a new home.

Much of the trouble with bees in Roman law lay with the difficulty of categorizing them. For Roman lawyers, there were two basic categories of animal: wild animals (such as lions or tigers) and domestic or tame animals (such as cows and dogs). Bees did not fit easily into either of these categories. Pliny the Elder argued that bees were a middle, indeterminate, category, 'neither tame nor wild';[56] though interesting, this idea hardly helped clear things up. These categories mattered because they determined property rights. In Roman law, you could fully own only animals which were tame. Wild animals could be possessed, but only temporarily. If your cow strayed on to the field of a neighbour, it was still your cow. But if, for whatever reason, you had captured, say, a wolf and brought him into your house, you would lose any claim on him as soon as he escaped. A wild animal that escaped was restored to its natural liberty.

This was all very troubling for people who wanted to own bees. The Roman lawyers said that you could turn wild animals into domestic ones by either taming them or enclosing them, but this was no good for bees either. No amount of tender loving care in a man-made hive can render bees cuddly and docile; nor can they really be enclosed – unless you are happy to kill them – because their honey-producing power depends on their leaving the hive to forage for nectar. Bees, it seemed, were a law unto themselves. New legal concepts had to be explored before men could own them.

The lawyer who provided much of the legal justification for bee ownership was Iuventius Celsus, 'a peculiarly irascible jurist of the early second century A.D.', who took violent exception to the notion that bees were simply wild.[57] Celsus argued that bees are not like wolves but like doves: while they will often leave human control, they will also habitually return. On account of this tendency to return, bees are not straightforwardly wild. To own bees, therefore, depends on separating the concept of ownership from the concept of possession. You can own a swarm of bees without physically possessing them all at any given moment.

This definition is still tricky, however, because bees are in fact *not* like doves. As individuals, bees may leave the hive in search of food with the intent to return. But when they leave their dwelling as a whole swarm it is for good, because they are looking for a new habitation. This raised an additional set of legal dilemmas. Does the owner of a swarm have the right to trespass on someone else's land if his bees go there? Who is liable if your bees sting someone else's animals?

Celsus had another argument, which dealt with these questions much more effectively than his dove analogy. A beekeeper, he argued, continued to own bees even when they swarmed out of his control, simply because he was the person who profited by their existence. The basis for ownership of bees in Roman law was ultimately economic and pragmatic. Beekeeping was an extremely profitable activity in the Roman world, and so it made sense for the law to act as if it were possible to own bees, whatever the complications. Ownership of bees was justified because it was practical. The beekeeper was the person who took on board both the profit of honey and the liability of bee stings. He worked for the bees, and they worked for him. The law would tame them for its own purposes.

And yet the magical thing about bees is that, after 8,000 years of attempts to domesticate them, they never really do work for men. They are industrious, but never industrialized. Large honey producers in advanced industrial countries often treat their bees as if they are slaves. Yet it is impossible to enslave them. The very biggest industrial beekeepers may manage as many as 10,000 colonies of bees at a time (though small-scale beekeepers can only manage up to 300). They drive as many as 120,000 km a year, extracting the maximum honey from their hives and moving the hives large distances to collect the maximum amount of nectar. Unlike the IBM gurus genuflecting before the brilliance of the 'waggly dance', the industrial beekeeper treats the worker bees as so many economic units. In the winter, he may use cyanide gas to kill off as many as 6,000 colonies of bees, as if they are just cogs in a machine he can treat as he likes. He may convince himself that the bees are working at his command. But this is not so. No amount of diesel and cyanide can deflect the bees from the purpose of their own industry.

Even if we steal their honey and wax at the end of the summer, they did not make their honey and wax to gratify us. Bees will never be made to love us, like dogs. We can never become part of the working colony. The old motto about industrious bees said, 'We work, but not for ourselves.' It should really have been, 'They work, but not for us.'

2

Sex

And tell with honeyed words the tale of love.

Erasmus Darwin, *The Botanic Garden* (1791)

How would human beings ever have made love to each other, without honey and bees to help them? It is scarcely an exaggeration to say that, in all cultures and at all times, honey and love have enjoyed a special relationship. Not only has honey been the literal food of lovers, it has provided them with the words for expressing their love – the honeyed kisses, the honey-sweet feeling of falling in love, the lover-like devotion of the bees to flowers and to their combs and queens – and even the day-to-day honey of 'Honey, I'm home.' And it is one of the peculiarities of bees and honey – both of which are at once deadly and innocent – that they have seemed just as appropriate in the service of sacred love as profane love. Psalm 119 speaks of 'Thy promise in my mouth, sweeter on my tongue than honey'. The love in question is pure and godly. Yet the words themselves are not very different from those used to express the utterly secular and lascivious love celebrated by Richard Barnfield in *The Affectionate Shepherd* (1594), with his desire that 'my lips were honey and thy mouth a Bee'.[1] The fact that honey is to be found in celebrations both of sexual ecstasy and of chaste worship is not just because different poets put their subject matter to varying uses. It is also because, although we cannot always articulate it, there is something genuinely weird and contradictory for humans about the love in the hive, something irreducibly puzzling, mysterious and strange.

In a beehive, love seems at once to be everywhere and nowhere. Honey is one of the most tempting substances known to man; yet the bees themselves, while surrounded by all this sweetness, have always appeared free from the burdens of lust and greed. 'Why', asks Maeterlinck, do the bees renounce 'the delights of honey and love, and the exquisite leisure enjoyed, for example, by their winged brother, the butterfly?'[2] For men, bees are at once the exemplification both of sex and of the denial of it. And, in the denial of sex, bees have promised to teach men about a higher love than the kind which usually ensnares them in the human world. But this promise is never realized. Try as we might, we are not like bees; and carnal passion, like honey, is still endlessly seductive to us.

Honey Love

Kama, the Hindu god of love, who gives his name to the *Kama Sutra*, is often shown riding on a kind of bee fused with a lion. This is how he appears on the side of honey jars in India. Kama's bee symbolizes the sweetness of love as well as its sting. He also uses strings of bees as missiles from the 'bow of love'.[3] As the fifth-century Indian poet Kálidása writes:

> A stalwart soldier comes, the spring,
> Who bears the bow of Love;
> And on that bow, the lustrous string
> Is made of bees . . .[4]

This brings to mind that other god of love, Cupid or Eros, who fires arrows at his victims, sometimes dipped in honey. Cupid also steals honeycomb. This was an irresistible subject for the old masters, some of whom painted it over and over again. Lucas Cranach the Elder produced nine versions in a single year, from 1530 to

1531. Cranach's paintings vary in size, but the scene is always more or less the same. The viewer's eye is dominated by a slender and naked Venus, standing, knowingly, with her left leg thrust confidently towards us. She is holding the merest wisp of white material, which only accentuates her nudity. In the background

The Indian god Kama riding a bee

are trees and a city. Next to her, but not commanding any of her attention, is her son, Cupid. He, a chubby child of two or so, is carrying a luscious-looking crag of dark golden honeycomb, but whining because some bees are stinging him. Most mothers, if their naked toddler were being viciously attacked by insects, might break away from displaying their porcelain body for a minute; they might at least look a little troubled; they might even comfort their child or go in search of some bandages. Not Venus. In this story, it is all Cupid's fault. He ought not to have stolen the honey in the

Cupid the Honey Thief by Lucas Cranach the Elder, 1530

first place. Besides which, the pain he feels in being stung by the bees is as nothing compared to the pain he inflicts with his own amorous arrows. In a depiction of the same myth by Albrecht Dürer in 1514, the Venus looks even more serene, though she is wagging her finger a little at poor swollen Cupid, as if to say 'Tut-tut.'

The earliest version of the story of Cupid and the bees comes from the fifth century BC, from the verse of a poet named Anacreon, a pleasure-seeker who was said to have died choking on a grape. Anacreon wrote astonishing poetry on how one might blot out the horrors of death and war with the joys of wine and the beauty of boys and women. He was also fond of bees and honey: 'A broken cake, with honey sweet / Is all my spare and simple treat,' begins one of his odes.[5] The thirty-fourth of his odes is a paean to this 'sweet insect', and the thirty-fifth is all about Cupid and the bees. Almost all subsequent versions of the story are copies of Anacreon, except that, in Anacreon's original, Cupid is not actually guilty of stealing the honey: he is merely lazing in some roses when a 'slumbering' bee awakens and like a 'snake with wings' attacks him. He runs to Venus. 'Oh mother – I am wounded through / I die with pain – in sooth I do!' To which, she replies:

> My infant, if so much
> Thou feel the little wild bee's touch,
> How must the heart, ah, Cupid! be
> The hapless heart that's stung by thee![6]

This ancient ode spawned countless imitators, particularly among the Elizabethan love poets. But, for the Elizabethans, the heart was not the only organ that the bee summoned up. More suggestive still was the mouth – a mouth which is capable of sucking, tasting, kissing and murmuring either sweet nothings or lies. This example, from Thomas Lodge (1558–1625), is typical:

> Love guards the roses of thy lips,
> And flies about them like a bee;

> If I approach he forward skips,
> And if I kiss he stingeth me.

The thought that love, like a bee, can sting heightens the poet's pleasure in the foreplay to the kiss. Lodge goes further in another of his poems, a madrigal of 1590:

> Love in my bosom like a bee
> Doth suck his sweet;
> Now with his wings he plays with me,
> Now with his feet.
> Within mine eyes he makes his nest,
> His bed amidst my tender breast;
> My kisses are his daily feast,
> And yet he robs me of my rest.
> Ah wanton, will ye?[7]

Honey and bees have allowed poets to move very quickly from airy talk of harmless flowers to disguised obscenity, which is often barely disguised at all. Take Richard Barnfield's bucolic shepherdess, who begs her love to 'sucke my sweet and my fair flower / That now is ripe and full of honey-berries'. She is probably flattering herself in pretending that the thing she wants him to suck will taste of honey. For here, as in so many other love verses, honey is used to stand in for the fluids of the human body, and to sweeten their appeal:

> Then would I lead thee to my pleasant Bower
> Filled full of Grapes, of Mulberries, and Cherries;
> Then shouldst thou be my Wasp, or else my Bee,
> I would thy hive, and thou my honey bee.[8]

But you can have too much of a good thing, and this syrupy substance has also signified the dark side of human desire. As well as being sweet, like true love, and delicious, like carnal love, honey can be treacherous and sticky, like false love. In the biblical Proverbs, 'the lips of an adulteress drip honey and her tongue is smoother than oil'.[9] Hamlet's mother, Gertrude, is 'stewed in corruption, honeying and making love / Over the nasty sty'.[10] Honey is a trap, designed to snare the innocent. In a Greek poem from 200 BC, Venus complains of Cupid, 'an evil heart and a honeyed tongue has he, for his speech and mind are at variance. Like honey is his voice, but his heart of gall.'[11] Naive diplomats who get into bed with sweet-looking girls, only to have incriminating photos pushed under their door next morning, are still said to have fallen into a honeytrap. Yet pure honey is precious and good, like married love. 'Or will ye be my honey? / Or will ye be my wedded wife?' asks Rob Roy.[12]

Hence, also, the honeymoon, so pure, so carnal, the true meaning of whose name cannot be agreed upon. Some believe it refers to an ancient Viking custom in which the bride and groom would eat honeyed cakes and drink mead for the first month of their betrothal. But, whatever the origins of the honeymoon, the use of honey in marriage rites has been a constant throughout the Indo-European world, and beyond. In an ancient Egyptian marriage contract, when the husband married the wife he would say to her, 'I take thee to wife . . . and promise to deliver to thee yearly twelve jars of honey.'[13] During Swedish wedding feasts of the sixteenth century, huge amounts of the stuff were consumed. At one wealthy wedding in 1567 they ate no fewer than 453 jars of honey. In Morocco, even now, the newly married groom is supposed to feast on honey for its aphrodisiac effects.

Apart from its nutritive properties, the use of honey in weddings has had a symbolic dimension, recalling the sympathy of humans with bees, and hinting at the desired harmony to come. During old Hindu wedding ceremonies, the bride's forehead, mouth, eyelids, ears and genitals were anointed with honey. As the bridegroom kissed the bride for the first time, he would say, 'This is honey, the speech of my tongue is honey, the honey of the bee is dwelling in my mouth and in my teeth dwells peace'. In Poland they used to sing a song at weddings that goes, 'Diligent is the life on a farm, like the life of the bee, and marriage is sweet as honey.' When the Polish bride got home, she would be blindfolded as she entered the bridal chamber and honey would be rubbed on her lips. In Bulgaria, wedding cake baked with honey is rubbed over the face of the bridegroom. The woman who performs this cere-mony has to exclaim, 'Be fond of each other as the bees are fond of this honey.'[14]

It would be easy to go on like this – about the honey crosses they smear on the newly-weds' door in Rhodes, or the wedding ribbons they used to tie on beehives in Brittany. The links between bees and love seem almost infinite. Yet the aspects of bees' lives invoked in the human language of love almost always fall outside the hive itself. The bees of love are the bees of the human garden, the bees of stinging, of flying, of sucking, the lovers of pretty flowers, the collectors of nectar, the bees of the air. Love in the hive, however, is an altogether different matter. While bees and honey are used incessantly to signify and to enhance the love of humans, for most of history humans have been utterly mystified about the sex lives of the bees themselves.

The Mystery of Reproduction

'None of them has ever been seen copulating', claimed Aristotle.[15] He had clearly never witnessed the queen bee copulating so hard with one of her drones that his genitalia get left behind and he dies, copulating so vigorously that the queen stores up enough sperm to lay hundreds of thousands of eggs. But then Aristotle would not have understood it even if he had seen it – he didn't know that the queen bee was female.

The mystery surrounding how bees reproduce themselves has been responsible for much of man's admiration for them. These strange, wonderful, honey-giving creatures, which, as so many of the ancients observed, clustered like 'bunches of grapes', seemed more fruit-like than animal in the way that they grew. Some ancient Greeks thought that the bees simply found their young inside plants – perhaps in olive flowers, since swarms of bees were most numerous at times when the olive harvest was most abundant.[16] The Greeks, for whom olives and honey were both fundamental foods, saw something olive-like about the bees' burnished little bodies. But still they were puzzled. Bees were enigmas left from nature, or from God – living, breathing creatures untouched by the mechanics of sex. This, along with the glorious golden combs they produced, was what made them sacred. Bees were both improbably fertile (of honey, of wax, and of themselves) and miraculously chaste – a combination unmatched in the animal kingdom. These qualities were admired by the ancients and were admired afresh and in new ways by the early Christian fathers; and there are still vestiges of this sexual mystery in much of our admiration for bees today.

Our ancestors were not fools to think about bees in these ways. Most of us, if we were left alone in a state of ignorance with nothing but a hive and the naked eye, would get a good deal less far than Aristotle did in the fourth century BC in unravelling the mystery of how bees reproduce; and we would surely end up agreeing with him that 'There is much difficulty about the generation of bees.' The hive contains not one but three different kinds of bee, none of which appears to have sexual intercourse (since the queen copulates away from the hive, and only a handful of times). Where on earth did they all come from? Aristotle broke the problem down into three basic possibilities. The first was that bees fetched their brood 'from elsewhere', for example from olive flowers, in which case they must either be spontaneously generated or be 'produced by some other animal'. The second possibility was that bees generated their young themselves. The third possibility was a mixture of the first and second: maybe the bees fetched the young drones, but generated the workers and the leaders themselves. But Aristotle discounted the possibility that bees ever 'fetched' their young: if this were the case, then young bees ought to spring up even where there were no mature bees to fetch them. This made no sense. Besides, what possible motivation could the bees have in collecting these young 'if they are neither their own offspring nor food'? Therefore, he concluded, the bees must generate themselves: possibility two was right.[17]

But Aristotle saw that the problem did not end here. If bees did generate their own young, it must be either with or without copulation. And, if copulation did take place, were bees created from the union of drones with workers or from the union of leaders with either drones or workers? None of the answers involving sexual intercourse seemed plausible to Aristotle, not least because he was unable to see how any members of the hive were straightforwardly one sex or another. It is here that his reasoning on the bees, so far watertight, starts to break down, thanks to his prejudices about human females. To Aristotle's mind, the workers could not possibly be females, because they have stings and 'Nature does not give weapons for fighting to any female.' But nor, he reasoned, could the drones be female and the workers male, since 'No males are in the habit of working for their offspring' as the workers do. Therefore, he wrongly decided, the workers must contain in themselves 'both sexes as plants do': the generative power of females and the fighting power of males. Nor could the leaders be entirely female, he thought, 'for the leaders are like both kinds at once, like the bees in possessing a sting, like the drones in size'. The bees must be like certain fishes, which lay eggs without having sex. By a process of elimination, Aristotle then came to his convoluted conclusions about how honeybees are made, which were more wrong than right: (1) None of the bees copulate (wrong). (2) The leaders generate more leaders, but also generate the ordinary bees (right). (3) The ordinary bees generate the drones (mainly wrong). (4) The drones do not participate in generation (wrong).[18]

Aristotle was the first in a long line of observers of the hive who have projected their image of human sexual relations on to the society of bees. In his case, deep-held convictions about how men and women should divide up their labour led him to false assumptions about insect life. His solution to the question of bee reproduction was as much political theory as entomology. In Aristotle's

Politics, women are relegated to the household along with children and slaves; only men fight and participate in the *polis* (or state). Aristotle could no more contemplate a fighting woman than he could envisage a man doing housework. Either scenario would be *unnatural*. This otherwise brilliant zoologist therefore missed the fact that numerous female insects, not just bees, *are* endowed with offensive weapons, and that many males do work for their offspring. And, from this false start, Aristotle shut off the only really plausible solution: that bees do engage in sexual intercourse after all.

To our modern eyes, Aristotle's theory of the fish-like androgyny of the bees looks like an absurdly elaborate way to get to the wrong answer. But we should remember that it is scarcely more fantastical than reality. Who on earth could have guessed the truth about the bees? That the queen is the only true female; that the workers are undeveloped females; that the drones are the only true males; that the queen lays some eggs before she has been fertilized by a drone, by a process of parthenogenesis; that these eggs result in drones; that the queen then copulates only during her few flights away from the hive, with carefully selected drones; that during a single encounter a drone fills her with enough semen to lay tens of thousands of eggs, before dying a hideous death; and that the rest of the queen's life is a process of unceasing egg-laying, after which the grubs that develop can be made into either workers or queens, depending on the way they are fed. It was not until 1771 that the mating flight of the queen was first proved, when a Slovenian beekeeper, Anton Janscha, observed the queen returning to the hive with a distended abdomen, carrying off with her 'the genital organs of the male'.[19] And it was much longer before this would be accepted as scientific fact. As late as 1776 the distinguished Royal Society could publish research from a Mr John Debraw, apothecary of Addenbrooke's Hospital, Cambridge, protesting that the microscope had 'blasted' people's belief in the necessary chastity of the bees[20] and arguing, in terms not far removed from Aristotle, that 'no real junction of the sexes takes place in bees', but that the queen lays eggs which are then impregnated, like those of fish.[21]

But seeing bees as like fish, or olives, was not the strangest answer that was devised to the question of how bees are made. The mystery of their origins provided fertile breeding ground for much more spectacular creation myths. If bees didn't make themselves, maybe they came direct from the sun, or from paradise? Were they human souls transformed into insects by the gods? Or were they the spontaneous production of death itself?

Bees have often been identified with gods. In one of the very earliest creation myths, the human race itself was born from a bisexual king bee. In early Christian lore, bees were meant to come from the wounds of Christ; or from his navel; or from tears which he shed while on the cross; or from the blood that dripped from his wounds – blood which the bees sucked like nectar from roses.[22] Similarly, in ancient Egypt, which was known as the Valley of the Bees, these sacred insects were said to come from the tears of the god Re. A papyrus in the British Museum reads:

> The god Re wept and the tears
> From his eyes fell on the ground
> And turned into a bee
> The bee made [his comb]
> And busied himself
> With the flowers of every plant;
> And so wax was made
> And also honey
> Out of the tears of the god Re.[23]

Thus the bees, having been created, at once become creators themselves.

For many early peoples the conundrum of the bees held out the promise that man could grasp the mystery of divine creation. Perhaps he could then even participate in that creation. In some cases the birth of bees seemed to give man the chance to fulfill his desire to create life and negate death. The clearest example of this desire can be found in the strange, troubling story of the oxen-born bees.

The Ox-Born Bee

Perhaps the oddest of all the various theories about the origins of bees is the belief that, instead of generating themselves, bees were spontaneously fashioned out of the dead body of an ox. As the Latin poet Ovid (43 BC–AD 18) put it, 'Swarms rush from the rotten ox; and one extinguished life produces a thousand.'[24] To us, the theory that a dead ox could give birth to living bees seems frankly nuts. Yet its oddity did not prevent it from being an accepted explanation for the existence of bees for more than 2,000 years. This was in part a reflection of the yearning of men to control these miraculous creatures, and thereby to control death itself.

In Greece they called this process of creation *bugonia*, meaning 'birth from an ox'. Since both oxen and bees were revered as sacred and useful animals, why shouldn't the death of one give rise to the life of the other? In the first century AD the poet Archelaeus called bees the 'factitious progeny of a decaying ox', and the agricultural expert Columella even believed that oxen and bees were related.[25] In Rome, they spoke of *apes facere*, the practice of making bees, as if men could manufacture them at will. Ovid writes of using a rotting ox to recover dead bees 'by art'.[26] Creating bees in this manner meant that man could dream of standing in relation to the bees as gods did to man. In Roman myth, the discovery of how to create bees from cattle was indeed a gift of the gods, coming via Aristaeus, the pastoral 'Honey Lord', who was meant to have first taught men the art of beekeeping. Here is how the poet Ovid tells the story: 'Aristaeus was weeping because all his bees had died, leaving the unfinished combs. His mother, Cyrene, tried to console him, and told him that Proteus [the sea god who could change himself into any shape he liked] would tell him how to obtain fresh swarms.' Eventually they find

Bugonia: making bees out of dead oxen. Wenceslaus Hollar's
illustration to Dryden's translation of the *Georgics*, 1697

Proteus sleeping near the mouth of the Nile and bind him in fetters so that he can't escape. 'Thus captured he was forced to speak and told Aristaeus that he must bury the carcass of a slaughtered ox, and that from it he would obtain what he wanted, for when the carcass decayed, swarms of bees would issue from it.'[27] The same story of death and resurrection is told in more elaborate form in Book IV of Virgil's *Georgics*, where Aristaeus's discovery of *bugonia* is mingled with the myth of Orpheus and Eurydice. Such was the enduring status of Virgil that Church fathers in the Middle Ages still treated *bugonia* as the literal truth.

But the superstition that the life of bees derives from the carcass of dead animals long predates these Roman poets. Versions of both the belief and its putting into practice seem to have begun in ancient Egypt, where the bull (the sacred 'kine') was worshipped for its fertility and the bee for its honey, and where belief in the reincarnation of the soul was strong. In the third century BC the Alexandrian poet Antigonos of Karystos was certain that *bugonia* was originally Egyptian, noting that 'In Egypt, if you bury an ox in certain places, so that only the horns project above the ground and then saw them off, they say that bees fly out, for the ox putrefies and is resolved into bees.'[28] In ancient Arabia there was a similar practice involving a dead horse.

But perhaps the best-known early variant on the *bugonia* legend is the biblical story of Samson and the bees, which is still referred to on the green-and-gold label of Lyle's Golden Syrup. In this case, it is a lion, not an ox, that creates the bees, but the message of one life giving rise to many is the same. 'Out of the strong came forth sweetness' reads the legend on the label (quoting Judges 14:14), which adroitly sidesteps the fact that the sweetness Samson was meant to have got from the dead lion was pure wild honeycomb, not man-made syrup.

The story of Samson, like the story of Aristaeus, is an allegory; but it does not follow that the ancient attachment to *bugonia* was merely fanciful or symbolic. People may have embellished its origins, but *bugonia* was not generally seen as a fairy tale. Killing a fresh

The famous label of Lyle's Golden Syrup refers to the story of
Samson and the lion

young ox was an expensive as well as a gruesome business – not
something you would undertake in a spirit of fancy. Much of the
writing on the subject is coldly practical, explaining exactly how
to kill and treat the animal. The most detailed account is from the
Geoponica, an anthology of ancient Greek and Roman farming
advice.[29] It states that the best time to perform *bugonia* is when the
sun enters the sign of Taurus, because this is when the weather and
plants are most favourable. Having chosen your ox, a good young
bullock of two to three years old, you should stuff his nostrils and
every orifice with rags and confine him to a narrow chamber ten
cubits (equivalent to the length of ten forearms) square, with four
windows and a door. Next, you should beat the poor creature until
his flesh and bones are crushed, but without drawing blood (as
Virgil puts it, 'pound his flesh to a pulp but leave the hide intact').
Then, you should lay his body on a heap of thyme, close the doors
and windows with mud, and leave the ox to rot for thirty days.
Finally, you should open the chamber for another eleven days to
air the carcass out, after which time miraculous clusters of bees will
be found 'pouring out, like a shower from summer clouds',[30] while
the ox himself is reduced to horns, bones and hair.

The point of the blocked nostrils, the small confined space and the clinically careful cudgelling was to do everything possible to trap the soul inside the ox after his elaborate death. That way, the soul could transfer direct to the bees. Sometimes, however, the animal would be simply buried in the ground instead of encased in a chamber, which was cheaper. Pliny recommended covering the ox in dung.[31] There were many different twists on the belief. It was sometimes said that the 'king bee' was produced from the brain or spinal marrow of the ox, and ordinary worker bees from the flesh, though of course no one could be sure.

The real puzzle, however, is why the *bugonia* superstition should have continued in any form, when its efficacy seems all too easy to disprove. So far from growing out of rotting oxen, bees loathe carrion and shun decaying animals. Surely it would take only a few fruitless experiments with rotting oxen to see that bees really were not produced in this manner. Yet, instead of dying out, the *bugonia* belief persisted well into Renaissance times and beyond. And it persisted not just as folklore but as current practice. *Bugonia* was transferred straight from ancient poetry to the prosaic British animal husbandry of early-modern Cornwall. In the 1650s an 'old Mr Carew of Anthony', a Cornish countryman, was claiming to have successfully manufactured bees from the carcasses of year-old calves. Carew, who kept his bees in hogsheads instead of hives, insisted that burying a dead animal at the end of April would produce honey-making bees in time for summer.[32] Beekeepers became very excited by Carew's claims, professing pleasure to discover that the stories of Virgil could be confirmed by 'modern English experience'.[33] Shakespeare, too, refers to the bee leaving 'her comb in the dead carrion'.[34] Ben Jonson wrote in *The Alchemist* (1610):

> Beside, who doth not see, in daily practice,
> Art can beget bees, hornets, beetles, wasps,
> Out of the carcases and dung of creatures,
> Yea, scorpions of an herb, being rightly plac'd?[35]

Even in the seventeenth century, an ox-born bee was for many not fiction but unremarkable 'daily practice'.

How is this possible? The first thing to acknowledge is that the plausibility of *bugonia* went with a general belief in spontaneous

Another picture showing *bugonia*. Here the bees are born from a lion as well as an ox. The man is trying to call the bees into the hive by 'tanging' them or making a loud banging noise

generation – a belief which was not challenged by science until later in the seventeenth century, and which actually recurred in various forms until well into the twentieth century. Spontaneous generation meant that living beings could be created from non-living matter. It was a common assumption, for example, that if you left pieces of cheese wrapped in rags in the corner of a dark room you could actually generate new mice, their lives springing from the cheese itself. By the same token, the stinking maggots found swarming on meat that was past its best were supposed to have emerged out of the meat itself, rather than simply feeding on its surface. It was also believed, both by classical and by

Renaissance thinkers, that you could generate wasps from asses, drones from horses, and hornets from mules. Spontaneous generation gave rise to all manner of weird cross-species breeding. There were even those who held that the vertebral column of a dead man could sometimes be converted into a snake.[36]

But in 1651 the English physician William Harvey, the genius who two years before had discovered the circulation of the blood, published a book which cast doubt on this entire way of thinking (though this was not in fact Harvey's intention in writing the book). In *Anatomical Exertations Concerning the Generation of the Animals*, Harvey used his researches into the development of chicken embryos to argue that the origin of the embryo of all living creatures was to be found in the egg: '*Omne vivum ex ovo.*' Harvey's work implied that no animal life could be generated without either sperm or egg. You could not produce something living out of something non-living. In 1668 Harvey's work was continued by the great Italian naturalist Francesco Redi, a man now better remembered for his poetry celebrating wine. In his *Experiments on the Generation of Insects*, Redi published the conclusions of his work with meat and maggots. Having put meat in various flasks, some sealed, some unsealed, Redi discovered that only in the unsealed flasks did maggots form. The maggots must have got there through flies laying eggs on the meat; if the flies couldn't get at the meat, no maggots could form. The idea that putrescence could engender maggots was therefore utterly false.

Redi reserved especial contempt for the 'ancient falsehood' of *bugonia*. He observed that numerous modern men – even men of science – were 'convinced that bees originate in the flesh of bulls'; but it simply could not be true. 'Bees are very dainty animals,' he pointed out; 'they not only do not eat dead flesh, but they loathe it extremely.' The story of Samson, Redi thought, might conceivably have some kind of basis in truth, because if the lion's carcass had been left long enough in the sun to become baked and desiccated – 'a mere dried skeleton' – the bees might indeed have built their combs in it. But in this case the story of Samson becomes an example not of *bugonia*, but of the ingenuity of bees. As for those Greek and Roman writers who thought you could really manufacture bees from enclosed and putrefying oxen, they were going about their experiments in exactly the wrong way: enclosing the carcass would actually mean that no insects could gather there, least of all fastidious bees.[37]

Redi's science was unarguable; but still the mystery remained. In fact the mystery grew. While Redi had refuted *bugonia*, he had done nothing to explain why people had believed it in the first place. It would take two more centuries before a satisfactory solution to this conundrum would emerge. Then, in 1894, a German scholar called C. L. Osten-Sacken argued that the 'contemptuous sneer' with which Redi and others treated *bugonia* was misplaced. Though it might appear stupid to us, 'A superstition so universal and so persistent . . . must necessarily have some foundation in fact.'[38] The ancients were not idiots. In reply to the question of why they didn't try to verify their belief in *bugonia* by experiments, Osten-Sacken argued that many did try the experiment, over and over again, and believed it to be successful. While their enclosure of rotting oxen was a 'preposterous' way to go about obtaining bees, it was a 'perfectly rational' way to produce an altogether different insect, the *Eristalis tenax*. This insect, commonly called the drone-fly, lays its eggs on putrescent animals and, crucially, looks remarkably like a honeybee in colour, shape and 'hairy clothing', the main difference being that it has only two wings to the honeybee's four. Moreover, Osten-Sacken noted, the hermetic sealing of the ox, which Redi had ridiculed, would actually encourage the growth of the *Eristalis tenax*, since its larva are aquatic and require a pool of stagnant water in order to flourish.

Not everyone has been convinced by Osten-Sacken's theory. Several classical scholars of the twentieth century have pointed out that, even if the ancients had succeeded in producing drone-flies, surely their belief in *bugonia* ought to have vanished as soon as they discovered that these fake bees produced no honey?[39] But Osten-Sacken had already provided an answer. Practitioners of *bugonia*, he wrote, both ancient and modern, were suffering from the 'mental inertia' to which all human minds are prone.[40] They were trapped in a syllogism. They knew that honey came from bees. They believed they had created bees. Therefore they could not but believe that honey would eventually follow. And when it didn't, there were enough charlatans around to persuade them that it had – like Mr Carew of Cornwall, who must have been simply lying.

As an explanation for why otherwise rational men performed this bizarre experiment for so long, Osten-Sacken's masterly account cannot be bettered. And yet *bugonia* cannot be entirely explained by reference to reason. For this belief was not simply a delusion: it was also an outlet for one of the most profound human desires – the desire to conquer death. Virgil understood this. The description of *bugonia* in Virgil's *Georgics* is, at first, quite literal and practical. But later it becomes grafted on to the myth of Orpheus – 'piteous Orpheus', who loses his beloved wife, Euridyce, to the shades of the underworld, and rages with a bottomless grief. When, at the end of the poem, Virgil depicts Aristaeus slaughtering four bulls, they are offered in honour of dead Euridyce; and when the 'huge and trailing clouds of bees' emerge from the oxen's bellies it is 'a miracle strange and sudden to tell of' – the miracle of resurrection, the realization of the ardent hope that repellent destruction can lead to fresh life.[41]

The nineteenth-century French historian Jules Michelet called the fourth *Georgic* a 'song full of immortality, which, in the mystery of the transformations of nature, contains our dearest hope: that death is not death, but a new life beginning'. It was a hope that Michelet himself knew well, having lost his father and, four years later, his son. In his work *L'Insecte*, he recalls wandering through the cemetery of Père Lachaise in Paris, in the year 1856, in a disconsolate mood, looking for the tomb shared by his father and son, longing hopelessly for his dear relatives to rise from the dead like Lazarus. He imagines their living faces coming back to him. As he approaches their tomb, he sees a cluster of what seem to be about twenty bees. For a moment he imagines that these unthreatening creatures are offering him friendship in his time of misery. They seem to be consoling the spirits of his father and his son, even reanimating them. But, looking a little closer, Michelet suddenly perceives that these are not bees at all. They are too luminous, and they have only two wings, not four. Forty years before Osten-Sacken, Michelet's epiphany in the cemetery gave him the idea that Virgil must have been mistaken about oxen-born bees: that the bees in question were a different insect. Unlike Osten-Sacken, however, he focuses less on the mistake than on the poetry it created. These fake bees, these 'noble Virgilian bees', might not be able to create any honey. Yet they are the 'daughters of death', capable of bestowing the 'honey of the soul, the hope for the future', which is more precious still.[42]

We may laugh at the *bugonia* of the ancients, or recoil from it. But no one who has ever lost a beloved is entirely immune to the human impulse that it feeds off.

Chastity

Their seemingly miraculous creation has not been the only aspect of generation that men have praised in bees. For most of history, bees have been revered for possessing another faculty missing from humans: a preternatural ability to abstain from sex. Cole Porter, needless to say, took exactly the opposite line:

> Birds do it. Bees do it.
> Even educated fleas do it.
> Let's do it,
> Let's fall in love.[43]

But our ancestors, though they knew less, were closer to the truth. Bees don't fall in love, and most of them don't even 'do it'. It is positively perverse that parents explaining the 'facts of life' to their children are said to be talking about 'the birds and the bees', given that the birds, unlike humans, hatch out of eggs, and most of the bees do not indulge in sexual activity at all. For teenagers acquainted with entomology, this euphemism could result in no end of sexual confusion. Certainly the bees provide a very curious and not very encouraging model for adolescent love – one in which all the boys want to sleep with a single girl, but the only ones who manage to do so are castrated and killed in their moment of success, while everyone else dies a virgin.

Almost all ancient observers noted the unsuitability of bees as a guide to human sexual relations. The passionlessness of these creatures, while admirable, was what made them fundamentally unlike men. As Virgil writes in Book IV of the *Georgics*:

> Most you shall marvel at this habit peculiar to bees –
> That they have no sexual union: their bodies never dissolve
> Lax into love, nor bear with pangs the birth of their young.
> But all by themselves from leaves and sweet herbs they will
>   gather
> Their children in their mouths, keep up the [kingly] succession
> And the birth-rate, restore the halls and the realms of wax.[44]

While he invites the reader to 'marvel' at this spectacle of selfless virginity, Virgil is not inviting us to follow it. Their very chastity means that the bees cannot be a model for mankind, since men and women are unavoidably committed to having sexual union, and women to having labour pains. For Virgil, sex and childbirth are imperfect devices, but thoroughly human ones. The whole of the *Georgics* can be read as a plea to understand the limitations of mortal human flesh. The chaste perfection of the bees is not, ultimately, to be emulated, because we are human, and bees are not.

For the early Church fathers, on the other hand, the chastity of the bees *could* be a model for humans, both literal and allegorical. Monks and nuns have always been among the most enthusiastic beekeepers (it has been said that the art of beekeeping in Britain never quite recovered after the Reformation), and their attachment to the bees who supplied them with their honey and mead resonated with their own vows of chastity. In his *De virginibus*,

St Ambrose (*c.* 340–94), whose emblem was a beehive, exhorts Christians:

Let, then, your work be as it were a honeycomb, for virginity is fit to be compared to bees, so laborious is it, so modest, so continent. The bee feeds on dew, it knows no marriage couch, it makes honey. The virgin's dew is the divine word, for the words of God descend like the dew. The virgin's modesty is unstained nature. The virgin's produce is the fruit of the lips, without bitterness, abounding in sweetness. They work in common and their fruit is in common.[45]

For medieval Christians, bees came to represent that combination of productivity, order and chastity towards which the monastic life aspired. Around 1260, Canon Thomas of Cantimpre, a French Dominican canon, wrote an influential text, *The Book of Bees*, in which he presented the chaste community of the hive as an example for those in holy orders.[46] Monks could learn from the bees' attachment to a single 'king' (a single pope), from their unity, and, above all, from their supposed virgin purity. Cantimpre, like many other medieval Christians, implied that bees themselves were actually practising Christian chastity – that their restraint was holy.

St Ambrose, who commended the chastity of bees

Looked at rationally, the belief that insects are capable of religious action is also perfectly ridiculous. You might say that these early Christians, like so many others before and after, were doing little more than projecting their own values on to the hive. But consider for a moment why it is that they might have chosen this particular vehicle – the hive – as a medium for expressing these particular values. It was not just that the early Christian fathers had read their Virgil and knew – or thought they knew – that bees have 'no sexual union'. It was not just that monks enjoyed honey on their bread and wanted to justify their pleasure as holy. It was also that the bees supplied the Church with one of its most important props of holiness, the waxen candles without which Catholic rites could hardly take place and churches would be places of darkness. And this wax, produced in such fertile profusion by the chaste bees, came to symbolize the most significant chastity of all: that of Mary, mother of God. As it says in an Old English Christian text, 'Wax bitokeneth the maydenhed of Marie, Cristes modir.' Like Mary, the wax-producing bees possessed a mystical combination of fecundity and virginity. Bees 'produce posterity, rejoice in offspring, yet retain their virginity', says the hymn that is sung on Holy Saturday in honour of the paschal candle.[47]

The medieval holiness of wax lost some of its glow from the sixteenth century onwards, under the combined pressures of the Reformation and the growing sugar industry. On the other hand, the link between the cult of the Virgin Mary and the cult of beeswax lingered on well after scientists in the eighteenth century discovered that bees were less chaste than had been previously thought. Even as late as 1907 *The Catholic Encyclopedia* stated that beeswax was the most appropriate symbol for the flesh of Jesus Christ born of a virgin mother.[48] Yet, as always, the products of the bee are in human hands instruments both sacred and profane. It was this same beeswax that was said to be used by brothelkeepers to reseal the hymens of prostitutes wishing to offer their clients a virgin experience of an altogether different kind.

In a sense, the Catholic cult of virgin beeswax continues an older, pre-Christian, set of beliefs in which bees are supposed to loathe the debauchery of men. According to the first-century Greek essayist Plutarch, bees are irritable towards men who have enjoyed sexual intercourse with women, and seek to punish adultery. Columella, likewise, advised the would-be beekeeper that 'Above all he who takes the pains to keep bees must have the precaution, when he wishes to examine the combs, to abstain from the pleasures of love the night before.' The Italian writer Giovanni Rucellai, in his sixteenth-century work *Le Api*, commented that bees could not bear to smell the breath of an unchaste person. The same belief has been found among the tribes of the Sema Nagas and the Angami Nagas in Nagaland, near Burma, where honey-hunters insist on not having sex the night before going on an expedition to take a bee's nest. If anyone breaks this rule, the bees supposedly will sting him. In the Yemen it is said that bees love the pure of heart. Well into the twentieth century it was still thought in much of eastern Europe that bees were able to discern whether a girl was a virgin or not. In a humiliating ritual not unlike a witch test, before she got engaged a young woman would have to walk through an apiary. If she got stung she was clearly a slut and must be rejected. But if she emerged unscathed her fiancé could marry her without fear that he was getting damaged goods.[49]

The bees' apparent hatred of lust has been linked to their hatred of all things unclean. Numerous writers, ancient and modern, have observed how carefully the bees clean their hives in spring, and believed that they recoiled from bad smells, such as garlic and onion. The Revd Charles Butler told the beekeeper, 'Thou must be chaste, cleanly, sweet, sober, quiet and familiar, so will they love thee, and know thee from all others.'[50] Again and again, men have used the hive to stand in moral judgment over themselves.

In the early twentieth century, however, the Austrian Rudolf Steiner came up with a new take on the sexual restraint of these insects. The bees were actually denying themselves sex in order to suffuse human beings with their love. Steiner, a wearyingly prolific writer, is mainly remembered now for starting the Steiner schools and for founding, in 1912, the Anthroposophical Society, a movement which tried to put man in touch with his higher spiritual consciousness. Bees provided one vehicle for this journey of the soul. Steiner, like hundreds before him, had noticed that the sexual element in bees was 'very strongly suppressed', and that this set them apart from other insects such as ants and wasps. For Steiner, nothing in the universe was accidental, and the reason that the sex drive of the bees was repressed must be in order to achieve a higher kind of love:

The whole beehive is permeated with life based on love. In many ways the bees renounce love, and thereby this love develops within the entire beehive. You'll begin to understand the life of bees once you're clear about the fact that the bee lives as if it were in an atmosphere pervaded thoroughly by love. But the thing that a bee profits from the most is that it derives its sustenance from the very parts of the plant that are pervaded by the plant's love life. The bee sucks its nourishment, which it makes into honey, from the parts of a plant that are steeped in love life. And the bee, if you could express it this way, brings love life from the flowers into the bee-hive. So you'll come to the conclusion that you need to study the life of the bees from the standpoint of the soul.[51]

Where does this leave humans? Answer: with honey to spread on our bread. But for Steiner, honey is not just a sensual pleasure like jam or marmalade. It is higher food. The chaste bees are doing more than feeding us. Through their chastity, they are somehow giving us back our souls. 'At the moment when you eat honey, it creates the proper connection and relationship between the airy and fluid elements in the human being.' Thus, Steiner reasons:

By means of the honey, the bee colony returns to humans the amount of effort the soul needs to expend in their bodies. Whenever someone adds honey to their food, that person wants to prepare the soul element for properly working upon the body, for breathing, as it were. This is why beekeeping can be a great aid to human culture: it makes human beings strong.[52]

This is wacky stuff, by anyone's standards. Thinking that bees are choosing to transfer 'soul' from flowers to honey to humans is in many ways odder than thinking that bees can be born from dead oxen. But Steiner's writing on the bees is expressive of a deep yearning to revert to an older way of thinking, unspoilt by reason and science – to go back to that long period, far before the songs of Cole Porter, when most of western Europe believed that bees were chaste, and that their ruler was a king. In fact both Steiner's soul food and the ancient lore of the king bee indicate a hankering for natural order – for the way things used to be.

The Āb *or Father Bee*

In the part of the Arab world which we now call Yemen they have long produced honey of fabulous quality, even by Arab standards, though the region is more famous globally for its coffee. If you drank a cup of coffee any time between the sixteenth and the eighteenth centuries, in the coffee houses of London or Paris or Amsterdam, the chances were that it came from the Yemen city of Mocha. In comparison with its desert neighbour, Saudi Arabia, Yemen was Arabia Felix, Fortunate Arabia, a fertile place with a strategic location at the entrance to the Red Sea. Its middle high-lands were perfectly suited to coffee plantations. Nowadays these highland areas are increasingly planted with *qat*, a mild stimulant whose leaves are chewed, and the economy of Yemen is powered more by oil than by coffee, which is another story. But further to the south, in the ancient valleys of Hadramaut, they still produce not coffee but luxury honey, which the rich men of the region consume in copious amounts – 'lovely golden round combs almost too beautiful to cut'.[53]

For a long time, north and south Yemen were divided; they joined up only in 1990, a fallout from the end of the Cold War. Previously, the north had been under separate Muslim rule, first as part of the Ottoman Empire and then, as the Yemen Arab Republic, by independent imams. For twenty years the south had been a Communist state, the People's Democratic Republic of Yemen. Before that, from 1839 to 1969, the south of Yemen was under British control. The man largely responsible for keeping southern Yemen British for so long, for good or for ill, was Harold Ingrams, who brokered the so-called 'Ingrams Peace' in the 1930s, bringing some 1,400 tribes who had been warring for generations to agreement under a British protectorate. Ingrams was a scholar of the region as well as a diplomat, and wrote a travel book called *Arabia and the Isles*, which exudes the kind of imperial serenity it was impossible to replicate after the Second World War – a combination of romantic love for the beauty and wisdom of Arabia with a rugged confidence in his own Western values.

Arabia and the Isles contains a discussion of the sex life of the bees that is as revealing about British attitudes as about Yemeni ones. Ingrams describes being shown round a lovely kitchen garden in the Du'an area of the Hadramaut, the honey-producing heart of Yemen. His host, Ahmed Ba Surra, leads him through a shaded haven of 'dates, elbs and lime trees, and neat beds of carrots, onions, lady fingers, tomatoes and pumpkins', before stopping to look at a beehive 'consisting of circular sections about a foot in diameter' fitted into a wall, with a small hole for the bees to enter and leave the hive. Ba Surra remarks that 'the bees have an *āb* (father) . . . Sometimes a new *āb* arises and it leaves the hive and goes away a short distance followed by some of the others'. Ba Surra then shows Ingrams how he swarms the bees to a new hive by removing this '*āb*' in a little wooden cage, at which Ingrams exclaims:

> 'Why, it's just what bee-keepers do in England . . . Only we call the *āb* the queen, for she is the mother of all the bees. We put her in a cage, too.'
>
> But Ba Surra could not understand this. 'But it is the leader,' he said, 'and whoever heard of a woman leading an army like that?'
>
> 'Ah well, you know, the children always go after their mother. It's just that this mother has so many children.' I thought of the old woman who lived in a shoe but did not see how she would help the story. 'With the bees it is the women who are important; as a matter of fact all the bees who gather the honey are women, but they don't breed.'
>
> 'But they are the soldiers,' said Ba Surra, 'they have the swords to sting with. The bee women are bigger and don't sting.'
>
> 'We believe they are the males,' said I, 'the strongest of them marries the queen and then is killed by her. The workers kill the rest.'
>
> This was sheer revolution. I could see how his mind was working. 'There are tribes in other parts of the world where women do the fighting,' I added. Ahmed was too polite to contradict me. He just shook his head in doubt.

The punchline of this delicate cultural exchange, in which each man is tempering his beliefs for the sake of the other, comes with Ingrams thinking to himself that it was not so very odd that Ba Surra could only conceive of the queen bee as male. 'After all, we once thought the same thing . . . If some wise fool had not discovered the truth, women might never have thought of votes.'[54]

Ingrams's conversation in the lovely valley of Du'an echoes the evolving pattern of Western ideas about the sex of the leader bee over the centuries. At first men assumed, like Ba Surra, that the leader bee was a 'father': that leaders were men, and so the leader bee must be male. Then the microscope told them that she was female. Some, like Ba Surra, just wouldn't or couldn't believe it. Others came to terms with this cataclysm by ceasing to think of the largest bee as a leader and by instead playing up her role as a mother, like Ingrams invoking the old woman who lived in a shoe. But still others, like Ingrams too at the end of the exchange, thought of 'parts of the world where women do the fighting' and wondered if the hive didn't offer an image of a society with very different roles for women from those prescribed in modern Europe. If the hive wasn't patriarchal, perhaps it was a matriarchy – a matriarchy which might even teach human women to dream of a better world. A lot depended on the sex of the bee at the top.

The King Bee

'They have a king,' wrote Shakespeare of bees in *Henry V*.[55] In this, he wasn't taking artistic licence: he was simply agreeing with almost every writer on bees who came before him, from Pliny to Chaucer. The Romans referred to the biggest bee in the colony as '*rex*', '*dux*', '*imperator*', '*ductor*' – all masculine terms for the masculine role of ruler. In Greek, this remarkable creature was usually *basileus*, another masculine word for a male ruler. The big bee – so different in appearance from the rest, and so central to the buzzing lives of all the others in the hive – has always stood out. And to human eyes it has seemed obvious that this singular creature must be the ruler of life in the colony, in the same way that human rulers command human states. And, just as it has more often than not been assumed that human rulers must be male, so it was assumed that this long, regal bee must be masculine too.

Not everyone in ancient times thought the queen had to be a king.[56] But those who treated the big bee as female usually dropped the ruler analogy at the same time. Aristotle tells us that some of his contemporaries called the ruler bees 'the mothers, from an idea that they bear or generate the bees'.[57]

The ancients also sometimes revered bees in general as feminine beings. In the ancient world there were numerous bee-goddess cults, the most famous being the cult of Artemis of Ephesus. In Greece, *melissae* were female bee-nymphs. This association of bees and mothers reoccurred in the Middle Ages. Welsh laws of the 1200s refer to the *modrydaf* or 'mother of the bees'. Anglo-Saxons called the queen bee the *beo-modor*, or bee-mother, and in Russia she was the *mat* or *matka* – the mother or little mother.[58] St Ambrose, who was so in awe of the chastity of bees, admired the 'blessed and marvellous mother bee'. In various popular medieval 'swarm charms' – the incantations that beekeepers used in order to control their hives – the largest bee was also called a 'mother'. 'Humble little bee / little womb-mother,' says one from Austria.[59] We should not assume from these scattered references, however, that people actually *knew* that the leader bee was female. More often than not these 'bee-mother' motifs were no more than symbolic. They had no greater significance than references to 'mother nature', and did not affect the general orthodoxy of the king bee.

The reign of the king bee persisted for centuries. As one historian has described, the 'embarrassing discovery' in science that the king had female genitalia 'remained controversial until the 1740s. "A Queen-Bee", explained an encyclopedia in 1753, was the "term given by late writers to what used to be called the King-Bee".'[60] Despite having lived under the reign of the virgin queen

Elizabeth I, the entomologist Thomas Moffett took it for granted that the ruler of the hive must be a king, since males were more 'strong and able' than females.[61] William Lawson's work of 1618 on the husbandry of bees likewise refers to the 'master bee', as does John Levett's of 1634: 'These master bees are absolute in their authorities and command.'[62] Moses Rusden, who was the bee-master to Charles II of England, unsurprisingly also revered the masculinity of the king, this 'fair and stately bee'.[63] Until the microscope definitely proved otherwise, the hive was usually a patriarchy.

In Renaissance times, however, a number of writers had already begun to guess, surmise or in some cases even observe that the queen bee was female. The first to observe it was probably the Spaniard Luis Mendes de Torres, in 1586, though he still believed that bees were chaste.[64] He was followed, in the seventeenth century, by a whole series of English bee experts – Charles Butler, Richard Remnant, Samuel Purchas – who, without knowing it for sure, asserted the femininity of the leader bee. It might be expected that, having recognized this sublime creature as female, these writers would also come to change their views of the potential of human women to play a great role in society, and even hold high office. Interestingly, however, it usually went the opposite way. Even when they saw the hive as 'Amazonian', the bee-men were frantic to show that the sexual order of the hive need not disrupt that of the human colony.

The Amazonian Hive

The hive was an 'Amazonian or feminine kingdom', wrote Charles Butler in 1623, referring to the mythical tribe of female warriors. With the publication of Butler's *The Feminine Monarchy*, British bee writing entered a new era, discarding many of the old wives tales through which it was previously approached.[65] Butler was a true Renaissance man, who had also penned works on logic, music, English grammar and the vexed question of marriage between cousins. Though he fully shared the traditional admiration for the bees, swooning before their industry and the beauty of the honey cells, he also brought a fresh rigour to his subject. 'Every living thing doth breed Male or Female of his kind and experience doth teach us that bees do yearly breed.' Butler was fairly sure he had seen testes in the drone – 'two lawful witnesses of his masculine sex' – and also noticed that 'the more the Drones are, the more and greater are the swarms'. From this he concluded that the apparently useless drone was actually 'the Male-Bee', which he believed (wrongly) mated with the female worker bees. These 'lady-bees' managed everything in the hive, under the rule of their lady queen, this being a kingdom of 'Viragos' or 'Amazons'.[66]

Aristotle was wrong, complained Butler, to call the governor a *'basileus* or *rex'*. In fact 'the males have no sway at all', being entirely subject to the females. The drones are 'but vassals to the honie-bees, which as they do excel them in vertue and goodnesse, so do they also in power and authoritie, ruling and over-ruling them at their pleasure'. Though he admitted that it went against the grain, Butler insisted that the fact of the queen bee was true. He was adamant, however, that the sexual set-up of his hive was not to be mimicked by humans: 'Let no nimble tongued sophisters gather a false conclusion from these true premises.' The beehive did *not* license women to 'arrogate to themselves the like superioritie'. Besides, if human women wanted the power of the female bees, they should also emulate their 'singular virtues' – their 'temperance, chastity, cleanliness'. If by any chance women should find themselves saddled with a husband as useless as the drones, they should 'use the poor Skimmington as gently as they may; especially in private, to hide his shame'. And nature had not entirely turned itself upside down in constructing the bee's society. Butler noted approvingly that, while the females had the sovereignty, the males had the 'louder voice', just like the crowing cock. This was because 'nature teacheth that silence and soft voice becometh [the female] sex'.[67] Butler hadn't noticed that, just before the swarming of the hive, the queen makes a shrill, piping cry, louder than any other sound emanating from the hive.[68] Or, if he noticed it, he ignored it.

Richard Remnant, another early modern bee expert, was, in his discourse on bees of 1637, still more explicit about what messages human women could read in the hive. Yes, Remnant argued, the head bee was a female. But she was also 'a very gentle and loving Bee, and will not sting'. In other words, the queen bee might be a ruler, but she never forgot her feminine virtues. And did it follow from her example that women could govern states? Sometimes – but only in cases when 'nature' had disabled men from governing. As for governing in their own households, there was nothing more unnatural than 'obeying husbands' and 'commanding wives'. The true wisdom of the hive pointed in an altogether different direction. Beekeepers, Remnant ingeniously proposed, could use the 'experience of ruling bees' to teach them 'how to rule most women', for, like the bees, women were sensitive, passionate creatures who could be 'very industrious' if 'kept in good order' by their master, but the cause of great 'hurt and trouble' when mishandled.[69]

The logic of Butler and Remnant continued in bee writing of the eighteenth century, after entomologists' discoveries had confirmed that the king was a queen. Some used the queen bee as an excuse to flatter contemporary queens, but few wanted the 'Amazonian kingdom' of the bees to be replicated among humans. Now that surmise had become fact, it was all the more imperative that women should not get the wrong idea about what queen bees signified. In *The Female Monarchy* (1744), John Thorley – yet another English clergyman beekeeper – noted that God had subjected women to men in Genesis. He was dismayed by the injustice of the hive, where the female was crowned with 'regal dignities and all the ensigns of royalty', while the men were 'downgraded, treated with the utmost contempt'. He took some small comfort, however, in insisting that at least the queen preserved her chastity, the most 'precious possession' of every female. It was scandalous to imagine, as some did, that the drones had sex with the queen, as if she were some sort of 'common prostitute, a base, notorious, impudent strumpet, the most hateful and abominable whore with gallants by the hundreds'.[70]

Those who saw the bees as moral exemplars could not bear it if the sexual practice of these insects departed from the most exacting human norms. For Jean-Baptiste Simon, a French bee-lover writing in 1740, the 'republic of the bees' – this 'charming school' – offered a humbling message from nature about how men should live: in civil and industrious harmony. The bees represented all the 'principal virtues' in a state of absolute 'perfection'. Having set the bees up as paragons like this, it would have been rather a blow to Simon if their sexual arrangements had been anything less than perfect. And so he made sure that they weren't. It was quite wrong, he argued, to suppose there was just one royal bee in the hive – a '*roi*' or '*reine*'. This would be unnatural! Clearly there must be both a king *and* a queen: the king to rule, and the queen to act as mother. Together this noble couple would perpetuate the 'royal race', and only the royal race, leaving the reproduction of lowly worker bees to the workers themselves, and of drones to the drones. In this way the classes of the hive could be kept rigidly apart, and all the sexual and social proprieties could be preserved. Simon saw those who believed there was just one ruler bee, which might perpetuate the whole hive, as altogether fanciful. 'It is not possible that a single bee . . . could carry enough eggs to produce forty or fifty thousand little bees.' Besides, it would be beneath the dignity of the queen to behave in this filthy way.[71]

But, as the eighteenth century progressed, the facts about the queen bee became more and more undeniable. One reaction to the news that the king was actually a queen was to downgrade her altogether: if she was female, she must not be so special after all. In 1780 John Keys, who called himself a 'practical bee-master', complained about the mystification of the queen bee, comparing her to Eve, whose power over Adam had made him do a 'very foul thing'. Whereas most other observers had praised the beauty and 'stately' grace of this creature, Keys saw her as an ungainly figure, 'not unlike a tall woman in a short cloak'. She was not truly a queen in any case, wrote Keys, but simply an undignified breeding machine. She certainly did not sanction women at large to enthrone themselves. Similar views were expressed in 1790 by the Abbé della Rocca in France, who insisted that the queen was not 'responsible for the government, nor for public order, nor for the maintenance of the laws'.[72] Such protestations are proof, if proof were needed, that when we search for social truths in the natural order we generally find exactly what we are looking for. And not many men in the seventeenth and eighteenth centuries were looking in the beehive for proofs of female superiority.

A notable and possibly unique exception, however, was the French poet Jacques Vanière (1664–1739), who followed Virgil in making poetry out of the bees, but did not follow him in treating the queen as a king. In Vanière's poem *The Bees* the beehive is a standing rebuke from nature to French society for mistreating its women. Vanière was familiar with the scientific work of Giacomo Maraldi, whose *Observations on the Bees* (1712), based on work done with a glass observation hive, had announced the queen as unequivocally female. But for Vanière the implications of this work went far beyond the laboratory. In France, women were prevented from ruling by the Salic Law, which insisted on a male succession. Among the bees, however, 'no *Salique* Law excludes the female line'. These insects showed the 'same sound policy' as the Amazons in elevating women. What makes Vanière's poem so remarkable is that he reveres the queen bee not only as a holder of sovereignty, but also as a prodigious lover, reversing the usual pleas of chastity:

> She has her am'rous train;
> Proud of her charms, of her attraction vain,
> She boasts the male seraglio; unconfined
> Her favours grants, and multiplies her kind

> When in the apt season her intrigues begin,
> No law has made polygamy a sin.

Vanière's queen bee is a splendid, voluptuous creature, with wings of 'glistening gold' and 'jet black' face, who rules with great mercy and efficiency. Only the useless male drones threaten the perfection of life among the bees, but these 'lazy sluggards' are soon dispatched by the female 'sword of state'.[73]

Vanière gazed into the hive and found an idyll of free love coupled with sound government. In factual terms, his picture of bee society is strikingly closer to the truth than Virgil's. He was right, for example, about the queen becoming impregnated through multiple unions (though he didn't know that these took place away from the hive) and about the subsequent dispensability of the drones. But this was still just guesswork, based on what he wanted to be true. At heart, Vanière's poem was an appeal to a nature more fictitious than factual. It took men of science, not poets, to uncover the real story.

The Natural History of the Bees

The first person to establish definitively that the queen, and the queen alone, was the mother of the other bees was a Dutchman, Jan Swammerdam, who was born in 1637. His life, like that of many geniuses, was one of toil and torment, and he achieved only posthumous glory. Seventy years after his death, it was said by fellow scientists that Swammerdam's treatise on bees was a work of 'perfection . . . a work which all the ages from the commencement of natural history to our own times, have produced nothing to equal, nothing to compare with it'.[74] His drawings of bees are still admired as virtually unimprovable. But in his own lifetime he went more or less unrecognized and was a bitter disappointment to his father.

Swammerdam senior was a respectable Amsterdam apothecary who just wanted his son to earn a decent living, preferably in the

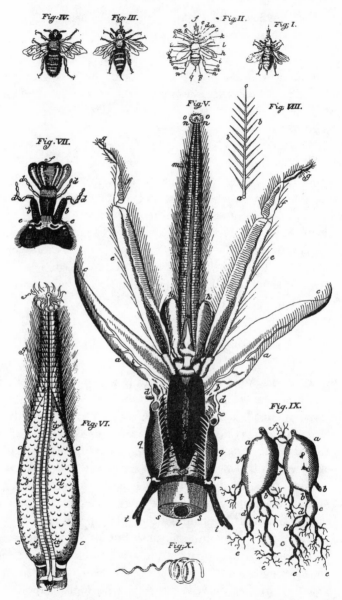

Drawings of bee anatomy by Jan Swammerdam

Church. Without intending it, however, he had stirred up an altogether different vocation in the boy. Mr Swammerdam was famous throughout the city for his remarkable collection of 'curiosities': a personal museum crammed with porcelain from China, fossils, strange vegetables, and above all insects. Princes passing through Amsterdam would come to visit and stare in wonder at the strange little things in cabinets. Young Jan was often given the job of cleaning his father's curiosities, and as he did so he developed a lifelong passion for natural history.

He soon felt unequal to his intended life in the Church, and his father allowed him to change careers to medicine, sending him to Leyden University to study to become a doctor. Again, things didn't go according to plan. It was not that Swammerdam lacked talent for medicine; but that he had too much. Formidably intelligent and 'incomparably dextrous', he soon distinguished himself in anatomy and was noticed by the greatest Dutch anatomists for his 'extraordinary skill in dissecting frogs'. He also obtained permission to dissect the bodies of 'such patients as should happen to die' in the Amsterdam city hospitals.[75] His doctoral thesis on respiration was a triumph, and he was welcomed into the Amsterdam college of physicians. A glittering career lay ahead of him. The trouble was, he didn't want it. Swammerdam was almost pathologically unworldly, and rejected such opportunities to make money as came his way. Besides, fascinating as he found human bodies, he was still more preoccupied with those of insects, busying himself over the copulation of the hermaphrodite house snail, or dissecting cocoons to reveal the butterflies hidden within. To his father's chagrin, and despite his constant nagging, Jan never became a practising medic, and was still relying on his meagre family allowance when he finally died of dropsy and melancholy aged forty-three.

His life had been devoted almost entirely to the dissection and microscopic examination of insects – an expensive and thankless occupation – without any patron to support him. (The duke of Tuscany had offered to finance him at the court at Florence, but

Swammerdam, wilfully independent as ever, had refused.) At least Swammerdam lived at the right time and in the right place for pursuing his passion. It was in the Netherlands in the seventeenth century that the wonders of the microscope first expanded what the human eye could see, through the work of men such as Anton van Leeuwenhoek. Swammerdam himself used relatively simple microscopes to view his insect subjects, but what he did under the lens uncovered a whole new world.

Working from six in the morning until late into the night, he constructed tiny dissecting knives and minuscule scissors that could be sharpened only under magnification. With these scissors, it was said, he could 'dissect the intestines of Bees with the same accuracy and distinctness, that others do those of large animals'. He also developed techniques for filling the smallest veins of the insects with air, and tracing the paths with wax or dyed liquids. Swammerdam cast his zealous eye over the insect kingdom, from moth to gadfly, from caterpillar to rhinoceros beetle, but the creature that attracted him like no other was the honeybee. The bee was both his comfort and his ruin. Five whole years of his life were devoted to studying the hive, after which he suffered a nervous breakdown and did no further scientific work of any kind. The bee even tested his faith, causing him, he would say, 'a thousand agonies of heart and mind'. So miraculous did he find bees, he constantly struggled to remind himself 'that God alone, and not these creatures, was worthy of his researches, love and attention'.[76] In other words, the bees were so perfect that it was hard to believe in anything better – not even God.

His great discoveries did not reach the public until nearly sixty years after his death, when Herman Boerhaave finally gathered all Swammerdam's insect work into *The Book of Nature* (1737), a work later prized by both Erasmus Darwin and Charles Darwin. While Swammerdam was alive, however, the world neither honoured nor rewarded him. Before he died, he was forced to sell his precious collection of insect specimens for a fraction of its true value. But Swammerdam's work on the bees suggests none of this personal sadness. It is all serenity and beauty, including the most exquisite drawings of bee anatomy. As drawn by Swammerdam, the bee's hairy legs are more lovely than a peacock's feather, and the bee's guts look prettier than a rose. These exquisite pictures exemplify the hope of his happier moments: that in studying nature he was studying the works of God.

Swammerdam's admiration for the bee was never greater than when it came to sex. His microscopic scissors exposed to view the ovaries of the queen, thus puncturing all the king bee theories of the past several thousand years. 'From one female,' he wrote, 'which is the only one of that sex in the whole hive, are produced all three kinds of bees.' But Swammerdam reserved his greatest excitement for the genitalia of the drone, which, he tells us, he once 'shewed to his serene highness, the grand duke of Tuscany, among other wonders of nature, in the year 1668, when he graciously condescended to approve of my labours'. Three whole pages of drawings in *The Book of Nature* are given up to the drone's male organs, in various stages of unfolding and thrusting, appearing like exotic sea monsters. Swammerdam cherishes, as only a connoisseur can, the way that the testicles of the drone fill up the entire belly. And as for 'the little part which appears like a penis in the Bee', it is 'wonderfully small and delicate, and of a very beautiful structure; and hence I preserve it in my collection as a thing very worthy of contemplation'. He goes on, 'If the reader views the admirable structure of these genital organs, and the exquisite art conspicuous therein, according to their worth and dignity, he will indeed see that God, even in these minute insects, and their parts, has concealed from the incurious eye stupendous miracles.'[77]

But, while he exposed the bee's private parts to full view, Swammerdam still had not penetrated the mystery of how the queen conceives her offspring. He was deeply puzzled by the fact that, while the males are 'provided with a penis fit for coition, yet they never have an opportunity of copulating with the female'.[78] The only possible explanation, he thought, was that the sperm reaches the queen without the drones needing to touch her. Perhaps he was so in awe of the drone's potent male organs that he allowed himself to imagine that just the presence in the air of the sperm of 400 male drones might be enough to impregnate the queen – the so-called *aura seminalis* theory. Bees, he speculated, might be conceived 'odoriferously', through the atmosphere, without the need for any sexual activity to take place.

As we now know, the odoriferous explanation was wrong, but a hundred years after Swammerdam's death, as the eighteenth century neared its close, entomologists were still no nearer to explaining how the queen becomes a mother. A German scientist called August Schirach had shown, controversially, that, contrary to what almost everyone previously had thought, queens themselves were raised from the same kind of larva as the workers, simply by dint of a different, special, diet. Meanwhile Swammerdam's proof of the queen as sole mother was accepted as gospel. But 'on these two facts a host of theories, some more plausible than others, had been built up'.[79] Apart from the odoriferous theory, one of the strongest hypotheses about the fecundation of the queen remained unchanged from ancient times: that bees reproduced like fish. An English naturalist named John Debraw asserted that the queen laid eggs in cells, and that these eggs were then fertilized by the drones, who sprinkled each egg with seminal liquid. He even claimed to have observed this semen – a whitish fluid at the bottom of some of the cells.[80]

But, before the eighteenth century was finished, both Swammerdam's and Debraw's theories would be proved impossible and the mystery of the queen's fecundation would be solved. The man usually credited with this is a Swiss beekeeper named François Huber, still worshipped by many beekeepers as the greatest beekeeper of all time – and all the greater for the fact that while he was undertaking his bee researches he was more or less completely blind.

François Huber was born in 1750 into a rich family, blessed with all the privileges of the Age of Enlightenment. Huber's

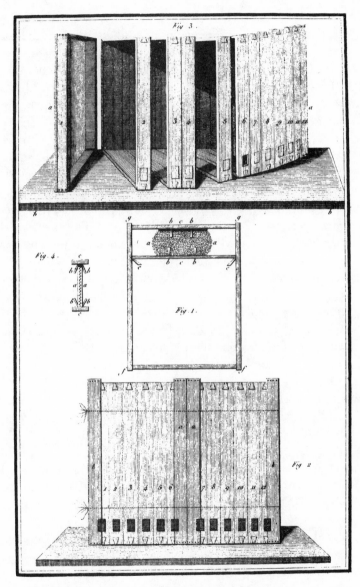

The Huber leaf–hive invented by François Huber, the scientist
who also discovered how the queen was 'fecundated'

father, a friend of Voltaire while the latter lived in exile in Switzerland, could afford the luxury of whiling away his time as a minor poet and musician. In contrast with Swammerdam's father, Huber's did not expect him to earn a living. The boy was destined for a life of gracious intellectual pursuits. To this end, he read passionately, and long into the night. But all this enlightenment put a strain on his eyes. At the age of fifteen François Huber was taken to an oculist, who advised him to lead a quiet country existence and told him that before long he would be completely blind. In the Swiss countryside, where he learned how to plough and studied wildlife, Huber discovered two passions: natural history (particularly honeybees) and a girl called Maria Lullin, whom he met at a dancing class. They fell violently in love. For seven years Maria's parents prevented them from marrying, not wanting her to be saddled with a blind man. But she remained constant, and they were eventually to enjoy a long and happy marriage. Huber later remarked, 'As long as she lived, I was not sensible of the misfortune of being blind.'

Apart from the other pleasures she must have given him, Maria did all Huber's reading and writing for him, and through her eyes he was able to keep abreast of the very latest literature on the subject of bees. As for the practical business of examining bees in the hive, Huber delegated this to his faithful servant François Burnens, a man of little or no education but an acute gift for scientific observation, who would sometimes work for twenty-four hours at a time without stopping for nourishment, enduring terrible stings with uncomplaining fortitude. Huber paid tribute to him as a 'natural-born observer', a man of almost infinite courage and patience.[81] When we speak of Huber's discoveries, Burnens should always be credited too.

It took Burnens and Huber only one experiment to disprove the theory that the queen was inseminated 'odoriferously' through sperm in the atmosphere of the hive. Burnens simply confined all the drones of the hive in a perforated box 'which would allow the passage of odour without permitting the passage of the organs of generation'.[82] The results were conclusive: the queen remained barren. Swammerdam's theory of the *aura seminalis* was wrong.

As for Debraw's theory that the drones fertilized eggs by sprinkling them with semen, it was dispensed with in a similarly clear-cut way. Huber asked Burnens to confine all the bees to the hive so that none could escape, and to eliminate all the drones. The bees 'were kept prisoners for four days and at the end of that time I found forty worms newly hatched'.[83] This confirmed Huber's suspicions that the eggs laid by the queen were already fertile and did not need sprinklings of seminal liquid from the drones. As for the whitish substance that Debraw claimed to have found at the bottom of cells containing eggs, the eyes of Burnens and the mind of Huber exposed it as nothing but a trick of sunlight. Burnens and Huber dispatched many other theories about the 'fecundation' of the queen in this way.

Eventually, having eliminated all the other possibilities, Huber was left with the real answer to the conundrum of reproduction in the hive: that the female bees must be 'fecundated' outside the hive. The sexual activity so long denied among bees actually did take place, in a mating flight almost impossible to observe. Now he and Burnens just needed to get proof positive by means of direct experiment. One day Burnens noticed the queen leaving the hive and returning with the lower part of her body 'filled with a thick whitish substance' very similar to the liquid found in the genitals of the male bees.[84] Two days later he saw that the stomach of the queen was visibly enlarged, and she began laying eggs. From 1787 to 1788, under Huber's direction, Burnens repeated the observation countless times in their tranquil Swiss garden, while in a country next door a real king and queen were nearing their doom. Burnens experimented with queens of various ages: twenty days old, twenty-five days old, thirty days old. Each time the result was the same: the female was impregnated after a single mating flight and returned coated in the whitish substance, along with the severed sexual organs of the drone with which she had coupled. Why did nature demand such a brutal sacrifice from the drones? This was a 'mystery' of nature which even the great Huber did not pretend to understand.

In the twentieth century, bee historians found out that Huber was not so original as had previously been thought. Unknown to him, most of his discoveries had actually already been made nearly twenty years earlier, in 1771, by the Slovenian beekeeper Anton Janscha, who like Burnens had seen the queen flying out of the hive and returning fertilized, carrying away with her both the semen and the genitalia of the unfortunate male. There are those who now contend that Huber's uniquely honoured place in bee science is therefore not altogether deserved. But, even if his originality was less than had previously been thought, nothing can detract from the enlightened thoroughness with which he and Burnens conducted their experiments, trusting no information which they had not tested with their own senses; Huber's book on bees is still consulted by scientists. Nor can anything dim the romance of this blind naturalist. No fewer than two novelizations of his life have been published in recent years – *Blind Huber* by Nick Flynn and *The Beekeeper's Pupil* by Sara George – and a movie biopic will surely follow, given Hollywood's penchant for glamorizing disability.

But, however great their achievements, neither Janscha nor Huber had solved all the sexual riddles of the hive. Neither had ever managed actually to witness the pitiless moment of copulation itself – what Maeterlinck called that 'unique kiss of an instant' which weds the drone 'to death no less than to happiness'.[85] It was not until the 1850s that an observer caught bees in the act, when the queen chanced to fall to the ground in the middle of her mating flight: in 1859 a Reverend Millette of Whitemarsh, Pennsylvania, witnessed the queen and a drone plunge earthward in close contact, before the drone expired, having lost the 'speciality of his sex', those organs so admired by Swammerdam.[86] It was later still that it was discovered that the queen usually mates with more than one drone, albeit on a single mating flight. It was also only over the course of the second half of the nineteenth century that scientists began to unravel the puzzle of how the bee colony determines the sex of the eggs that the queen lays, according to the needs of the society as a whole.

For some time after Janscha and Huber made their discoveries, the hive remained a place of sexual mystery, whose secrets were unlocked only bit by bit. But at least, by the close of the eighteenth century, it could no longer be claimed that the queen was immune to sex; nor could it be denied that the hive was, above all, a feminine environment. The age of the queen bee had arrived.

3

Politics

Where's the state beneath the firmament
That doth excel the bees for government?

Guillaume du Bartas, *Divine Weeks and Works* (1578)

'I'LL TELL', SANG Virgil, sometime around 30 BC, 'of a
tiny / Republic that makes a show well worth your admiration – / Great-hearted leaders, a whole nation whose work is
planned, / Their morals, groups, defences.'[1] That tiny and perfect
republic was a hive of honeybees.

The beehive is perhaps the most enduring of social utopias.
Sooner or later, wherever people have dreamed of a better life for
the oppressed, they have also considered whether the beehive
might help them in their labours. After all, it looks like the perfect symbol of brotherly or sisterly co-operation: here you have
thousands of workers toiling away in useful industry, all happy and
harmonious, all working in a state of freedom towards the
common good, without any apparent coercion. The beehive
ennobles the worker's life – makes it seem golden, not grimy. If
you glance at it fleetingly, with its sweet whirr of activity, it resembles the most productive of factories, only without the factory
bosses. As soon as working-class political movements began to be
organized, in the nineteenth century, they invoked the straw beehive as their vision of the perfect society of the future. (They
didn't worry that such beehives actually had exploitative propri-
etors, in the form of man.)

In France, one of the main worker newspapers of the 1840s was called *La Ruche Populaire* – The People's Beehive. In Britain, the most influential weekly worker's newspaper of the 1870s, a mouthpiece for trade unionism and radical politics, was *The Bee-Hive*, edited by an agitator called George Potter, who had led the London builders' strike of 1859. Just from the name, readers knew what to expect inside: *The Bee-Hive* stood for a co-operative system of government, sanitary reform, and a radical restructuring of Parliament to take account of workers' needs. The dream of the British co-operative movement was to enable workers to save money as well as to earn it. Worker bees seemed to exemplify this principle, producing more honey than they needed immediately, to help them in hard times.

The beehive seemed a utopian society because it was such a wonderful combination of unity and freedom – impossibly wonderful, from a human standpoint. Compared to the competition and misery of ruthless industrial progress, the hive was blissfully harmonious. Such was the view of the influential French utopian socialist Charles Fourier, writing in 1826. Fourier, whose extraordinary writings are mostly forgotten now, was full of weird ideas about the secret symbolism of the universe. He believed that cabbages, with their twisted green leaves, symbolized illicit love affairs (peel away to the bitter heart), while proud white cauliflowers stood for the joys of free love. He also thought the sea would one day turn into lemonade. But Fourier's ideas about the beehive were relatively conventional. Fourier argued that the wasp and the spider were symbols of evil – the wasp because of its 'useless nest' and the harm that it caused, and the spider because it was 'the image of lying commerce and the snare of free competition'. The beehive, by contrast, with its splendid production of both wax and honey, was an image of the joys and usefulness of work in the future. Honey, he thought, indicated the 'wealth' of the future. Wax, a 'source of light', was a symbol of social enlightenment. Fourier argued that bees, by working together so hard in visiting flowers, proved that humans, too, were destined for 'social harmony'.[2] Later socialists, inspired by Karl Marx, thought Fourier terribly naive. But Fourier, who understood human needs better than Marx ever did, believed that human beings could learn to live together only if they could learn to work together despite their differences; and that meant learning from the bees.

What, though, of the rules that would govern this co-operative paradise? Fourier, like many socialists, was stronger on why we had to get along than on how. In this respect the innate order of the beehive was endlessly seductive. Human beings have all too often been dazzled to find another social animal in nature, and one that actually surpasses us in its sociability. As the entomologist Karl von Frisch once wrote, it is pretty amazing that while you can own a single cow, horse or dog, you cannot own a single bee: the smallest unit is always the whole colony.[3] When a honeybee is separated from the rest of its community it dies. The whole always comes before the parts in the hive. This is all the more remarkable given the existence in nature of numerous species of solitary bees, such as *Andrena* and *Halictus,* who raise their larvae not in colonies but in isolation, in hollow stalks or tunnels. Then there are the bumble bees, who are social in a vague and blundering kind of way, rearing eggs in messy cells of wax and earth, without ever coming close to the single-minded togetherness of the honeybees. The honeybees, like other members of the Hymenoptera (including the wasps and ants) are imprinted with a profound sociability. And, of these insects, it is the honeybees whose society men have admired the most.

'Man', as Aristotle remarked, 'is a social and political animal.' And this is where the trouble starts. Having admired the bees as *social* beings like ourselves, the tempting next step is to think that bees must also be *political* animals. Such is the breathtaking complexity of the bee colony that men have on countless occasions deluded themselves that a bee politics must follow naturally from a bee society. This is a mistake, but a very easy one to make. It takes an unusually rational mind to dissent from it. Thomas Hobbes (1588–1679), the author of *Leviathan* – a defence of sovereignty against anarchy – was one of the most unflinchingly rational men who ever lived. Hobbes noticed that Aristotle counted bees as 'political creatures' because they 'live sociably one with another'.[4] But Aristotle was wrong. There is no real politics in the hive. Bees, wrote Hobbes, lack the qualities on which men founded politics. They lack language and reason; and, more than that, they lack strife and envy and the 'troublesome' quality of men. Human politics, argued Hobbes, arose only as an artificial mechanism to deal with conflict (and Hobbes knew a thing or two about conflict, having lived, horrified and terrified, through the bloodbath of the English Civil War). The bees, however, needed no such mechanism. The covenant by which they governed themselves was natural. Thus the very qualities which men so admired in the beehive – the spontaneous agreement, the apparent lack of discord – meant that bees would never need politics. There were no civil wars in the hive.

Hobbes's view seems unarguable, but it has seldom been heeded. For as long as there has been human politics, there has been an assumption that bees have politics too. Someone or something must be telling the bees – so loyal, so obedient – what to do. Bee politics has taken almost as many forms as human politics, shifting with the changing values of different places and times. The hive has been, in turn, monarchical, oligarchical, aristocratic, constitutional, imperial, republican, absolute, moderate, communist, anarchist and even fascist. As so often in politics, we see whatever it is we want to see.

Yet even political fantasies of the hive have their limits, and the limit comes with democracy. It is true that the political philosopher and educationalist Jean-Jacques Rousseau, author of *The Social Contract* (1762), believed that in societies where honey-hunting took place, such as the lovely wilderness of Corsica, democracy would follow. Corsica was poor, Rousseau observed, yet its mountainous and well-wooded terrain was richly supplied with food: Corsicans were rich in 'meat, milk and honey'. This gave them independence – one of the preconditions of democracy.

Another essential for democratic life was a 'spirit of equity', which Corsicans also luckily had, thanks to a culture of gathering honey from mountains and hollow trunks of trees. Rousseau wrote that: 'Honey can be distinguished in no other way than by the mark of first occupier; ownership of it can neither be created nor preserved save through public good faith; and it is necessary for everyone to be just.'[5] Hence a society founded on honey would probably have both the independence and the justice which democracy needed. By contrast, Rousseau argued that true democracy was impossible in large, decadent, sugar-eating nations. Sugar is unthinkable without commercial life. And it was Rousseau's Spartan opinion that commerce – which fostered both dependence and injustice – would mean the death of democracy.

But while honey could encourage democracy, democracy is the one form of government that no one, to my knowledge, has ever tried to imprint on the honey-makers themselves. The hive is too hierarchical and gilded for democratic politics: the contrast between the single bee at the top and the masses at the bottom is just too great. If you want an insect democracy, you must turn to ants (hence the success of *Antz* and *A Bug's Life*, two films of the late 1990s, which idealized the democratic potential of the little darlings). Perhaps this also explains why, from the twentieth century onward, as democracy became the world's favourite idea, the old utopia of the beehive began to turn nasty. Bee politics was all much simpler in the days when human beings, like bees, could be happy with just one ruler reigning from a golden cell.

Monarchy

In the beginning, bee politics was always perfect, and perfectly monarchical. As early as 5,500 years ago, in the time of the First Dynasty of pharaohs, the bee was a hieroglyph meaning both 'Egypt' and 'King'. Luscious honeycomb was a highly valued commodity in the Nile Delta. Honey was the food of the rich and greedy, and who could be richer or greedier than the king? The king of Upper Egypt was known as 'The One of the Bee'; the king of Lower Egypt was 'The One of the Reed'.[6] Around 3200 BC the two dynasties united under one pharaoh, and a papyrus rejoiced, 'He hath united the two lands, / He hath joined the Reed to the Bee.'[7]

Egyptian hieroglyphs for both 'bee' and 'king'

To put it kindly, the Egyptian bee hieroglyphs were not very lifelike. The bee was always drawn in profile, with a head, antennae, thorax and abdomen all visible, but looking more like a bird or a grasshopper than a bee. Hieroglyph-painters always got the number of legs wrong, too.[8] At first the bee hieroglyphs for pharaohs had three legs; later four; but never six. A couple of thousand years later, in China, the Shang Dynasty emperor Trou Yu put bees on his flag as 'an auspicious emblem'.[9] Yet these were always simply generic bees. The ancient rulers who chose the bees as emblems must surely have noticed that there was one bee larger and more prominent than all the others; but, if so, they did not make much of the fact.

Bee politics really started to get interesting only when the ruler of the bee colony began to be identified as a king in his own right. 'They have states like ours, with king and government and organized society,' observed the Roman writer Varro, who wrote about farming in the first century BC.[10] Plato also spoke of king bees being like rulers of a human community.[11] But it took the development of medieval kingship for the ruler bees to come into their own. For apologists of feudal society, bees provided a useful example in arguing that being ruled under a king didn't necessarily mean being unfree. This is how one anonymous bestiary writer of the twelfth century put it:

> [Bees] arrange their own king for themselves. They create a popular state, and although they are policed under a king, they are free. For the king does not merely hold the privilege of giving judgment, but he also excites a feeling of allegiance, both because the Bees love him on the ground that he was appointed by themselves and also because they honour him for being at the head of so great a swarm.[12]

Because they admired the king so much, claimed this writer, the worker bees were not oppressed. Their love made them free. But being free was emphatically not the same as being democratic. In medieval Europe, democracy was often synonymous with a random lottery. As our bestiary writer goes on, 'The king [bee] does not become their leader by lot, for in casting lots there is the element of chance rather than of good judgment, and often by the irrational misfortune of luck somebody who is worse gets preferred to better men.' This twelfth-century author warmed to a theme which would be used again and again by admirers of the bee monarchy: the ruler bee was marked out as superior by his very different appearance. His rule was therefore *natural*. As St Basil had put it in the fourth century, the king bee 'commands respect by superior size, beauty and character'.[13] The medieval mystic Thomas of Cantimpre, who wrote a whole book recommending the politics of bees to men (*The Book of Bees*), noted that the king bee was 'honey coloured, as if fashioned from choice flowers'. Charles Butler, writing in 1609, was even more poetical: 'The Queen is a fair and stately bee, differing from the vulgar both in shape and colour: her back is all over of a brighter brown; her belly even from the top of her fangs to the tip of her train, is of a sad yellow, somewhat deeper than the richest gold'.[14]

Another theme in the twelfth-century bestiary that would

become a frequent refrain was admiration for the remarkable clemency of the ruler bee. Clemency or mercy was what distinguished kings from tyrants. The ruler bee was seen as merciful because he had a sting but did not use it (it was not then known

The beehive as a symbol of royal clemency from a
sixteenth-century book of emblems

that queen bees do sometimes use their stings, against other queens). As our bestiary writer expresses it, 'the peculiarity of a king is the clemency of his character, for even if he has a sting he does not use it in punishment – since there are unwritten laws in Nature, not laid down but customary, to the effect that those who have the greatest power should be the most lenient'.[15] Only tyrants and usurpers used punishment excessively: kings were secure enough in their power that they didn't have to be always showing it off. In 1230 Bartholomew the Englishman said the same about the king bee: as well as 'highness', the king had 'mildness', and, although he had 'a sting, yet he useth it not in wreck'.[16] Xanthippus, the general of the Carthaginians in 255 BC, was said to have remarked that he would rather be placed under the command of bees than rule an army of ants, because the bee commander did not use his sting.[17]

Other admirers of bee rule were under the impression that the king bee had no sting in the first place. These included the Stoic philosopher Seneca, the foremost ancient theorist of clemency. Seneca was the teacher of Nero – in the end the bloodiest of all the Roman emperors, but early on a young man of whom many had high hopes. After Nero assumed office in AD 54, aged seventeen, Seneca wrote *On Mercy*, a deeply wishful text urging Nero to see that being merciful would be far more powerful than being vengeful. Nero took no notice, poisoning and punishing all those closest to him. But it is easy to see why, early in Nero's reign, Seneca should have sought inspiration from the king bee. To start with, the bee gave Seneca a way of flattering Nero's bottomless vanity: 'Kingship has been devised by nature herself, as you can see from bees.' Just as Nero cosseted himself in the most ornate rooms of his palaces, the king bee had 'the most spacious cell in the central and safest place'. Then, having buttered Nero up, Seneca tried to urge mercy. The king bee, he insisted, 'has no sting'. The reason was that nature didn't want him to be 'savage' and so 'took away his weapon and left his anger unarmed. A mighty example for great kings!'[18] But not, unfortunately, for Nero, who eventually instructed Seneca to commit suicide, which he did uncomplainingly, in true Stoic fashion, by slashing his veins.

In 1516 the Renaissance humanist Erasmus took up Seneca's arguments, and elaborated them in his own book on how monarchs should behave, *The Education of a Christian Prince*. This time

the bees were to offer a model to Charles V, emperor of the
Habsburgs and ruler of an empire as great as Nero's. What really
mattered, wrote Erasmus, was to be a legitimate ruler and not a
despot. Yet again, nature had pointed the way through animals. In
nature, the lion, the bear, the wolf and the eagle were tyrants 'who
live by mutilation and plundering', but their doing so exposed
them to the hatred of all the other animals.[19] The king bee is a far
better model, thought Erasmus, because, despite lacking a sting,
he is actually safer in his office and less likely to be attacked. This
same thought was very well expressed by the bee writer Moses
Rusden 150 years later: 'The Lion and the Eagle have no subjects
but what are in rebellion because they do not protect, but devour
them. But the King-Bee, though the most absolute monarch, yet
is attended with all the love and loyalty imaginable from his
people, because he devoureth none, but is a cherisher of and bene-
factor to all.'[20]

But love and loyalty weren't always enough for kings and
queens. What they wanted was obedience, even from those who
didn't love them, and regardless of how they themselves behaved.
As monarchies across Europe emerged from the feudal world of
the Middle Ages into an age of absolutism, so bee rule evolved
new meaning. The bee state was still a monarchy, but the emphasis had changed. The real issue was no longer just the good
grace of the monarch but the absolute devotion that he – or she
– could inspire in the citizens of the hive. By the time of Charles
Butler's *The Feminine Monarchy*, in 1609, the bees' form of government was no longer just 'the most natural': it was also 'the most
absolute'.[21]

Charles Butler (1559–1647), the first great bee writer of modern
times, wrote his book six years after the death of Elizabeth I,
whose forty-five years of glorious rule had made the English state
stronger and more centralized than ever before. Now James I, that
'wisest fool in Christendome', was on the throne, with an adamant
belief in the divine right of monarchy that was in part a way of
covering up his own personal silliness and physical inadequacy.

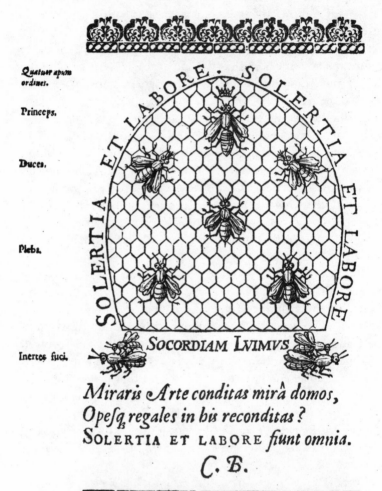

The political structure of the beehive, as drawn in Charles
Butler's *The Feminine Monarchy*, 1609

Superior size, beauty and character were not James's strongpoint, so he had to rely on God's blessing instead. The same year that Butler's bee book appeared, King James gave a speech to Parliament in which he called the state of monarchy 'the supremest thing upon earth; for Kings are not only GOD's lieutenants upon earth, and sit upon thrones, but even by God himself they are called gods'.[22]

Charles Butler had lived most of his life, as a vicar and musician, adoring Elizabeth. Now he had to adapt to James. Butler's writing on the 'Feminine Monarchy' of bees is torn between a wistful yearning for the days of the Virgin Queen, when you could love your monarch for her own personal qualities (his bees 'love' and 'revere' their queen), and the realities of Jacobean times, when you could respect the sovereign only if you saw that you had no choice. A sign of his political schizophrenia is that Butler veers erratically between calling the ruler bee 'Queen', 'Sovereign', 'Stately Prince' and 'Governour'.[23] Ultimately, however, it was only prudent to come down on the side of the divine-right rule of James. Bees, marvelled Butler, live 'under the government of one Monarch' whom they obey 'in all things'. Butler was very admiring of the fact that bees obeyed one 'prince' and not two, and spoke approvingly of how they killed any pretenders to the throne. 'For the bees abhor polyarchy, or anarchy, God having showed in them unto men, an express pattern of a perfect monarchy.' The bees were above all else obedient. Their orderliness, thought Butler, should be 'a pattern unto men'.[24]

However, absolute monarchs do not rule alone: they need help from hierarchies of officials who do their bidding. This posed a problem, because there were no obvious parallels for these in the hive. Nevertheless, the more absolute the bee monarchy was taken to be, the more subsidiary officers the bee monarch was credited with, regardless of what actually took place amidst the honeycombs. Pliny had given the ruler bee guards and *lictors* or Roman magistrates. Seventeenth-century advocates of divine-right monarchy multiplied this court well beyond the point of absurdity. Butler imagined he saw bees in his old wicker hives who had special 'tufts', 'tassels' and 'plumes' to distinguish their different ranks.[25] You might think that Butler's eyesight must have been failing if he 'saw' such marvels, except that he was not the only one. The 'Master Bee', wrote John Levett in 1634, was guarded by not just by a 'whole multitude of common soldiers' but also by supreme commanders, generals, marshals, sergeants, colonels and captains.[26] This was clearly nonsense. But nonsense doesn't always stand in the way of political imperatives, especially in an age of absolute power.

As the English seventeenth century progressed, the obedience of bees and men to their rulers became all the more urgent. After the English Civil War, in 1655, with the monarchy abolished and Oliver Cromwell occupying the post of Lord Protector, Samuel Hartlib published a book on bee husbandry called *The Reformed Common-Wealth of Bees*, as if the bees had somehow adapted to the Puritan politics of the times. His work was subsidized by the government, and it is not clear if he had any specialist knowledge of bees.[27] In 1657 a more expert writer, Samuel Purchas, brought out *A Theatre of Politicall Flying-Insects*, which also emphasized that the beehive was a commonwealth, ordered by a 'Commander', who, like Cromwell, was neither a hereditary monarch nor a democratically chosen governor, but for whom the bees would 'be anything, go any whither, stay anywhere'. Purchas was very careful to avoid the vocabulary of kingship, yet he was no less amazed by the obedience of bees than the monarchists had been. The difference was that Purchas's bees were obedient to the common good, under the guidance of their commander. These bees demonstrated the 'invincible' power of the multitude: 'Bees are political creatures and destinate all their actions to one common end; they have one common habitation, one common work, all work for all, and one common care and love towards all their young, and that under one commander'. Bees, argued Purchas, were 'most perfect creatures' who would 'conserve community unto their last'. The polity of the bee was 'admirable and imitable'. Their citizens were valiant fighters, who surpassed all other creatures in courage and yet – the contrast with the warring English here was stark – were very patient when it came to internal disputes. Men, wrote Purchas, should 'borrow a civil life from the bees'.[28]

THe Parliament is held, Bils and Complaints
Heard and reform'd, with severall restraints
Of usurpt freedome ; instituted Law
To keepe the Common· Wealth of Bees in awe.

John Daye's *The Parliament of Bees*, 1641. This was a political allegory about the actions of 'Good and Bad men'. Here we see 'Mr Bee' the 'Pro-Rex' or leader of the Parliament of Bees

Unfortunately, the new British commonwealth of men did not last, and when it ended, three years later, so did the commonwealth of bees. After the monarchy was restored with Charles II, the absolute beehive was back with a vengeance. Perhaps the most insistent hymn of praise to the monarchical bees was published in

1679, a year when the restored monarchy was being severely tested by the Exclusion Crisis, a battle over whether Charles would be succeeded by his Catholic brother James as king. Meanwhile Charles was very ill, and royal prerogative was looking distinctly shaky. In this atmosphere of faction and rebellion, Moses Rusden produced the innocuously titled *A Further Discovery of Bees.* Rusden, an apothecary, had landed himself the job of personal bee-master to King Charles II, a unique office which had never been held before. He was determined to use his publication on bees to restore lustre to the British monarchy. Viewed from Rusden's royal apiary, the hive was a political idyll free from all unrest and disobedience. There was no Exclusion Crisis here.

In the preface to his book, Rusden insists that 'My business is to shew Nature and Truth, naked and unadorned with Metaphors and Suppositions.' In fact Rusden's panegyric to bee monarchy is more fanciful than any medieval bestiary. King bees, like human bees, Rusden claimed, rule by unquestionable divine right. They belong to 'The Royal Race of King Bees, being natural Kings'. One king bee equals 'the value and worth of all the rest'. But the king's subjects apparently like it that way, being quite astonishingly and squirmingly obedient, ready to defend him at any moment. Without a king, they would 'pine away and die'. The bees have 'an excessive love' for the body of the king, and therefore hate 'Rebellion and Treason'. The king's authority is absolute. He is supported by a court and a 'retinue' of special courtier bees, and makes his throne at the top of the hive, 'to which he always hastens when any disturbance happens'. The king bee has the authority and therefore the power to be as harsh as he likes. 'His government is severe, just and absolute . . . like that of the Grand Seignior towards the race of the blood Royal, for, as soon as swarming time is fully past, all the younger princes being kept in . . . are expelled or executed by the King's orders.'[29] (This likens the drones being dispensed with at the end of summer to the practice whereby brothers and cousins of a new Ottoman sultan were murdered to prevent them from becoming a focus for conspiracies.) The gist of Rusden's book was to pretend that poor, unwell, womanizing, compromised Charles also had such power to control his destiny, even though Rusden must have realized with some part of himself that this was not so.

A Further Discovery of Bees is a shining example in a long line of implausible bee books offered as obsequious tribute to royalty. In 1712 Joseph Warder dedicated his *The True Amazons or The Monarchy of Bees* to Queen Anne, in a particularly wormlike manner: 'There is nothing [that] can excuse the presumption I am guilty of, in thus approaching your sacred hands with so mean a trifle, but the subject here treated of, which is of princes and potentates, Kingdomes and territories, Prerogative and Property, Dominion and Loyalty, War and Peace.'[30]

Warder's book is a chaotic gallimaufry of husbandry, science, cookery, farming and literature, but uniting them into some kind of whole is Warder's abasement before his monarch. Anne was at war with Spain for much of her reign. Hence, in Warder's mead section, we get a jingoistic recipe for 'English Canary, in no way inferior to the best of Spanish wines'. Warder insisted that he found among the bees 'so many things that resemble your Majesty's happy state and government, that all the while I was writing of this book I could not forbear wishing I might dedicate it to Your Majesty'. It is so easy to get acclimatized to the idea of a bee state that you have to remind yourself now and then how very odd this really is: that it could be considered gratifying to accuse a human monarch of approaching the perfection of an insect smaller than her thumb. Yet Warder found the parallels between Anne and the queen bee to be numerous. He even imagined that the bee was wearing something like 'a velvet cape or fur gorget', as was the fashion at the court of Anne, and he admired the largeness of her cell. Then came the rub:

> The Queen Bee governs with Clemency and Sweetness, so doth Your Majesty, she is Obeyed and defended, out of choice and Inclination by her subjects, so is your Majesty. And here I cannot but wish that all your Majesty's Subjects were as unanimously loyal

as the subjects of the Queen Bee, in whose Nature there is so strongly (as well as strangely) plac'd a Principle of Obedience, whereas I doubt here your Majesty is not altogether so happy: for though all the Thousands of your Britannick Israel esteem your Majesty's Person as sacred . . . yet I fear 'tis not hard to find . . . unquiet spirits.

In other words, the only point at which the analogy of bee politics broke down for Warder was with the subjects: worker bees put humans to shame. Warder admired the way in which bees fended off the attacks of mice, moths, earwigs and hornets – pests who perhaps corresponded to the Continentals bothering Anne's kingdom. He had reason to hope that one day, 'Your Majesty's subjects may be as Affectionate and Dutiful to your Majesty, as my bees are to their Queen'. Anne's subjects could learn a lot from the 'undivided fidelity' of the bees and abandon 'faction' once and for all.[31]

Much of Warder's argument sounds very similar to that of Rusden three decades earlier. But, given Warder's attachment to Anne, it was crucial that he make it clear that the queen was a queen and not a king. Warder therefore referred to Rusden's theories on the sex of bees as 'ridiculously false'.[32] The fact that Warder was scientifically right was almost beside the point. What mattered was that he was politically right.

After the British monarchy passed once more out of female hands, and as science made it increasingly clear that the ruler of the hive could not possibly be a man, the scope for bee dedications lessened. It became more the custom to dedicate bee books to the wife of the reigning monarch; but somehow this was unsatisfactory, since a king's wife was not the same thing as a real queen. Nevertheless, in 1768 Thomas Wildman dedicated his treatise on bee management to Queen Charlotte, the wife of King George III. In 1832 Thomas Nutt dedicated his *Humanity to Honey Bees* to 'Her Most Gracious Majesty, Queen Adelaide', the wife of William IV. Compared to the political engagement of Purchas, Rusden and Warder, this seemed rather flat. When at last Victoria was crowned, in 1837, and the sceptre passed again to a woman, there was occasion to renew the apiarian grovelling. In 1838 Edward Bevan rushed out a new edition of *The Honey-Bee*, dedicating it to his new sovereign, commenting that 'The queen of every bee community has been destined to fill her high station from a very early age.' Bevan was far from the only person to call Victoria a queen bee. But the image of bee monarchy no longer seemed so urgent. The politics of the beehive had moved on, in many different directions. Calling Victoria a queen bee was a nice touch, a pretty embellishment to her monarchy; but no one really believed any more that the hive provided a natural justification for her rule.

Republican Bees and Consumer Bees

Over the course of the eighteenth century – the age of Enlightenment and of Revolution – both the authority of the queen bee and the virtue of her citizens were challenged. The bee monarchy, it seemed, just didn't add up. In 1740 a Frenchman, Jean-Baptiste Simon, published *The Admirable Government, or the Republic of Bees*.[33] In it, he praised the republican morals of the bees – their frugality, the regularity of their conduct. If only French mothers were as tender as bee mothers, he lamented. In 1744 the republican hive gained more ground when the most widely read French bee writer, a Monsieur Gilles Augustin Bazin, asserted that the old belief that the mass of bees in the hive were following the orders of the queen made no sense. It was not that Bazin thought that bee politics per se was nonsense, as Hobbes had said. It was simply time for the form of government to change. If the beehive was a monarchy – and even this was not certain – then it was a republican monarchy, and not an absolute one. In Bazin's bee book we have one of the typical stirrings of the times against absolute rule – stirrings which would lead, fifty years later, to its overthrow. 'If [the queen bee] reigns,' Bazin wrote, 'it is over subjects who every moment know, that the good of their society demands what they perform; and who never fail to do it.' The unified action of the bees now had a new twist. It no longer signified obedience, but republican virtue. 'They never have occasion to receive orders. In this state, every one, whether monarch or subject, pursues their original design, from which they never vary.'[34]

French republicans grew bolder and bolder in adopting the beehive as the century progressed. Many enlightened minds of the time had an obsession with nature. Natural law was the foundation of all rights, including those specified in the Declaration of the Rights of Man and the Citizen, the founding document of the French Constituent Assembly following the revolution of 1789. French republicans were therefore extremely troubled by the view that the queen bee should be taken to provide any justification for monarchy in nature. After the revolution, intellectuals in the newly founded Ecole Normale, which would become the most prestigious institution of higher education in France, staged a debate to sort this problem out once and for all. Already the revolutionaries had dispensed with the notion that the lion was the 'king of animals'. The lion could not be the king of animals, because 'in nature there is no king'. But then a student called Laperruque piped up, full of anxiety about the beehive. 'I see in nature', he confessed, 'something worse than a king; that is to say, a queen. And what is even more extraordinary, a queen in a republic!' All was not lost, however. The head of the Ecole Normale, Professor Daubenton, had an answer. The queen in the beehive was no Marie Antoinette. In fact she wasn't a queen at all. The real power lay with the workers. This had to be so because 'it is obvious that in Nature there can be neither king nor queen'.[35] By 'Nature', of course, he meant France.

With that cleared up, the virtuous beehive could now be allowed to exhort republicans to ever greater acts of civic duty. Sometime around 1793, in the middle of the Terror, with the king executed and many of his drones having followed him to the guillotine, the French republic adopted the hexagon as its symbol, as if the nation were now a single cell in a honeycomb. This regular geometric shape was meant to reflect the geographical contours of the country. But it also reflected the political contours of Jacobinism: regular, pitilessly logical and unyielding. Later in the

A French republican beehive

1790s the leading school in France, the Pritanée Français (formerly the Collège Louis-le-Grand) was depicted with a rustic beehive outside it, alongside a stone tablet engraved with the Rights of Man and the Citizen. For the revolutionaries, the beehive was itself a school of liberty (the hive bowed to no one), of equality (all worker bees were equal) and of fraternity (bees all worked together). On 3 Brumaire, Year IV, the Committee of Public Instruction even proposed in the national assembly that the national seal and all national buildings should bear an emblem of a hive surrounded by bees. The idea was rejected, amid much sniggering, when one of the 'deputies' of the French assembly pointed out that bees had a queen and therefore 'cannot be an emblem of a republic'.[36]

The queen was not the only problem for the virtuous republican beehive. There was also the little matter of Bernard de Mandeville, whose bestselling *The Fable of the Bees* (1714, with many subsequent editions) had blazed a trail throughout the eighteenth century, and remains the most celebrated book about bees and politics ever written. It was once called 'the wickedest, cleverest book in the English language'.[37] Mandeville, an émigré Dutch physician and satirist who settled in London, had set forth a disturbing paradox, and a brilliant riposte to republicanism. What if the success of the beehive had nothing to do with virtue at all? What if the overall 'luxury' of the honeycomb was actually obtained through the vice and corruption of individual bees? What if, as Mandeville's most famous phrase stated, 'private vices' could yield 'public benefits'?

Readers were as startled by Mandeville's politics as earlier generations had been by Machiavelli. What shocked them was his deep, unflinching worldliness. Mandeville did not deny that virtue made men lovable. But he did deny that a mass of virtuous citizens would make for a prosperous nation. On the contrary, in Mandeville's view, great nations were founded on 'Fraud, Luxury and Pride'. Mandeville's worker bees were not republicans but voracious consumers, whose 'Crimes conspired to make them Great'.[38]

In 'The Grumbling Hive', an earlier poem incorporated into *The Fable of the Bees*, Mandeville describes:

> A Spacious Hive well stockt with Bees
> That lived in Luxury and Ease.

He first cunningly lures the reader in by offering some very typical and familiar platitudes about the bee state:

> They were not slaves to Tyranny,
> Nor rul'd by wild Democracy.

This ideal beehive was also, true to form, comfortable, glorious, populous, fruitful. But then comes the real break with tradition, which so appalled Mandeville's contemporaries. This admirable beehive, he reveals, was founded not on virtue but on vice, on 'vanity' rather than 'frugality'. The bees' sociability – so much praised by the moralists – was founded on 'evil'. None of the workers in Mandeville's hive was honest. This was a workforce of 'Sharpers, Parasites, Pimps, Players, Pick-pockets, Coiners, Quacks, Sooth-Sayers'. The bees were all fraudsters – even the judges and the ministers of state, who would rob the Crown itself if they could get away with it. What made this even more shocking was that Mandeville refused to condemn this den of thieves. Even though 'every part' of Mandeville's hive was 'full of vice', the whole mass was 'a Paradise'. Each of the seven deadly sins contributed to the life of the nation in some way: Avarice in the form of Luxury

> Employ'd a million of the Poor,
> And odious Pride a Million more.

The hive began to lose its happiness only when its inhabitants suddenly – stupidly – decided that they needed Honesty, at which point commercial life was destroyed:

> In half an Hour, the Nation round,
> Meat fell a penny in the pound.

Without lust, and the greed for luxury goods, the hive was destroyed. The few, deluded bees who remained had to leave their comfortable hive and swarm into a hollow tree. It was the end of civilization.[39]

In contrast to all the other political hives that preceded his, Mandeville's seems remarkably truthful. He was right to say that our fickle and 'ridic'lous' love of fashion encourages trade – though Adam Smith was also right to observe that Mandeville was exaggerating somewhat by calling a taste for pretty clothes a 'vice'. But the reason why Mandeville's hive seems more plausible than other bee states, for all its hyperbole, is that he was really dealing not with bees, but with human beings and all their contradictions. He can speak the truth about human relations because he does not even attempt to speak the truth about the bees. It is a fable. (The rest of *The Fable of the Bees*, in which he expanded the ideas set out in 'The Grumbling Hive', actually mentions bees hardly at all.) The usual moral of bee politics was the impossible one that men should aspire to be more like bees. No one would try to copy the bees of 'The Grumbling Hive' – they are already like us.

> These Insects lived like Men, and all
> Our Actions, they performed in small.[40]

In other words, they are not insects at all. You can tell that Mandeville was an admirer of Thomas Hobbes. Though he went about it in a more roundabout way, he, like Hobbes, threatened to explode the very possibility of a bee politics.

Mandeville posed a real problem for republican admirers of bees, in America as well as in France. One historian has noted that Mandeville 'wrought psychological havoc among patriotic Americans', who, after 1776, wanted to adopt the republican hive as a symbol of their new nation but certainly did not want to be seen as a nation of fraudsters. Many simply rejected Mandeville's hive outright. For the self-righteous Virginians and Pennsylvanians, 'The Grumbling Hive', like those aristocratic drones, was part of cynical, corrupt Britain. In the new society of the USA, public benefit would be created out of private virtue. 'Nothing but virtue can constitute the happiness of society,'[41] exclaimed a Philadelphia newspaper in 1780, in direct contradiction to Mandeville. The American beehive would persist as a commonwealth, by ignoring any information which did not fit with it, and ignoring the rest of the world too. This was just as well. For while Americans were busy forging a new world of republican virtue, back in Europe some old bee dreams were dying hard.

Autocracy

Both republicans and autocrats like social unity in a state, which is why they like the beehive. The difference is that, whereas republicans prefer to achieve unity from the bottom up, autocrats, by definition, impose it from the top down. Bees had been associated with the some of the most autocratic rulers the world had seen: popes and emperors. As the eighteenth century turned into the nineteenth, Europe still had its popes; and it was about to acquire a new emperor.

What linked the bee to the papacy? Pretty much everything. Wax and honey were the sacred substances of the early Church; the supposedly beneficent pope, like the supposedly beneficent king bee, was a ruler without a sting; the hierarchy of the hive, like the explicit and towering hierarchy of the Church, culminated in a single, resplendent figure. There was another thing that cemented the association: the papal tiara looked remarkably like a tall straw skep beehive. This was a coincidence, but it didn't seem that way to contemporaries. Enemies of the pope noticed it, and in 1569 a biting Protestant satire was published, *The Roman Beehive*, condemning the 'Babylonicall Beast' of Rome, with a title page featuring a beehive-mitre.[42]

The bee–pope connection became more explicit still during the papacy of Urban VIII (1623–44). Urban VIII, born Maffeo Barberini, was a deeply unpleasant man, authoritarian to his fingertips. It was under his leadership that Galileo was pressured by the Inquisition into denying that the earth went round the sun, even though Galileo had been his friend.

The papal mitre depicted as a beehive, from Filips van Matrix's
satirical work *De Roomische Byen-Korf* (1581)

Maffeo Barberini was calculatingly ambitious from an early age.
The Barberinis were a rich Florentine family of merchants. Bit by
bit, they had scrabbled up the social ladder from peasant begin-
nings, until Maffeo himself became a cardinal. Originally the
family coat of arms had been three ordinary black horseflies, on
a sky-blue background. (The family had once been called by
the vulgar name of 'Tafani', which meant 'Horseflies'.) As the
Barberinis became richer, they upgraded both their name and the
horseflies, painting them gold instead. But, whatever its colour, a
horsefly is still a horsefly – not the most dignified of beasts. Being
known as the 'horsefly family' did not suit the Barberinis any more.
So Maffeo cannily changed the three golden insects on the crest to
bees. It was a brilliant touch. This was not the virtuous bee, or even
the kingly bee, but the bee as winner-take-all – the most untrump-
able of insects. With this new noble crest, Cardinal Barberini
seemed positively papal already. In 1623 Pope Gregory died, providing Barberini's opportunity. After a 'sweltering, contentious
conclave', he was elected by 50 out of a possible 55 votes.[43]

As pope, Urban VIII set about his corrupt business, enriching his closest relatives, and covering Rome with Barberini bees. He commissioned swarms of expensive baroque images of the golden creature all over the city to ensure a permanent legacy of his reign. Gianlorenzo Bernini, who designed most of the interior and colonnades of St Peter's for Urban VIII, became adept at sculpting the fat, symmetrical bees on the papal coat of arms. In the Piazza Barberini you can still see both the so-called Fountain of Bees and the Tritone Fountain, which is also adorned with the autocratic insects. The whole of the Palazzo Barberini, where the family lived, might as well have been called the Palace of Bees, so pervasive is the motif. Most striking of all is Pietro da Cortona's painting *Triumph of Divine Providence*, which covers the ceiling of the great vault. It is one of those frescos that gives you vertigo the minute you see it, a baroque explosion of velvet robes, heavenly rays and allegorical figures. Here is an angel holding what looks like a crown of fairy lights – actually the ring of Providence, calling Barberini to his papal vocation. At the very centre of the picture are three stolid-looking golden bees. These are meant to represent the Barberini family flying up to heaven, but they look much too well fed to fly anywhere. This is the exact opposite of the earlier Catholic tradition of humble, pious awe before bees. Here the insects are entirely emblematic: status symbols for rich, powerful, ruthless men. They are magnificent, aloof, untouchable, and they remained the official symbol of the papacy well into the nineteenth century.

It was for this kind of buzz that the bee also became the chosen symbol of the greatest autocrat of them all, Napoleon Bonaparte. When Napoleon was crowned emperor of France in 1804, the whole of Notre-Dame was decked out in golden bees. As one historian has written, bees legitimized the Napoleonic regime 'by linking it with the French past and the lost but not forgotten worlds of antiquity'.[44] The bee that Napoleon chose as his badge was the heraldic golden bee pictured *'volant en arrière'* – flying away from the viewer. Napoleon's advisers knew that bees had

Napoleon in his bee-studded coronation robes, borrowing the
glory of the Merovingian bees

represented the kings of Egypt. They also knew that 300 golden bees had been found in the tomb of the Merovingian king Childeric (*c.* 436–81), forerunner of the kings of France. There was even a theory – wrong, as it happened – that the fleur-de-lis depicted on the old regime's royal clothes was really a bee. Bees were therefore a way of making the transformation of Corsican peasant into supreme ruler of the French nation seem less preposterous. Autocracies, more than any other kinds of government, depend on maintaining confidence. Napoleon's rule was an illusion, like the emperor's new clothes. To keep up appearances, he covered his own new clothes with bees, donning an ermine-lined mantle with a purple field scattered with golden bees, to go with his Roman crown of laurels, his lace ruffles and his eagle-topped sceptre, just in case any one didn't get the message. Meanwhile his wife, Josephine, whose own power over Napoleon was extremely fragile, since she couldn't give him an heir, used bees as a decorative motif all over their home at Malmaison, in the hope that some of the magic might rub off.

In the end, the eagle became the Emperor's official badge (he had also considered the lion, the elephant and the cockerel – all virile creatures), but bees came next in order of imperial honour. In 1804 there was even a suggestion, by Cambacérès, the chief justice, that a swarm of bees should become the emblem for the whole French nation. Jean Jacques Cambacérès urged that the swarm would be the perfect symbol for Napoleon's system of government, since the bees exemplified a republic but with an all-powerful chief. Napoleon himself was not particularly interested in how the bees ruled themselves. The question was how they could help *him* rule. It has been suggested that Napoleon's adoption of bees was a vestige of his Corsican childhood, when he would have feasted on the lovely wild honey of the mountains.[45] But any lingering nostalgia for the foods of his boyhood seems unlikely. For one thing, Napoleon was not a man ruled by his stomach. He was impatient with meals, and chose to eat rations of soldier's bread even as a child, to prepare himself for a life of battle.

For another thing, the bees of Napoleonic heraldry were not real bees. These were baubles, not honey-makers. Napoleon's bees were entirely honorific, wholly detached from the crawling, swarming, propolis-sticky life of the hive.

As emperor, Napoleon established a complex hierarchy of heraldic entitlements. Only those of the rank of High Officer of the Empire and above were entitled to decorate themselves with bees; mere dukes had to make do with stars, and those below the rank of duke were entitled to neither bees nor stars. This was pure power politics, and it had nothing to do with the life of the bee-hive. Both Urban VIII and Napoleon Bonaparte made bees into toweringly autocratic beasts, but only to uphold their own pretensions. Ultimately, the reputation of bee politics was not enhanced by such self-aggrandisement. It was not a huge step from Napoleon glittering in his bee-spangled robe to the idea that the beehive represented all that was bad in politics.

Dystopia

As we saw at the beginning of this chapter, the beehive provided a benign image for early socialists and workers' movements. But, as time went on, neither socialism nor beehives seemed so benevolent. By the beginning of the twentieth century, some people saw socialism not as a harmless dream of co-operation but as sinister social engineering. In 1908 the bestselling bee author Tickner Edwardes wrote that the hive was 'a living example, a perfect object-lesson of what socialism, carried out to its last and sternest conclusions must mean', both to bee communities and to human ones. The hive, he declared, was governed by the principle of everyone working for 'the greatest good of the greatest number'. Population growth was accelerated or retarded according to the estimate of the food supply. The proportion of the sexes was varied 'at will'. This was a kind of eugenics in action. All the wealth of the state was held in common. 'The rule that those who cannot work, must not live, is applied with ruthless consistency.'[46]

The socialist beehive was partly a by-product of developments in bee science, which had downgraded the influence of the queen bee in the hive. In 1901, in *The Life of the Bee*, Maurice Maeterlinck wrote of the hive as a society where private life was eroded in a sacrifice of 'the individual to the common interest'. Bees were governed not by the queen, but by a mysterious power, the 'spirit of the hive', which controlled the very minds of the bees.[47] The queen now seemed a rather helpless figure. Here is Tickner Edwardes again:

> The truth is that the queen-bee is the very reverse of a monarch, both by nature and inclination. She possesses only the merest rudiments of intelligence. She has a magnificent body, great docility, certain almost unrestrainable impulses and passions, a yielding, womanish love of the yoke; but she is incapable of action other than that arising from her bodily promptings. Her brain is proportionately smaller than that of the worker. In a dozen different ways she is inferior to the common worker-bees, who rule her absolutely, mapping out her entire daily life and using her for the good of the colony, just as a delicate, costly piece of mechanism is used by human craftsmen to produce some necessary article of trade.

So far from being an absolute monarch, the queen bee was a kind of slave in her own bee commonwealth. As for the workers, they too were all brainwashed. They were no longer individuals but machines, programmed to produce the common good. This was the anarchist dream turned into a nightmare. The hive represented an order without any need for 'law or penalty': all the law had been internalized in the personality of the bees themselves, and 'every worker-bee is herself the State in miniature, all propensities alien to the pure collective spirit having been long ago bred out of her by the sheer necessities of her case.'[48]

The beehive, in other words, had become a totalitarian collective, and this is a view that has persisted to the present day. What has changed is that the nightmare no longer includes Tickner

Edwardes's concept of the queen bee as the mindless slave of the workers. This is because of the discovery in the mid twentieth century of 'queen substance', the pheromones emitted by the queen which trigger certain activities in the colony. Queen substance means that the workers do take their lead from the queen – but only in the sense that chemicals from her body trigger them to act in certain ways and not others. Scientists still marvel at bee colonies achieving 'co-ordination without central planning', but they also emphasize that, for a colony to be effective, it must have a fully functioning queen. This leaves the field for nasty forms of politics wide open.

DC Comics supervillain Queen Bee™ & © DC Comics.
All rights reserved. Used with permission.

Just how nasty is shown by the appearance in 1999 of 'Queen Bee', a DC Comics supervillain, and the most dystopian bee politician yet imagined. Queen Bee's real name is Zazzala. She is a vision of evil loveliness in black and yellow. You know she is an insect because she wields a gauntlet filled with venom sacs and a stinger, and she has multifaceted eyes, but otherwise she is all woman, as only a comic-book woman can be – an improbable combination of jutting curves and tight abdominal muscles. Zazzala's title is the Royal Genetrix, since she is the mother of an entire insect race. She lives in the hiveworld Korll, where she rules trillions of swarming 'drone-slaves', whom she subjugates with her mind-numbing 'hypno-pollen'. Her henchmen are the so-called Bee-Troopers, a band of male warrior drones reared in collective crèches, who remain fanatically faithful to her cause and who happily sacrifice their lives by stinging her enemies using their bioelectric stinger cannons. Her mission, like that of any other self-respecting supervillain, is to rule planet Earth – starting, needless to say, with New York. 'There are almost six billion independent mindzzz on thiszz planet', she buzzes. 'By tomorrow, there will be none.'

It is stating the obvious to say that Queen Bee is not intended as anything other than fantasy. She is no more a serious contribution to entomology than is Spiderman. What is interesting, however, is that even the most serious entolomogists now write about the dystopian politics of the beehive in terms not entirely removed from those of DC Comics.

Probably the most influential and brilliant honeybee entomologist currently working is Professor Francis Ratnieks of the University of Sheffield, England. His speciality is understanding the ways in which the honeybee colony polices itself in order to manage conflict. The key to policing in a honeybee colony is the strange method of sex determination, called haplodiploidy. Honeybee workers are not sterile, as was previously thought. They have ovaries, and under rare circumstances they can lay eggs, which are always male drones. However, Ratnieks has found that workers will do all they can to 'prevent each other from reproducing. If one worker lays an egg, that egg will almost certainly be eaten by another worker within a few hours.'[49] Workers do this, he argues, to maintain order in the colony. It is better for the workers collectively if they prevent each other from laying drone eggs, because while they are closely related to all drones descended from the queen (they share the same mother, after all), they are much less strongly related to the sons of worker bees. Hence, the gobbling-up of workers' eggs – the workers in general don't want a new breed of drones complicating things. 'I think it's the best example of conflict resolution in nature,' says Ratnieks.[50]

To promote his work, Ratnieks has frequently compared the discipline of the bees to human politics – the police state in particular. Bees, he writes, even use 'prisons' of wax to trap alien infestations of beetles.[51] When Ratnieks's latest findings were written up in *Nature* magazine recently, it was said that the honeybee 'police force' is 'so pervasive that it rivals the former East Germany's infamous Stasi'.[52] The queen is the dictator at the top; the workers are the Stasi apparatchiks, so thoroughly indoctrinated that they carry out political repression without having to be told. The article (not by Ratnieks himself) begins, 'Murder, torture and imprisonment – these are the standard tools of repressive regimes. But if you imagine that human societies have a monopoly on such tactics, think again. Social insects perfected the police state long before people got in on the act.' Honeybees, the article goes on, are 'the most advanced insect police state so far discovered'.

Scientists have, however, discovered some bee colonies where the policing breaks down – where worker bees begin to reproduce en masse – and the usual rules do not apply; these are known as 'anarchies'. One science writer claims that the beehive offers a face-off 'between authoritarianism and anarchy'. An evolutionary geneticist has been quoted as saying that worker policing in the hive is not just a 'metaphor' – that it might even provide some kind of model for resolving human conflict.[53] Yet Ratnieks himself has said that all conflict in the bee colony is essentially about 'reproduction'. If this is the case, scientists ought to see that it cannot be political conflict, and it cannot teach humans how to resolve anything. The comparisons between the hive and the police state *are* just metaphors, and not particularly good ones. (Not even the Stasi was so pervasive that every worker was a signed up operative.) But the truth is that scientists – even the kind of rational, peer-reviewed scientists who write for *Nature* – are no more immune

to the pull of the political beehive than were the various lickspit-
tles, fantasists and megalomaniacs who went before. The twenty-
first-century bee state is a darker, more repressive place than the
golden realm of the seventeenth-century bee monarchists, but that
doesn't make it any more real. It is still just a beehive, and, as
Thomas Hobbes said, there is no politics in the beehive. But
Hobbes is as little heeded as ever.

4

Food and Drink

Figs and fat cakes,
Soft oil and honey sweet,
And a wine cup, strong and deep.

Plutarch, *Life of Theseus* (first century AD)

THERE IS NO great cuisine (with the partial exception of that of the Chinese, who have never been very sweet-toothed) which has not used and praised honey. Honey has always been a way to make nice things nicer. In ancient Egypt they candied melons in liquefied honey. The ancient Greeks ate milky curds with honey, just as the modern Greeks eat cool, thick yoghurt with honey for their breakfast.

Of course honey is also delicious on its own – thyme-scented honey, herbal eucalyptus honey, spicy leatherwood honey from Australia, or magical tupelo gold honey from swampy Florida, which never crystallizes. The bees who make

An advertisement for Be-Ze-Be honey

this glorious food are worshipped, but few people want to think about what the bees have to do to make it. As the food writer Jane Davidson once wrote, if you asked most people if they would like to eat insect spit, they would probably say no; yet few can resist honey.[1] With honey, there is always this rift between the divine and the disgusting.

The Food of the Gods: The Origins of Honey

It is hard to recapture now quite how special honey must have seemed, during the thousands of years when it was the only real sweetener available. When early man, like the men and women in

Virgin honey from the Pyrenees

those Spanish cave paintings of 10,000 years ago, discovered a lucky comb in a tree and managed to avoid death by stinging and take it home to a hungry family, they must all have felt it to be the most serendipitous of treats. If the sweetest thing you were used to eating was fruit, how rich and heady sweet honey must have tasted – enough to give you a kind of high, to make your head spin with stickiness. It is entirely natural that, in all the great mythologies of the world, honey should have become known as the food of the gods: the *mead* of the Teutons, the *amrita* of India. We call it 'nectar' because honey was the *nectar* and *ambrosia* eaten by Greek gods. 'Honey is the food of the gods,' says the Greek philosopher Porphyry (*c.* 232–*c.* 305).[2] Honey seemed like a food too good for mere mortals. To eat amber honeycomb was such a pleasure that man told himself it must be illicit – stolen from the gods to whom it properly belonged. Technically, honey *is* stolen food – stolen from the bees, which is why vegans today prefer not to eat it, seeing it as exploitative. And stealing from insects is not the most dignified of activities. For most of history, therefore, man told himself that he was stealing not from the bees but from the gods. The idea that honey was divine food led to great confusion about its origins. The very fact that honey was so revered prevented humans from understanding what exactly it was that they were eating.

Honey is really regurgitated nectar transformed by enzymes (chiefly invertase) in the bees' glands into an 'invert' solution, then evaporated in the wax cells through a fanning action into a concentrated syrup. This is the real 'secret' of honey: enzyme action and hard work.[3] Nectar is a more or less watery solution of sugars which vary depending on the flower involved but which always include sucrose. The bees use the enzymes produced by their hypopharyngeal glands to convert this sucrose into glucose and fructose, then condense them into a supersaturated solution which keeps well and packs in a lot of energy in the winter when the flowers are gone. At just three weeks old, worker bees know how to travel up to three kilometres (and in rare cases twice that) for a good source of food. They may visit as many as a thousand flowers on each foraging trip, sucking the nectar out and carrying it in their honey stomachs, before returning to the hive to deposit the load on to the proboscis of house bees, who disgorge the sweet liquid into waxen cells. In the heat of the hive, with other workers flapping their wings, the liquid ripens and condenses to the right consistency. It is then capped with wax, to stay fresh during the lean winter months. The magic lies in the bees' sheer, ruthless efficiency.

But, when all this was unknown, the origin of honey was supposed to be altogether more magical. Honey was thought to have
been regurgitated not by the bees but by the gods, whose spit,
being godly, was supposedly very delicious. This sweetener was
thought to be so perfect a food that it must have fallen from the
skies. Honey was so extraordinary, so ready to eat and utterly
unlike the other basic foods – consider how much more edible and
instantly nourishing a honeycomb is than a sheaf of wheat, a pig,
a cow – that it seemed it could be fabricated only in the heavens.
'For he on honey-dew hath fed, / And drunk the milk of
Paradise', as Coleridge writes in 'Kubla Khan' (1816).

Pliny believed he was writing straightforward 'natural history',
not poetry, when he wrote that the 'exquisite pleasure' that honey
gives us must be due to its 'ethereal nature and origin'. He wasn't
sure if honey was 'a saliva emanating from the stars' or 'a juice
exuding from the air while purifying it', or perhaps 'the sweat of
the heavens', but he was positive that this 'unctuous' liquid must
have descended from the skies: 'This substance is engendered from
the air, mostly at the rising of the constellations, and more especially when Sirius is shining; never, however, before the rising of
the Vergiliae, and then just before daybreak.' If only honey could
reach us direct from the heavens, it would be 'pure limpid and
genuine'. Alas, lamented Pliny, because it fell from 'so vast a
height', it attracted earthly corruption and was 'tainted by the
exhalations of the earth'. By the time that it reached the human
table, it had been 'accumulated in the stomachs of bees, then cast
up again'.[4] Thus, the bees were merely carriers of the food of the
gods, not the producers of it.

There was one type of honey that seemed to come directly
from above. 'Honeydew' was the name given to the sweetness of
heaven which fell to earth and covered plants with its sugar. In
1634 Charles Butler wrote of it as 'the purest nectar' which 'God
doth miraculously distil out of the air', a delicate dew which lands
on the leaves of oak trees.

> When there is a honey dew you may perceive it by the bees: for
> (as if they smelled it by the sweetness of the air) they presently issue
> out of their hives, in great haste following one another; and refus-
> ing their old haunts, search and seek after the oak; which for that
> time shall have more of their custom than all the other plants of
> the earth.

Butler speculates that this honeydew is 'the very quintessence of
all the sweetness of the earth . . . drawn up, as other dews, in
vapours into the lowest region of the air, by the exceeding and
continual heat of the sun; and there . . . condensated by the
nightly cold into this most sweet and sovereign nectar, which
thence doth descend in the earth in a dew or small drizzling rain'.[5]
Honeydew was a gift from nature, a way for man to eat the very
goodness of the earth itself. The Roman doctor Galen (born in
AD 129) said that, when honeydew appeared on trees, farmers
joked that Zeus had rained down honey on them.[6] When this happened, the people of Mount Libanus would spread out animal
skins on the ground to catch this 'air-honey' as it fell off the trees.

There is such a thing as honeydew – a sugary substance which
drips from certain plants. Unfortunately, the real honeydew is far
less poetic and appealing than the stories that men have built
around it. In fact it is revolting.

So far from being the saliva of the stars, real honeydew is the
excrement of small insects. Aphids and other related insects consume the sweet plant sap on resinous trees in very large quantities.
Most of this sap passes through their bodies unchanged and crystallizes on the plants. This excrement gathers on leaves, ready to
be collected by bees and made into honey. It drips stickily, more
so in hot weather. In the broiling summer of 1976, cars driving
down the tree-lined avenues of Paris were anointed with a thick
green aphid syrup.[7] Once this honeydew is on the trees, bees then
gather it and add their saliva to the mix of bodily fluids. Butler's
'quintessence of . . . sweetness' is in fact this ungodly substance.
Some honey-lovers prize honeydew, and you can buy it from
health-food shops and gourmet honey retailers, usually at consid-

erable expense. Sometimes it is euphemistically said that honey-dew is 'exuded' from the insects, as if we still wish to cling to the idea of a heavenly sweat. Insect poo does not sound so paradisiacal. I have tasted top-quality honeydew (imported into Britain by the Italian food specialists Seggiano), excrement from the very finest Etruscan aphids in the woodlands of Monte Cimino. The minute I lifted the spoon to my lips, I disliked the dark, crawling taste. Put politely, it tasted figgy, liquoricy and woody. Put impolitely, it tasted – well, it tasted of its true origins. Some honey advocates have cast doubt on whether 'honeydew' should really be considered fit for human consumption. Tickner Edwardes called it 'detestable'. Now that we know what it is, we may be tempted to agree.

What is Honey?

Honeydew is an extreme case of the difficulty that all honeys have posed when it comes to classification. Human beings have been persistently baffled about what exactly honey really is. In ancient Roman medicine, almost all foods could be placed into one of two categories: animal or vegetable. Honey was different. Just as the bee was seen as neither tame nor wild, honey was seen as neither animal nor vegetable, but of indeterminate status in between. It was vegetable because it came ultimately from flowers. Yet it was animal too, because it was apparently gathered by bees, which were animals. It must have been vegetable, because it was eaten by devout vegetarian Pythagoreans, who spurned all meat. On the other hand it must have been animal, because honey did not grow on plants or in the ground. It was near impossible to come down one way or another in this animal versus vegetable debate. Honey was *sui generis*. It confounded the usual rules. In both Islamic and Jewish law, bees were regarded as unclean beasts; yet honey itself was not unclean.[8]

Part of the problem was that people just could not make up

their minds whether bees made honey or just 'collected' it. The Latin name we still use for honeybees reflects this indecisiveness. The rules for naming different species and strains of animals and other living organisms come from the Swedish botanist Linnaeus (Carl von Linné, 1707–78), an obsessive classifier who tried to stamp a system on the whole universe. It was Linnaeus who invented the category of 'mammals' – from '*mammae*', meaning 'milk glands' – so that humans would for ever be classified by the capacity of a mother to breastfeed. When Linnaeus categorized the honeybee, in 1758, he called it *Apis mellifera*, meaning 'honey-carrying bee' implying that bees merely carried honey from flowers to comb. In 1761 Linnaeus (whose brother was a bee-keeper) spotted his mistake and changed the name to *Apis mellifica*, meaning 'honey-making bee'. It was too late. The earlier name somehow stuck.[9]

Now that chemists have identified most of the main components of honey, it only seems a more complicated substance than ever. About 70 per cent of honey is made up of sugar – the mono-saccharides fructose and glucose, to be precise, with smaller amounts of disaccharides, including sucrose, and trisaccharides. Up to 20 per cent of honey is water, in which the sugars are dissolved, giving liquid honey its syrupy consistency. So most of honey is sugar and water. But sugar and water are not what make honey honey. That secret lies in the remaining 10 per cent. There are close to 200 other different substances in honey: traces of vitamins and minerals, of proteins, of numerous different acids, of enzymes passed on from the bees' bodies, and, perhaps most crucially, of volatile aromas – a cocktail of alcohols, esters and other substances, which mean that, when you open a honey lid, what you smell is the unmistakable, heady smell of honey, of summer in a jar. (The fifth-century-BC Greek philosopher Democritus was said to have spent his last days staying alive by inhaling the fragrance from a honey pot.)

These volatile aromas vary dramatically from honey to honey, being influenced by the plants from which the bees get their nectar. Rape honey has a higher formaldehyde content than some other honeys, for example. Clover honey has a different mix of volatile compounds from lavender honey, and lavender in Provence will produce different chemicals from lavender in Norfolk. That different honeys have differing chemical compositions will also determine whether they are liquid or set in the jar. When first produced by bees, all honey is liquid; but over time it will crystallize to a greater or lesser extent. Honeys with a high water content and low glucose content – acacia, tupelo, milkweed – are the least likely to crystallize. Those with hefty amounts of glucose and less water – dandelion, rape – will crystallize extremely easily. Most honeys are somewhere in between. There are great differences, too, in the chemical pigments in honey that give it its colour. Honey can be red-brown from heather, or pearly-white from morning glory, or water-white from Alaskan fireweed; it can be straw-coloured from dandelion, or egg-yellow from sunflower, or teak-coloured from palmetto, or forest-black from buckwheat. Under rare circumstances, it can be psychedelic: I once saw some outlandishly multicoloured honeycomb taken from an apiary situated near a sweet factory: the bees, having run out of nectar late in the summer, had taken to eating seaside rock, whose colourings came out in the honey.

With all these variables, perhaps it is not surprising that our confusion about how to categorize honey lingers on. We are still in two minds as to whether honey is animal or vegetable. Honey gets sold in health-food shops that would otherwise shun animal foods. Yet, under European law, honey is now officially categorized as 'animal'. For British customs purposes, honey does not fit with 'sugars and sweeteners', nor with 'vegetable products', but with 'edible products of animal origin', along with 'meat and edible offal', 'dairy produce and eggs' and 'fish and crustaceans'. There is a big honey pot on the signs that greet you at British airports, alongside pictures of cheese, fish and meat: these things shall not enter.

Under the British Honey Regulations of 2003, the legal definition of honey is:

Honeycomb from a US beekeeper, emphasizing its purity

> The natural sweet substance produced by the *Apis mellifera* bees
> from the nectar of plants or from secretions of living parts of plants
> or excretions of plant-sucking insects on the living parts of plants
> which the bees collect, transform by combining with specific sub-
> stances of their own, deposit, dehydrate, store and leave in honey-
> combs to ripen and mature.[10]

This definition is certainly accurate, but it is not going to sell a lot
of honey. For most honey-eaters it doesn't much matter how the
bees make honey. It may have taken us a long time to discover
what honey really is, but people have always known they wanted
to eat it.

Honey's Heyday

Honey was not the only sweetener available before the trade in
sugar cane began around AD 700. But it was far and away the best.

Honey's competitors were all more limited in the way they provided sweetness. None gave the instant hit of a bite of swollen honeycomb.

The Romans, with their worship of the vine, had worked out how to extract sweetness from their beloved grapes, boiling down the juice of vine fruits into varying degrees of concentration. *Must* was basic, unfermented grape juice. *Carenum* was the same thing reduced by one-third. *Defrutum* was must reduced by half. *Sapa* was stickier still, being reduced by two-thirds. *Passum* was the sweetest of the lot, a thick, cloying raisin wine. In the Middle East they made similar grape syrups, called *dibs,* which are still prepared to this day. (In Turkey they call them *pekmez*.)[11] The ancient Arabs achieved even sweeter results by boiling down syrups from the sweet flesh of dates and figs. These dark, sticky concoctions were not unlike the pomegranate molasses still used in the cookery of the Levant, notably in the rich game dishes of Persia. You can still buy date syrup too. One brand is called 'Basra' date syrup, named after the Iraqi town, but made in the Netherlands. Such syrups are almost always delicious, in their way, but they have a very particular quality, giving extreme darkness and fruitiness at the same time as they dispense their sweetness – a bit like balsamic vinegar. Their sweetness is much more ambiguous than that of honey. In ancient Egypt, those of modest means would sweeten their food with fruit syrups; but honey was the food of kings.[12]

In other parts of the world there were other ways to satisfy the human taste for sweetness. Maltose, a kind of malt sugar, was sometimes made out of germinating grains. But this 'malt syrup' is far less sweet than honey (maltose is only one-third as sweet as sucrose), as well as having a rather tangy, bitter taste – good in milkshakes, but less appealing by itself. Then there were the sweet saps from certain trees, though these were confined to just a few lucky parts of the globe. The Chinese worked out how to use the sap of sagwire, a kind of sugar-palm tree; Indians in North America were blessed with the fudge-brown sap of the maple tree, which they tapped and made into gorgeous syrups. But by the time these reached the rest of the world the reign of sugar had begun.

All of which meant that, in pre-sugar days, nothing could hold a candle to honey – for those brave enough to collect it or rich enough to pay others to get it. Honey was prized not just for its own sweetness but for the sweetness it could impart to other foods. It was perhaps the most valued ingredient in the cookery of the ancient world.

There are Egyptian pictures on a tomb dating from 1450 BC which show cooks preparing fried cakes of date flour and honey. The ancient Greek playwright Euripides (writing in the fifth cen-

Ancient Egyptians baking 'honey cakes', from the tomb of Rekhmara

tury BC) refers to: 'Cheese-Cakes steeped most thoroughly / In the rich honey of the golden bee.'[13] *Placentae* was the name the Romans gave to these cheesecakes drenched in honey, whose appearance, according to a Roman-food expert, would have been not unlike modern 'baked cheesecake with an open texture which sucks up the honey'. The cheese would be sheep or goat. Around AD 200 the Roman food writer Athenaeus described these cheesecakes as 'streams of the tawny bee, mixed with the clotted river of bleating she-goats placed upon the flat receptacle of the virgin daughter of Zeus'.[14]

The happy marriage of dairy produce and honey is an ancient pleasure. There is still no better way of eating honey than dropped in shimmering beads over curds of yoghurt: the syrupiness of the honey offsets the sour-rich tang of the yoghurt. Few combinations are so nourishing and soothing at the same time, and few have such a long history. The Sumerians were making curds from cow's milk taken from their herds of cattle 4,000 years ago, and it can't have been long before honey was added, to make these primitive cheeses even more fortifying. Everyone remembers the promised 'land flowing with milk and honey'; but the Book of Job speaks of 'torrents of honey and curds', and the Book of Samuel refers to 'honey and curds'.[15] The Greeks sometimes elaborated the combination a little bit, making honey-curd puddings called *hypotrides*, where the milk and the honey were curdled together, then set in a bowl, like Italian pannacotta, and served with fruit. This is a delicious-sounding combination, not far off our modern tastes. But other things the Greeks and Romans did with honey sound a lot less agreeable.

Given that there was never enough honey to go round, wealthy gourmets liked to use as much of it as possible, simply to show that they could. The haute cuisine of the ancient world compounded this effect, by layering honey with other de-luxe ingredients. In Greece the best honey was *akapniston* – meaning taken from the hive without using any smoke, at high risk to the beekeeper. (Most honey tasted smoky on account of the smoke used by beekeepers to distract bees while they were taking the honeycomb.)[16] Foodies in both Greece and Rome valued this honey as a sauce for adding last-minute richness to already lush concoctions, which were neither wholly sweet nor wholly savoury but usually entirely decadent. By the time of Apicius, whose so-called 'first cookbook' came out of Rome in the first century AD, honey was being used in virtually all branches of cookery – including, notoriously, the preparation of edible dormouse. Apicius also puts honey in a sauce for fish (a concept which makes some of us today feel quite queasy) as well as for boiled ostrich and roasted crane. In another recipe, ham is boiled, skinned, anointed with honey, and encased in a flour crust before baking. Apicius also used honey to preserve meats. By immersing chunks of meat in honey, he writes, you can keep it fresh 'as long as you like without pickling'. He then points out that 'This is better in winter; in summer it will keep in this manner only a few days' – a rather alarming warning, which makes one think of the honeyed meat slowly going off in the Mediterranean heat.[17]

A century after Apicius, Julius Pollux, who was half Greek and half Egyptian and an expert on rhetoric, gives a recipe for stuffed fig leaves cooked in honey. This epitomizes the decadent school of honey cookery. First you take your fig leaves. Then you make a stuffing from flour, lard, eggs and brains (probably from a calf). Then you put little dollops of this mixture on to the leaves and roll them up as if you are making dolmades. You braise the little parcels in broth, made from either chicken or kid. Finally you drain them and cook a second time, briefly, in boiling honey – before expiring from the sheer richness of it all.

Honey was more than just a sweetener in pre-sugar times. It was also highly valued as an ingredient which could restore harmony to a dish, correcting faults in other components of the meal. In Roman Britain, honey was often smeared over meat or fish as it was cooking, as much to remove the taste of oiliness as to add that of sweetness. If your wine was too rough or too young, you might stir honey in 'to soften the wine's harsh flavour', as Virgil puts it.[18]

In the Middle Ages they became keener still on honey as a 'tempering' agent. The idea behind tempering was that certain foods contained 'evils' which must be 'allayed' or 'tempered' before the foods could healthfully be eaten.[19] To temper was to bring a dish to its proper temperament. Sometimes vinegar was used, sometimes mustard, sometimes honey. This was almost like exorcizing the demons of foods which were out of kilter with themselves or with us. For example, medieval cooks, especially in Germany and Austria, thought that honey had special powers to temper the evil of peas and make them more edible.

At the same time, the repertoire of really sweet dishes containing honey was expanding. In medieval recipe books, alongside the fruits preserved in honey of the Romans, you find 'composts' of pears, where the honey is mingled with wine and ginger and raisins and cinnamon, and 'confytes' made with quinces, honey, vinegar and anise. Apicius had dipped wheaten bread in milk, fried it in oil, and covered it with honey – like French toast soaked in maple syrup in New York diners. The medieval version was more complex. It was called 'panfoundew', and consisted of a coronary-inducing mixture of bread fried in 'grease', then pounded with red wine, raisins and honey. Then there was the *pain de gaulderye* of Dijon, a kind of solid mould made from gruel cooked with honey – which, as Maguelonne Toussaint-Samat points out, sounds like a kind of pudding they still eat in Tunisia (*hassidat b'el acel*), made from boiled semolina moulded with honey and dates.[20]

Yet the sweetest honey dish made in the Middle Ages was none of these bizarre and exotic combinations. It was gingerbread.

Gingerbread and other Honey Cakes

The name 'gingerbread' is extremely misleading. In its medieval version, gingerbread wasn't a bread and didn't always contain ginger. It was not much like our moreish damp, treacle-dark cakes. The one essential thing in the original gingerbread was honey.

Honey cakes are the oldest cakes of them all. At their most basic they were just honey mixed with flour and baked to hard golden bricks. Unleavened honey cakes were certainly made in biblical times. In the Book of Exodus the manna which God provides for the Israelites in the desert, during their flight from Egypt, is described as looking 'white, like coriander seed' and tasting 'like a wafer made with honey'.[21] Such honey wafers were probably cooked simply on the hearth, like pitta bread, and taken to supply energy on long journeys. Such cakes were very popular with nomadic peoples, because they kept almost indefinitely.

These biblical honey cakes turned into the European spice cakes of the Middle Ages. The *pain d'épice* of France – which has its counterparts in the *Lebkuchen* of Germany, the *couques de Dinant* of Belgium, the *taai-taai* of Holland – began as a flat cake of nothing more than flour, boiled honey and spices, usually including cloves, cinnamon and, most characteristically, anise. In modern *pain d'épice* the mix is considerably leavened with a lot of baking powder and sometimes even – *horreur*! – made with golden syrup instead of honey.[22] Having experimented with the older versions, which you have to gnaw at like a bone, so unyielding are they, I can see why you might want to modernize the recipe. But it is true that the old cakes keep extremely well, in so far as they never taste particularly fresh to begin with.

The secret of *pain d'épice*, which made it superior to the hastily made biblical cakes, was that the dough was ripened or rested for several months before baking. Over this time the honey would ferment slightly, lending the dough a more appealing texture and flavour. It was a skilled art, nurturing this 'mother dough' to just the right point. In 1596 the Corporation of Spice-Bread Makers was formed. Membership was only granted only to those who could produce a 'masterpiece . . . the mixture weighing 200 pounds, flavoured with cinnamon, nutmeg and cloves, of which there shall be three cakes each weighing 20 pounds'.[23]

'*Pain d'épice*' is often translated as 'gingerbread'; but gingerbread in its original incarnation was different – more of a honey candy than a cake. It was honey that had been boiled to a toffee and made thick with breadcrumbs and spices. One of the earliest recipes for 'gyngerbrede' reads:

> Take a quart of honey and seethe it and skim it clean. Take saffron, powdered pepper and throw thereon. Take grated bread and make it so stiff that it will be [cut in slices]. Then take cinnamon powder and strew thereon enough. Then make it square as though thou wouldst slice it. Take, when you have sliced it, and cast box leaves above, stuck in cloves. And if thou would have it red, colour it with sandlewood.[24]

This recipe produces a sticky-sweet candy, easily pliable, almost like playdough.[25]

All over Europe, gingerbread was forced into decorative wooden moulds, in alphabet shapes and other fancies, forerunners of our gingerbread men. Such moulded, candied honey cakes were prolific in the area around Nuremberg, which was known as

An eighteenth-century domestic scene with an apiary in the background

the 'bee-garden of the Holy Roman Empire'.[26] Gingerbread was the glorious highpoint of honey cookery – the point at which cooks revered honey enough to give it all their imagination and energy; when people loved it enough to mix it with their costliest spices and play with it, as they would later play with sugar. These gingerbreads – so intensely sweet, so whimsical – had a feeling of fun and joy to them, as most sweets do. This spirit is captured in Chaucer's *Canterbury Tales*, where the greedy Sir Thopas gets his minstrels to bring him

> . . . the sweet wine,
> And mead inside a maselyn
> And royal spicery;
> Some gingerbread that was full fine,
> And liquorice, and also cumin,
> With sugar that is so dainty.[27]

This is a platter of purest self-indulgence: assorted sweeties (the 'cumin' would really be candied caraway seeds) and alcohol. It is also captures the full honeyed flavour of the medieval world. What better to accompany the gluttonous knight's honey cakes than a bottle or two of honey wine, or mead?

Mead

Man's taste for wild honey was one he shared with beasts, but his taste for mead was all his own. Humans learned how to make mead before they learned how to plant seeds or keep animals. According to the French anthropologist Claude Lévi-Strauss, the discovery of mead marked the passage in human existence from 'nature to culture'.[28] Lévi-Strauss had studied the customs of the Chaco Indians of the Amazon, a people whose culture corresponds to that of the Stone Age. The Chaco told stories about how an old man invented mead by accident one night by mixing honey and water in a trough to ferment. Because this old Indian did not mind if he died, he risked poisoning himself and drank the strange new liquid. He fell down, as if dead. But, instead of dying, he woke up, and told everyone how wonderful it was to get drunk.

Fermented honey was the first way humans discovered of intoxicating themselves (it predates wine by thousands of years), and it probably did come about by accident. Honey ferments quite easily when mixed with water. It would take only some rain falling in a honey jar in warm weather for people to discover the magical sensation of tipsiness. Though it often made them behave like beasts, drinking mead made men feel like gods. The Greeks, the Romans, the Celts, the Slavs, the Scandinavians all saw mead as a divine drink. The importance of mead in early times may be judged by the fact that the same word was often used for mead and for honey: in Sanskrit, they are both *madhu*, which is related to the

Some Caucasian peasants of the sixteenth century enjoying the intoxicating effects of mead

medu of ancient Germany, the *midus* of Lithuania, the *mjod* of Russia, the *mjöd* of Sweden and the *mjød* of Norway.

The Romans had numerous different categories of mead: *hydromel* (a weak mead), *omphacomel* (made with grape juice), *rhodomel* (made with roses) and *oxymel* (made with vinegar and salt). Hydromel, according to Pliny, was made by mixing three parts rainwater to one part honey, and leaving in the sun for forty days at the rising of the Dog Star.[29] As well as making you drunk, this hydromel was supposed to cure small-mindedness.

We tend to associate mead with the drinking habits of the old Norsemen: we think of dead heroes swigging mead in Valhalla; of Beowulf supping from his mead-bowl; of rowdy warriors sitting on mead-benches, taking comfort in their foaming horns as the

cruel Danish weather beats on the walls outside. It is hard to imagine the Norse sagas without mead, and without the requisite
carved drinking vessels and horn cups. Odin, the leader of the
Norse gods, has a goat from whose udders mead flows eternally.

Yet the cultural significance of mead went far beyond
Scandinavia. It was not always a hearty drink for wassailing and
keeping out the cold: it could sometimes be quite refined. Well
after winemaking had become established, many discerning
drinkers showed a preference for mead. Few were more discerning than Sir Kenelm Digby, a suave Catholic courtier in Jacobean
England, who is now remembered mainly, and perhaps unfairly,
for 'writing a cookery book and for poisoning his wife', the beautiful Venetia Stanley.[30] The cookery book was *The Closet of the
Eminently Learned Sir Kenelm Digbie Opened* (1669), which was
published from his copious notes after Digby's death. It is really as
much of a mead book as a food book, containing more than a
hundred recipes for mead, metheglin (the name for certain
flavoured meads), hydromel and honey ale. Digby gives us mead
to drink with meals and mead to drink between meals, plain mead
and spiced mead, mead with marjoram and mead with winter
savoury, strong mead and weak mead and extra-weak 'small' mead,
'excellent' mead, 'very good mead' and mead which is merely
'pleasant', mead with 'Cherries or Morello-Cherries, or Raspes,
or Bilberries, or Black-Cherries', mead with primrose flowers and
sage flowers and borage flowers and bugloss flowers, white mead,
mead that is 'good for liver and lungs' and mead that is good for
'the colick and stone', mead from the best 'Hampshire-honey',
Antwerp mead and Moscow mead, and sweet mead for ladies.

Digby often uses his recipes as a vehicle for shameless social
climbing: there are sycophantic entries on The Countess of
Bullingbrook's White Metheglin and My Lady Morice's Mead.
His most famous recipe is 'Hydromel as I made it weak for the
Queen Mother', requiring eighteen quarts of spring water and
one quart of honey, flavoured with fresh ginger, rosemary and
cloves, to tickle the royal tastebuds. 'Thus was the Hydromel made

that I gave the Queen, which was exceedingly liked by every-body.'[31]

Whatever one thinks of his social tastes, Digby's culinary ones seem excellent. He puts together lovely flavourings, such as lemon rind and ginger, and points out that mead can stand up to 'strong herbs to make it quick and smart upon the Palate; as Rosemary, Bay-Leaves, Sage, Thyme, Marjoram, Winter-Savoury, and such like, which would be too strong or bitter in ale or beer'. Digby is very particular and practical in his methods, offering all kinds of pertinent advice, such as avoiding metal dishes when infusing gillyflowers and swimming a hen's egg in the mead to see if it is strong enough (if it is, the egg will stand up). It is hard not to warm to an author who advises morello cherries 'for pleasure and black ones for health'. Digby makes mead appear as a deeply desirable drink. He writes of one of his meads, 'It will be spritely and quick and pleasant and pure white', which makes me yearn to drink a glass of it.[32]

But, oh, the disappointment when you close the book and uncork a real bottle of mead! I have not tasted nearly as many meads as there were in Digby's closet, and I have not made my own; but I have tasted dry mead and sweet mead, spiced mead and unspiced mead, 'heritage' mead and mead for the modern palate. I have tried meads that taste of urine, and meads that taste of petroleum waste. What I have not tasted are any that are particu-larly nice. Bad mead is worse than the most mediocre wine, because of the expectations it raises. You are expecting the nectar of the gods, and what you get is cough mixture, if you are lucky.

Honey-lovers today sometimes lament that mead is now so neglected. The wonder is rather that anyone except beekeepers drinks mead at all; perhaps it is the success of films like *Lord of the Rings* and *Braveheart* that makes people think a hogshead of mead would be a fine thing. It is not that mead is always badly made. It is just that, even when well made, the honey gives it a weird after-taste, which is as unpleasant as fresh honey is pleasant. There are numerous independent meaderies in both Europe and the USA making interesting versions – dry ones and spiced ones and fortified ones like sherry. The *Honigwein* of Germany also has its admirers. The most filthy stuff is the kind labelled with quaint Celtic designs and cynically marketed at tourists in heritage spots, often in far-flung parts of the British Isles: this tastes like a mixture of Lucozade and the kind of cider that teenagers get so drunk on that they make themselves sick. If the invention of mead signalled the passage from nature to culture, as Lévi-Strauss thought, the victory of wine over mead is surely the passage to true civilization. The fact that drinkers have more or less abandoned mead is proof that, just sometimes, there really is such a thing as progress.

But should we feel quite so triumphant about the way we have abandoned honey as well?

Honey's Decline

One food historian observes that honey is now 'hardly used in cookery at all except for exotic effect'.[33] If any beekeeper should be kind enough to read this book, they may well harrumph in protest over this opinion, insisting that they and all their friends use honey in every kind of dish, from dressed avocado to baked gammon and Moroccan duck. But if honey on avocado isn't 'exotic' (and that's putting it nicely), then I don't know what is. It is certainly fair to say that when honey is used in Western cookery now it is predominantly as a flavouring, rather than a sweetener. The reason for this is clear. We have sugar.

We have no way of knowing exactly how much honey people ate in the distant past, but the best estimate seems to be that English honey consumption reached its peak around the 1100s, when it may have been as high as 2 kg per person per year.[34] At that time, when the Anglo-Norman kings were trying to maintain control over their unruly barons, average sugar consumption barely even registered. By 1975, almost a millennium later, when the factory bosses were trying to maintain control over the unruly trade unions, the British ate on average a mere eighth as much honey as their medieval ancestors – just a ¼ kg per person per year: a measly half a jar. But of refined sugar, imported from far-flung islands, they ate 53 kg per person per year. How did this turn-around happen?

It has often been said that British honey consumption was ruined by the Reformation, and particularly by the dissolution of the monasteries in the 1530s, which shut down one of the major sources of good honey. Monks and nuns had been important beekeepers, enjoying honey on their bread as one of their few lux-uries. In Catholic Spain and Portugal, honey remained an import-ant ingredient in cooking – in toothsome turron, that hard version of nougat, and eggy honey cakes – for much longer than in Britain. As Henry VIII's henchmen destroyed the monasteries, so they forced honey production into steep decline. It was bad timing, because, as it so happened, around the same time a new source of cheap sweetness was opening up with the Atlantic trade in sugar cane. Honey could not compete with this twin onslaught of Protestantism and sugar colonies. After the seventeenth century, honey all but vanishes from British cookbooks.

This economic explanation is part of the story, but it does not explain everything. Our preference for one food over another is only partly determined by supply. There is also the question of taste. You do not like one food more than another just because there is more of it on the market. Sugar cane had been available, albeit at a high cost and in only small quantities, long before the Reformation, through the Mediterranean sugar industry, which lasted from about 700 to about 1600.[35] Because of its expense and scarcity, it could not be used much. Almost all surviving European recipes for preserved fruit carried on using honey instead of sugar until the seventeenth century. And yet there are signs that, when cooks could get their hands on sugar from the Mediterranean, this 'honey from a reed' was preferred to real honey as an ingredient in the kitchen. As early as the mid-fifteenth century sugar is often suggested in written European recipes. There are several instances of honey being presented as an inferior substitute for sugar, much as a modern recipe might suggest margarine as an inferior substitute for butter. A recipe for custard tart from the mid-1400s says, 'Then take sugar enough and put thereto, or else honey for default of sugar.'[36] Increasingly, cooks came to see honey as very much second best to sugar. In 1287, during the reign of Edward I, the royal household used 677 lb (307 kg) of ordinary sugar, 300 lb (136 kg) of violet sugar and 1,900 lb (862 kg) of rose sugar.[37]

Honey is also virtually absent from the story of confectionery, as the historian of sweets Laura Mason has remarked.[38] Sugarcraft blossomed on the Renaissance table, but honey got left behind. As Mason explains, there were very good culinary reasons for this. If you are a confectioner by trade, honey, however lovely in itself, is a much less versatile tool than sugar. Its different chemical composition – with much higher levels of both water and fructose than sugar – means that honey candies can easily become soft and squishy. Honey is much harder to clarify than sugar. It never goes properly clear, and burns easily, giving off a nasty odour nothing like the delicious perfume of caramelized sugar. Sugar, on the other hand, with its equal amounts of glucose and fructose molecules, joined in sucrose crystals, responds well to boiling and cooling and moulding into fancy shapes.

In many cases, to cook with honey is to ruin it. Eva Crane points out that the most 'pleasing aroma components' of honey are those with low boiling points, which are evanescent and best appreciated fresh from the hive.[39] The most fragrant honeys are wasted on confectionery. But even the plainest honey is still too honeyish for most sweet-makers. The very characteristics which make honey such a glorious natural food – its particular aroma, its colour, its intensity – make it a poor vehicle for the sugarcrafter's art. There is too much art in honey already. Though it may be the finest of all sweets in itself, for those of us who like it, honey does not lend itself so well to making other sweets – except for sweets where the honey taste is the point, such as nougat, turron, halva or the delicious honey lollipops sold by the Maison de Miel in Paris.[40]

The taste for sugar is the taste for sweetness in its most potent form. Not all cultures have developed this taste to the same degree as others – in Bangladesh they consume a tiny fraction of the sugar they consume in Cuba, for example – but once the sugar bug infects a nation it is very hard to pull back from it.[41] We can see this happening now to an extreme extent in the USA, where each person eats, on average, about 75 kg of 'caloric sweeteners' per year – about a third in the form of refined sugar, a third in the form of corn sweeteners, and a third in the form of high-fructose corn syrup. Ever since sugar consumption began to skyrocket, there have been calls for domestic honey production to increase in competition. Honey represents the homespun and homegrown, while sugar is factory-made and imported. The irascible nineteenth-century reformer William Cobbett wanted country children to eat the honey of the parish, not the sugar of foreign 'slave-drivers'.[42] It is a nice idea, and one shared by the current critics of excessive 'food miles'; but it is hopelessly unrealistic, both about human tastes and about economics.

Human palates are very capricious. Just because you love the bitterness of chicory, it does not follow that you will love the bitterness of dark chocolate or of aubergines. Liking the sourness of lemons does not commit you to enjoying the sourness of tamarind. If you have a sweet tooth, you are bound to like sugar, because sugar is simply sweetness in its most general form.[43] But will you like honey? Maybe, maybe not. Honey is a more particular form of sweetness than sugar, even than brown sugar. There is more going on in it, both positive and negative. Before sugar, honey was the most general form of sweetness – more general, as we have seen, than the darkly aromatic date syrups and boiled grape juices. But once sugar has been tasted honey suddenly appears in a new light, and not necessarily a flattering one: it seems altogether more singular and less general.

For those who continued to prefer honey, sugar was the enemy. Towards the end of the sixteenth century, honey lovers began to complain about the growing popularity of sugar. One Robert

Southerne, a beekeeper, was very vocal on the topic in 1593, resenting the way that England's honey was being abandoned in favour of imported sugar:

> Such nice mouthes which are good for nothing but to taste lamp oil, cry, Oh honey fie it's fulsome: Sugar, I marry, that's the fellow: and why, forsooth? Because far fetched and dear bought is good for Ladies. No, no, England hath the blessings of God [in its honey], but the ingratitude of the people is . . . abominable.[44]

Though he is attacking it, Southerne presents the side of the sugar-lover more powerfully than he can have intended: 'Oh honey fie it's fulsome'. 'Fulsome' is exactly the word. In its old sense, 'fulsome' meant not just 'abundant', but 'overdone', 'effusive', 'cloying' and 'offensive'. This is just how honey tastes to those who dislike it: it intrudes in your mouth; it overwhelms you, as sugar does not. As Southerne goes on, 'Some . . . are afraid, that of the least drop of honey they shall surfeit'.[45]

Southerne's complaints fell on deaf ears. In 1633 James Hart announced, rightly, that 'sugar hath now succeeded honey' in esteem.[46] Part of honey's decline can be attributed to medicine. Sugar took over from honey as the apothecary's cure-all. 'So useful was sugar in the medical practice of Europe from the thirteenth to the eighteenth centuries that the expression "like an apothecary without sugar" came to mean a state of utter desperation.' One medical expert, Tobias Venner, writing in 1620, complained that honey 'annoyeth many, especially those that are cholerick or full of winde', whereas sugar 'agreeth with all ages and all complexions'.[47] Yet again, honey was too particular, too fulsome.

But in the end it was tea and coffee that ensured the out-and-out-victory of sugar – a victory that would endure long after sugar had ceased to be seen as curative, even after it became seen as harmful to health. Neither the coffee of the Arabic world nor the tea of the British working-classes is enhanced by the full-blown aroma of honey, which fights the volatile aromas of the drinks themselves. (Many beekeepers disagree, but on this question, as on so many others, they are in a minority.) Tea and sugar found popularity together. From 1750 onward, trade with the East Indies meant that the poorest labourer in Britain could afford to drink tea; and into this stimulating drink he put sweet calories from sugar.[48] Then, as the nineteenth century dawned, honey lost the last thing it had going for it in the battle with sugar: its cheapness.

Until about 1800, honey had always cost less than sugar – often a good deal less, because it was more plentiful and less labour-intensive to produce, not needing to be treated or imported. In the year 1250 honey was fifty times cheaper than sugar; in 1600 it was four or five times cheaper than sugar cane hauled all the way from the slave-fuelled Caribbean colonies. But sometime between 1800 and 1850 the price of sugar in England – the sweet-toothed nation par excellence – reached parity with that of honey. By 1850 all sugar, whether cane or beet, had become dirt-cheap, and suddenly it was honey that was expensive. The main reason for this was that the sugar market had suddenly become much more competitive, as world trade opened up. After England imposed a continental trade blockade on Napoleon in 1806, an unintended side effect was that both France and Prussia increased their production of sugar beet, so that they would not have to rely on the Atlantic trade in sugar cane. Meanwhile there was more competition from new sugar-cane producers in India, Australia, Brazil and, above all, Cuba. Honey would never again be able to compete with sugar on price. These days it costs many times as much as sugar (a recent scare over the safety of Chinese honey pushed the price up still further), and consumption of honey is a mere fraction of that of the processed sugar we guzzle so rapaciously.

Yet, even if it is now on a relatively small global scale, the taste for honey endures, as that for mead has not. Over the past ten years, world honey production has actually increased – not radically but steadily.[49] The rarer honeys have found a friend in the organic-food movement, both for their value as untampered-with food (to count as organic under British guidelines, apiaries must be placed with four miles (6.5 km) of organic land all round them) and for the role that honeybees play in sustainable agriculture. In some countries, notably Germany, honey is still consumed in quantities similar to those of medieval times (about 2 kg per person per year).[50]

Some nineteenth-century honey jars

Honey marketing people, of whom I've met a few while writing this book, tend to complain that 'the general public' is not more aware of the potential in using honey in savoury dishes. They would like to see us basting roast lamb in honey, and coating chicken legs in honey marinade for the barbecue, as if we were decadent Romans, thereby boosting sales. I disagree. Meat is sweet enough without honey to temper it. It is no tragedy that Julius Pollux's brain-stuffed fig leaves seething in honey have gone the way of all flesh. We now have other ways of showing off at table. If no one ever ate fish in honey sauce again, it would be no cause for tears – no more than the demise of mead. Honey cakes and puddings are a different matter. It would be a pity if we forgot the traditions of rye-rich gingerbreads and long-lasting honey cakes, of madeleines and cheesecakes steeped in honey. But their deliciousness alone will probably guarantee their survival. Anyway, the best way to eat honey has always been by itself, straight from the bees: on every kind of bread, on yoghurt or ricotta or clotted cream, on porridge, on pancakes, on fruit, or spooned straight from jar to mouth.

Viewed from a gourmet perspective, the recognition that honey is a more *particular* kind of sweetener than sugar has in fact been no bad thing. Even its expense counts in its favour. Honey is increasingly loved by connoisseurs precisely because it is not sugar; because it is natural and pure and raw; because it is special. Honey is now appreciated in all its fulsomeness; in all its wonderful variety.

The Varieties of Honey

What, then, makes a good honey?

Judges at modern honey shows tend to concentrate, rather sternly, on faults to avoid rather than qualities to achieve – something that competitors sometimes grumble about, quietly, when the judges aren't listening. The reason behind this negative judging is that honey shows were set up in the nineteenth century as a way of combating the widespread practice of adulteration. In the eighteenth century, honey was often adulterated using flour and other fillers, which could be disguised in jars of crystallized honey. This meant that if you found a honey that was clear and runny you could be pretty sure it was the real thing. This all changed when glucose syrup was invented in the following century: being transparent, this could be easily blended with honey without being easily detected. Sometimes fraudsters would even take an empty honeycomb and fill it up with glucose, a very sneaky deception. When the British National Honey Show started in 1874, in London, its aim was to discourage such malpractice by laying down stringent standards for honey offered for sale.

To win first prize at a honey show, you must produce honey that is without defect. Your honey must not smell or taste of any foreign matter. Its odour must not be strange, or smoky. It should not contain excess water, or be fermented. It must have a precisely determined composition of fructose and sucrose, with not too much sucrose. (There was a bit of a hullabaloo recently when British honey judges had to change the rules slightly to accommodate the fact that borage honey has a very high sucrose content which is natural and not procured by the deceitful addition of sugar.) Competition honey should not be stored in sticky jars: they should be spotlessly clean and neatly labelled. Whether it is clear or whether it is crystallized, the honey should be completely smooth and homogenous. No jagged crystals must spoil its uniformity. If it can avoid all these defects, it just might win.

The trouble with these criteria is that they tend to make for rather boring honey. For example, Honey Show honey must be strained of all 'residue'. But this residue, so far from being rubbish, is often the best bit of honey, the pollen-rich goo which gives honey much of its fragrance and health-giving properties. Beekeepers often save this residue for their own personal consumption. Competition honey is undoubtedly safe to eat, but – lined up in its neurotically hygienic jars – it is seldom great.

To say what does make a honey great is altogether harder. In AD 25, the Greek doctor Diascorides said that:

> The best, the most appreciated honey is sweet, penetrating and delicately perfumed, of a pale yellowish colour. It is not liquid but coagulated, thickening afterwards. It does not flow and sticks perfectly to the finger when one touches it. Spring honey is the best and so is summer honey. Winter honey remains very thick, it is a lot less pleasant.[51]

Many years later, in 1623, the English bee-master Charles Butler came up with a very similar formula for success. The best honey, wrote Butler, is clear, odoriferous, yellow like pale gold (but right Virgin honey is more crystalline at the first), sharp, sweet, and pleasant to the taste, of a mean consistence between thick and thin, so clammy that being taken up upon your fingers end, in falling it will not part, but hang together like a long string . . .[52]

In other words, what counted was colour, scent, taste and consistency. But there was also something more: something which corresponds to the *terroir* of winemakers, something which we might call the charisma of geography.

There were many famous honeys in the ancient world, all attached to particular places. Mount Hybla in Sicily was said to yield honey of 'perfect sweetness'.[53] The island of Calymnos, off Turkey, was also praised for its honey.[54] But most people agreed that the finest honey came from the Attic bees of Mount Hymettus, near Athens. Greek recipes tell us that Hymettan honey was white, thin and clear – which is odd, because nowadays the honey of Hymettus is golden brown. Perhaps it seemed white compared to the dark tree honeys of Greek pine forests. Hymettan honey developed a prestige which ran away with itself. This is illustrated by the character of Trimalchio, the most famous nouveau riche in ancient literature. In a satire by Petronius (a trend-setter at the court of Nero, who was forced to commit suicide in AD 66), Trimalchio throws a dinner party to show off his new-found wealth. Every detail is over the top. He showers his guests with pomegranates and peahen's eggs served with silver spoons. As for the honey, Trimalchio 'had bees brought from Athens to give him Attic [i.e. Hymettan] honey on the premises'.[55] This shows how potent the idea of Hymettan honey had become. Trimalchio was under the impression that the Hymettan bees could somehow carry with them the essence of their place, away from the thyme hills of Hymettus itself.

Other Romans thought they knew better. The agricultural writer Columella judged honeys not by their place of origin but by their plant source. All of Columella's favourite honeys came from the mint family: 'Thyme yields honey with the best flavour;

the next best are Greek savoury, wild thyme and marjoram. In the third class, but still of high quality, are rosemary and our Italian savoury . . .'[56]

In the marketing of honey, there is still a division between these two ways of thinking: labelling by place and labelling by plant source. You will find some honeys which are labelled simply 'Australian' or 'Greek', and others – the so-called monoflorals – which are labelled according to the flowers the bees mainly plundered: sunflower, chestnut, orange blossom, acacia. At the Maison du Miel in Paris, the greatest honey shop in the world (24 rue Vignon, near the Madeleine), they label honeys by both place and flower. There are 'polyfloral' honeys from every corner of France – Gatinais honey which tastes of cathedrals and candlewax, and alpine honey as toffeeish as *dulce de leche* – and 'monoflorals' including such rarities as carrot, dandelion and unctuous raspberry. Nowadays it is hard to say whether place trumps flower or flower trumps place.

Honey is a vehicle through which men have expressed the romantic attachment they feel for some places and not others. For a long while, until a scare about pesticide contamination killed its market, most honey sold in Britain came from China. But it was hardly ever advertised as Chinese. When honey comes from Spanish lemon groves, or the lavender fields of Provence, on the other hand, you can be sure that its retailers will make much of the fact.

In 1759 a certain English honey merchant called John Hill challenged this charisma of geography. Why, he asked, were his customers so in thrall to foreign honey, especially that of Narbonne in France? Hill owned a honey shop in Covent Garden, and so was well placed to comment on the honey industry. 'We have Honey from many parts of the world imported into England,' he wrote, 'and all of it is called, from the name of the place where the best is supposed to come, Narbonne honey.' Honey at this time mainly came from three sources: Switzerland, whose honey was thick but insipid; Italy, whose honey was often amber and fragrant; and France, where the 'true Narbonne honey' was of a 'perfect white colour; never at all cand'yd; somewhat thicker than a syrup; and of a smell which perfectly resembles a mixture of thyme and lavender'. Hill recognized that Narbonne honey was good, but he was unconvinced that it was better than honey he had once tasted 'on the edge of Battersea Fields' where they cultivated common lavender for the market – honey which 'seemed to have received the finest part of the essential oil of the lavender'.[57] English spring honey, Hill argued, could be just as good as that from more exotic locations, if only people could get over their prejudices against it.

Hill was fighting a losing battle. British beekeepers still make the same complaint today. They moan that consumers mostly prefer imported honeys to homegrown ones, even though British honeys are more rigorously produced than many others. But what we are seeking from honey is not rigour but romance. Much British honey is now thoroughly unromantic: we are a nation whose honey is now largely a by-product of cooking oil and premenstrual tension. The two major sources of British honeybee forage are oilseed rape and borage, otherwise known as starflower, which gets packaged by the pharmaceutical industry into capsules to relieve womanly cramps. Borage honey is thin and almost blueish, very sweet, undistinguished, watery and clear. Oilseed-rape honey, on the other hand, is extremely prone to crystallization. With most honeys, crystallization does not happen in the hive, because the temperature is too high. But oilseed-rape honey sets so quickly, to a milk-white solid, that if the beekeeper leaves it too long it will become impossible to open the hive, which gets completely gunged up. And if it is not beaten straight away after collection, to reduce the size of the crystals, the honey will be unpleasantly gritty. The other notable thing about rape is that it produces phenomenal quantities of nectar compared to other plants.[58] Bees can't get enough of those bright yellow fields, and they become far more prolific whenever rape is near. Human honeylovers have more mixed feelings about it. The best thing you can say about the taste of rape honey – overlooking its cabbagy smell – is that it is bland; mixed with other honeys it is all right.

The dominance of rape means that British city honeys – taken from bees enjoying the well-husbanded garden flowers of city parks and millionaire's residences – can now seem more special than country ones. There are exceptions to this, however, such as clover honey, with its milk-caramel scent and buttery taste, and the gleaming heather honey of Scotland, whose thick, jelly-like consistency has the same chemical properties as non-drip paint, being 'thixotropic'.

For true romance you have to travel further afield. A journey in a honey jar is as personal as any other kind. In many countries, especially hot ones, there is a strong feeling against set honeys, in favour of runny ones. Liquid honey and set honey are essentially the same; some honey types are more prone to crystallize than others, but any set honey can be rendered liquid if you stand the jar in a bowl of hot water. Creamed honey – that kind with an oozing texture but an opaque look – is made simply by whipping a little set honey into liquid honey. Left to itself, all honey will eventually crystallize. But in some cultures this candied honey doesn't seem nice. I have an Israeli friend who thought that British and French crystallized honeys – the kind we like to slather on our crumpets – were 'dirty' when she first arrived in this country.

Tastes in honey are as personal as any other kind. Some people love to crunch on the wax in segments of honeycomb, savouring the texture in the mouth like natural chewing gum, while others spit it out. There are those who adore the grown-up dirtiness of Italian chestnut honey (with its rotten-apple smell) drizzled over pecorino cheese; and the smoky tang of Rwandan honey; and the dark, resiny odour of Vietnamese jungle honey. I prefer things lighter: the civilized sharpness of French lime honey; the mild, herbal syrup of Californian sage honey; the citrus glow of Spanish orange blossom; the placid gel of Scottish heather and Australian jellybush. It is hard to dispute the ancient view that the very best honeys come from aromatic Mediterranean herbs. I have never had a lavender honey I didn't like, though mint honey is a different story (too minty), and thyme honey can be a brute if it comes from the wrong strain of thyme. About as adventurous as I go are the swampy honeys of Florida: deep burnished palmetto and especially the burnt-sugar-tasting tupelo, from the gum trees that grow alongside the Apalachicola, Choctahatchee and Ochlockonee rivers. Tupelo is the opposite of rape honey, both in its character and in the fact that it is almost impossible to crystallize.

The most expensive honeys are now those from Australia, New Zealand and the USA. At Selfridges in London, you can buy blueberry honey from California for ten times as much as generic supermarket honey – ridiculously pricey, but still cheaper than a flight to California. I doubt that I will ever visit Hawaii, but I can still buy rare white Hawaiian honey over the internet. Honeys now sell themselves on their ability to transport you to the limits of human civilization. To take one typical example, from Argentina you can buy 'Ché' honey, whose label boasts that 'Ché Honey is organically produced and harvested in a selected area of the uncultivated Chaco forest (The Impenetrable) in northern Argentina, hundreds of miles from cities and industries. This forest is free from pollution, artificial pesticides and GM crops . . . By purchasing this honey, you support the indigenous Wichi families involved in this product.'

Honeys make the human world seem larger and smaller at the same time. There is something exciting about opening a jar of honey from some province of New Zealand that you will never visit, from some plant you've never heard of but whose scent you become familiar with each day at breakfast. It's like owning a chunk of the moon.

The most thrilling honey I ever tasted came to me by a very circuitous route. It was bought by the food writer Fuchsia Dunlop in 1998, on the streets of Chengdu, the capital of Sichuan in China. It was a piece of honey as hard as rock and as large as a melon, which looked like no honey she had ever seen before. 'I wouldn't have believed it was actually honey,' she told me, 'except that a few bees and bits of papery comb-like chambers were embedded.' The people who sold it to her were itinerant traders who specialized in selling one-offs such as wild turtles. They said it came from Yunnan, but couldn't tell her any more. Dunlop never saw another honey rock for sale again. She took it home, and a for a whole year, while she was studying at the Chengdu cookery school, she would chip pieces off it for her morning rice porridge. When she returned to England she brought what was left of it with her.

Five years after she had first bought it, Dunlop sent what was left of this rare honey rock to me. By now it was more like an apple than a melon in size. When it came in the post I had a momentary thought that it was a bomb. My four-year-old son and I unwrapped it very slowly and gingerly. Suddenly the whole room was filled with the most enticing honey aroma. There, inside the bubble wrap, was what looked like a fossilized sponge, a hard purple-grey rock with holes in. Honey experts have since told me that it must have been a particularly crystalline kind of honey from a wild honeycomb, which had got compressed together and then solidified into this rock. Perhaps it got squashed together by Chinese nomads to help it keep better on long journeys, or perhaps it was just an accident. However it happened, it was a kind of miracle. We examined it for a long time, as if it were a scientific specimen. Then, tentatively, we chipped off a small grey crumb. We put it to our lips, not knowing what to expect.

It tasted sublime. We couldn't work out what it reminded us of, and then suddenly we realized. It tasted like sugar.

Food and Drink: Recipes

Notes on Baking with Honey

Don't do it! If you have some wonderful honey, the best thing you can do is to eat it in its unadulterated state, perhaps with yoghurt or good bread. But, in case you have some less exciting honey and feel like some baking, here are some suggestions.

Generally, items containing honey should be cooked at a lower temperature than other baked goods, because the honey will burn more easily than sugar. The right temperature can be hard to judge at first, because a little bit of a dark burnt taste is what gives many honey cakes their charm, especially those which also contain spices. If you wish to substitute honey for sugar in any of your own baking recipes, you should, as a rule of thumb, use 25 per cent more honey than sugar by weight (e.g. 125 g instead of 100 g) and reduce the added liquid slightly. Tempting as it is to discard sugar wholesale in favour of honey, in most sweet recipes, it is best – for texture as well as flavour – to retain some sugar. But just a little honey added to any of your favourite cake recipes can be very successful, making the crumb more tender and the cake keep better. Do not use your very finest honeys for cooking. They would be wasted. Use mild, all-purpose honeys such as acacia.

Conserved nuts (Confiture de noix)

A very delicious medieval sweetmeat. From *Le Ménagier de Paris*, adapted from D. Eleanor Scully and Terence Scully's *Early French*

Cookery: Sources, Social History, Original Recipes and Modern Adaptations (Ann Arbor: University of Michigan Press, 1998).

> 1 cup liquid honey
> 15 whole cloves
> 2 tablespoons slivers of fresh ginger
> ½ pound whole or halved walnuts

On a low heat in a small saucepan, warm together the honey and spices. Leave the ginger and cloves to steep in the honey for 5–10 minutes. Add the walnuts and bring to the boil. Cook, stirring occasionally, for about 10 minutes, until the honey seems thick and toffeeish (the soft-ball stage). Spoon out the walnuts and set them to cool on sheets of baking parchment. Warn people not to eat the cloves; but the candied pieces of ginger are almost the best bit. Like any kind of praline, this is good pulverized over ice cream.

Condoignac—Quince Jam

This is based on a medieval recipe (in *Le Ménagier de Paris*) in which the red wine accentuates the quince's natural pinkness and the honey brings out the quince's fragrance. It gives off a Christmassy scent as it is cooking, rather like mulled wine, and indeed would make a delicious Christmas sweetmeat, perhaps boxed in pretty containers.

> 2 pounds quinces (about 4 medium or 3 large)
> 2 cups red wine
> 2 cups honey
> 2 tablespoons superfine granulated sugar
> a pinch each of ground cloves, cinnamon and dried
>   galangal
> 3–4 tablespoons sugar

Peel and core the quinces, cut into quarters and cook them, covered in red wine, until soft. Drain, reserving the syrupy wine, puree the wine-dark quinces, and then press through a sieve. At this point the quince mixture will be a lovely Bloomsbury mauve. Add the honey and the caster sugar to the reserved wine, then bring to a boil. Add the pureed quinces and the spices. Boil until the mixture seems to have reduced by half and is leaving the sides of the pan. It should be thick and jammy. Pour into a greased 20-cm cake tin and leave to cool. Cut into bite-sized pieces and dip them in the granulated sugar. If you prefer, you can boil the mixture a little less long, pot it in jars, and use it as a divine quince spread.

Honey Ice Cream

Honey ice cream is a favourite of the people who run the Maison du Miel in Paris. Honey lends a wonderful texture to ice cream, as well as providing luxurious connotations of the land of milk and honey. I like to use lavender honey.

> 1 vanilla bean
> 2 cups heavy cream
> 1 cup milk
> ⅔ cup honey, preferably lavender

Split open the vanilla bean and scrape the seeds along with the bean into a large saucepan. Pour in the cream and milk and bring them just to a boil. Remove from the heat. Stir in the honey until it dissolves thoroughly. Cover the saucepan with a lid, and leave the mixture to steep until it is cool. When it has cooled, strain it to remove the vanilla bean, transfer the now-fragrant liquid to a jug, cover it with clingfilm, and chill in the fridge for at least an hour. Then churn it in an ice-cream maker, or freeze it in a shallow container in the freezer, whisking every so often to break down the ice crystals.

Spanish Turron

A Christmas delicacy related to nougat. The great honey historian Eva Crane notes that this is traditionally made with rosemary honey or orange honey.

⅓ cup (4 ounces) honey
2 large egg whites, beaten until stiff
6 ounces (about 1½ cups) blanched almonds, lightly toasted
4 ounces (about 1 cup) hazelnuts, roasted
rice paper

Put the honey and sugar in a saucepan and place over medium heat until boiling. Remove from the heat and beat the mixture until it seems to thin out. Stir in the egg whites, beating constantly, and return to a medium heat until a toffeeish consistency is reached. Stir in the nuts. Pour the mixture into a baking tray lined with rice paper. Cover it with more rice paper. Place under a weight for an hour or so, then cut into squares or diamonds, as you like.

Sour-Sweet Russian Bread

This dark, heavy bread is adapted from Lesley Chamberlain's excellent book *The Food and Cooking of Russia* (London: Allen Lane, 1982).

2 cups white bread flour
2 cups wholewheat bread flour
2 cups rye flour
1 package rapid rise yeast
2 cups water, just off the boil
2 tablespoons honey
1 tablespoon pomegranate molasses (optional—or another tablespoon honey)
1 teaspoon caraway seeds (optional)

Mix together the flours and the yeast. Pour over the water mixed with the honey and pomegranate molasses, mix, and knead well. Transfer to an oiled bowl and leave to rise in a warm place for an hour or until doubled in size. Knead again, adding the caraway seeds, form into two loaves, and leave to rise again. Meanwhile, preheat the oven to 430°F. When the dough has risen again, wet the loaves with wet hands and put them in the oven to bake, turning down the oven temperature to 360°F after 15 minutes. They will take about 40 minutes in total, depending on your oven.

Kodafa Drenched in Honey

This Middle Eastern cheesecake seems not unlike the ancient Greek cheesecakes steeped in honey mentioned by poets. It is rather intense, but good if you are in the right mood. Usually it is made with kadif, the shredded-wheat-like pastry, but this version, adapted from Marlena Spieler's informative *The Jewish Heritage Cookbook* (London: Lorenz Books 2002), uses couscous, which is easier to get hold of. I have changed some of the quantities slightly from the original recipe, using less cheese and butter.

> 1–1½ cups couscous
> 2¼ cups boiling water
> 1 stick unsalted butter, cut into small pieces
> 1 egg, beaten
> pinch of salt
> 1 cup ricotta cheese
> 6 ounces chopped mozzarella
> 1½ cups clear honey
> a pinch of saffron
> ½ cup water
> a squeeze of lemon
> a handful of chopped pistachio nuts (optional)

Mix together the couscous and the boiling water, then leave for half an hour. Stir with a fork, mixing in the butter, beaten egg and salt. Meanwhile, stir together the cheeses with a spoonful of the honey. Preheat oven to 390°F. Spread half the couscous on a round cake tin. (I used one with a diameter of 19 cm.) Add the cheese mixture. Top with the rest of the couscous. Bake for 10–15 minutes. Put the rest of the honey in a saucepan with the water and saffron, bring to the boil, and boil for five minutes, being careful not to let the syrup catch. Stir in the lemon juice off the heat. Once the cheesecake is cooked, put it under the grill until a golden crust forms. Pour some of the syrup over, and sprinkle pistachios if you like. Serve, cut in slices, with the rest of the syrup.

Thunder and Lightning

Take one piece of honeycomb and one tub of real clotted cream. Eat in alternate spoonfuls.

Breakfast of the Gods

Watermelon, Greek yoghurt and honey, eaten together early in the morning on a hot day.

Honey Bran Muffins

Honey-bran muffins are usually sold now as the 'healthy' breakfast choice – healthier than blueberry muffins or cranberry muffins, let alone double-chocolate-chip muffins: one more vestige of the belief in honey as the ultimate 'health' food. In fact, these butter-rich muffins are probably not particularly suitable for dieters (especially for those 'doing' Atkins), though they are delicious.

> 1 cup self-raising flour
> ½ teaspoon baking soda

½ teaspoon salt
½ cup brown sugar
¼ cup toasted wheat bran
⅓ cup raisins (or dried figs or apricots, chopped)
½ cup boiling water
5 tablespoons unsalted butter
¼ cup honey
½ cup milk or buttermilk
1 large egg, beaten

Preheat the oven to 340°F. Line twelve muffin cups with muffin papers or grease them well. Stir the flour, bicarbonate of soda, salt and sugar to combine. Put the bran and raisins in another bowl and mix in the boiling water. Meanwhile, melt the butter and honey together. When this has cooled, stir in the milk and the beaten egg. Then stir in the flour mixture – as always with muffins, do not overmix. Mix in the bran and dried fruit. Divide the batter between the muffin cases and bake for about 15–20 minutes, or until a skewer inserted into one of the muffins comes out clean.

Almond Baklava

Charles Perry, the food critic for the *LA Times*, and an expert on Arabic food, tells me that most baklava in Turkey is now made exclusively with sugar syrup in place of honey. Another illusion shattered. But baklava is good with honey added, and, even if not authentic, this recipe satisfies Western dreams of an aromatic East.

1 cup granulated sugar
⅔ cup water
5 tablespoons liquid honey
2 cinnamon sticks
the peel of a whole orange, removed with a swivel peeler
1 teaspoon rose water
just under a stick of unsalted butter, melted and cooled

12 ounces coarsely chopped almonds
½ teaspoon ground cinnamon
1 pound filo pastry, thawed if frozen

Put ¾ cup sugar into a saucepan with the water, honey, cinnamon sticks and orange peel and stir over a low heat until the sugar has dissolved. Bring it to the boil, then remove from the heat. Mix in the rose water and cool, then chill. This syrup can be prepared several days ahead. When you are ready to make the baklava, preheat the oven to 300°F. Brush a large baking tray with melted butter. Mix together the almonds, cinnamon and ¼ cup sugar. Fold one sheet of filo in half to make a rectangle. Place on the baking tray and brush with butter. Repeat until you have used up half the filo. Sprinkle the nut mixture over the top. Top with the rest of the sheets, folding each one and brushing with butter. Try to make the top layer nice and neat, and use a sharp knife to make diamond shapes on it. Bake until golden – about 40 minutes. Now strain the rose syrup to remove the peel and cinnamon. Spoon a scant cup of syrup over the baklava while it is still hot. Cut the baklava along the diamond lines. Let it stand for 4 hours before eating in very small pieces, with the rest of the syrup on the side, and a cup of strong black coffee.

The remaining recipes are for honey cakes of decreasing density.

Pain d'Épice

This, give or take a little sugar and baking powder, is the original article, as adapted from the *Larousse gastronomique*. It is an acquired taste. You couldn't accuse it of being light, but it has its charm: the honey, the flour and the spices all seem to bring out the flavours in each other.

1 pound honey
1 pound flour (white, rye or preferably a mixture)

4 ounces superfine granulated sugar
2 teaspoons cream of tartar
1 teaspoon baking soda
2 teaspoons aniseed
a pinch each of cinnamon and cloves
grated zest of a lemon
2 tablespoons milk
extra sugar

Heat the honey to boiling point, then skim it and mix it into the sifted flour. Leave to stand, covered, for at least an hour, and possibly a day. Knead in the sugar, baking agents and flavourings. Put in a buttered 23-cm square cake tin. Bake at 375°F for about 30 minutes. Then make a syrup by mixing cold milk with as much sugar as it takes to go syrupy. Brush this over the hot cake, then leave to cool.

Taai–Taai

This is the Dutch variant of *pain d'épice*. The name means 'tough-tough', which it is, but it is also very good, in a dark, spicy way. Dutch bakers have retained the tradition of ripening their dough, sometimes for many months. I have adapted this from Gaitri Pagrach-Chandra's *Windmills in My Oven* (Totnes: Prospect Books, 2002), a lovely book, simplifying the technique. Properly, *taai-taai* should be made over several days, but I make it in a single afternoon, as follows.

2 cups rye flour
2 cups all-purpose flour
¾ cup honey
¾ cup molasses
4 tablespoons water
1 teaspoon each ground cinnamon and aniseed
½ teaspoon ginger
a little grated nutmeg

¼ teaspoon baking soda
1 egg, beaten

Mix together the flours. Combine the honey, molasses and water in a saucepan and warm slightly until very fluid. Cool slightly, then mix with the flours, preferably in a mixer, beating well. Cover and leave for one hour. Then add the spices and bicarbonate of soda. Beat the mixture again. Preheat the oven to 430°F. Roll out the sticky brown dough into a rectangle, and cut it into about sixteen or more medium square shapes. Brush each one with beaten egg and bake on trays lined with baking parchment for about seven minutes, before cooling on a wire rack. The *taai-taai* will keep a long time in an airtight container.

Cardamom and Honey Pryanik

This recipe is also adapted from Lesley Chamberlain's *The Food and Cooking of Russia*. Chamberlain notes that *pryanik*, a spice cake with an important place in Russian cuisine, dates back to 'at least the ninth century, when it was a simple combination of rye flour, honey and berry juice. Spices were added and the preparation took its modern form in medieval Russia.' It survived in its traditional form until the end of the nineteenth century, when the Russian palate finally rebelled against *pryanik*'s killer combination of 'sweetness, stickiness and extreme density'. Russian cooks then adapted it by adding eggs and/or milk, until it became something 'light and foreign, somewhere between a tea bread and a sponge'. Chamberlain's recipe follows the lighter modern version. I have lightened her recipe still further, with a little brown sugar and an extra egg. But everything is relative, and even this 'light' version of *pryanik* may be rather overwhelming to those used to sponge cake.

1 pound honey
4 ounces brown sugar
4 ounces rye flour

¾ pound white flour
½ teaspoon ground cardamom
1 teaspoon cinnamon
½ teaspoon star anise
2 teaspoons grated lemon zest
½ teaspoon baking soda
½ teaspoon salt
5 eggs
1 scant cup crème fraîche or sour cream
½ cup milk

Preheat the oven to 320°F. Warm the honey and sugar in a large saucepan, then add the rye flour and beat well. Combine the white flour and the spices, lemon peel, baking powder and salt. Beat together the eggs, crème fraîche and milk before mixing into the white-flour mixture. Stir in the honey mixture. Pour into a greased 23-cm square baking tin and bake for about 45 minutes, following the usual precautions about burning. Serve cut into squares.

Lekach

This is the honey cake eaten at Rosh Hashanah or Jewish New Year. It is lighter than cakes of the *pain d'épice* family, with a pleasing bitterness from the dark coffee, picking up the slight bitterness in the cooked honey.

12 ounces all-purpose flour
1 teaspoon cinnamon
½ teaspoon cloves
zest of an orange
1 teaspoon baking soda
1 teaspoon baking powder
8 ounces caster sugar
2 large eggs
9 ounces clear honey

½ cup light olive oil
½ cup strong black coffee
a handful of sultanas and walnuts (optional)

Preheat the oven to 360°F. Sift the flour with the spices, orange zest, bicarbonate of soda and baking powder. Beat the sugar and eggs until creamy. Beat in the honey, oil and coffee. Gradually add the flour mixture to the honey mixture, beating well. If you like, you can add a handful each of sultanas and walnuts at this stage. Pour into two lined 2-pound loaf tins or one 23-cm square tin. Bake for 40–90 minutes, depending on your tin and your oven. It is done when firm to the touch on top.

Honey and Spice Cake

Adapted from Dan Lepard and Richard Whittington's *Baker and Spice: Exceptional Recipes for Real Breads, Cakes and Pastries* (London: Quadrille, 2003). This is a very clever recipe, because the rye flour and spice evoke the flavours of the older spice cakes, while the method and presence of butter, eggs and sugar ensure that the texture is airy and soft.

7 ounces runny honey
5½ ounces unsalted butter
2 ounces dark soft brown sugar
1 inch piece root ginger, peeled
2 large eggs
1½ ounces rye flour
4 ounces self-raising flour
½ teaspoon baking soda
½ teaspoon ground cinnamon
½ teaspoon allspice

Preheat the oven to 320°F and line a 2-pound loaf tin with baking parchment. In a saucepan over low heat, warm together the honey, butter and sugar until hot and the butter is almost melted.

Grate the ginger into this mixture. Then whisk it for 2½ minutes, either in a heavy-duty mixer or with an electric whisk. Add
the eggs and beat for 2½ minutes more. Then sift together the
dry ingredients and fold them into the wet mixture. Pour into
the loaf tin and set on a baking tray in the oven, baking until the
cake is a deep golden colour – about 40–60 minutes.

Madeleines

These are the polar opposite of the old gingerbreads: light, spongy
and sugary, with honey present only to add perfume and tenderness.
Many recipes add extra flavourings such as rose water or orange zest,
but I prefer the delicate taste of butter and honey by themselves. This
is a recipe which benefits from light and aromatic honeys, particularly citrus ones such as lime flower or orange blossom.

> melted unsalted butter
> 2 large eggs
> 5 tablespoons honey
> 2 ounces superfine sugar
> 6 ounces all-purpose flour
> 7 ounces unsalted butter, melted and cooled

Preheat the oven to 390°F. Brush the madeleine sheet (they seem
to come with either nine or twelve moulds, and either will do)
with melted butter and dust it with flour. Whisk together the
eggs, honey and sugar in a bowl set over simmering water until
just warm. Remove from the water and beat with a whisk until
pale and thick. This may take as long as 10 minutes. Fold in the
sifted flour alternately with the unsalted butter. When the batter is
all mixed in, spoon it into the madeleine mould, filling until three-
quarters full. This will not use up all the batter. Bake until springy –
about 10 minutes. Carefully prise out the madeleines and set them
on a wire rack, then wipe out the mould, brush it with more melted
butter, and bake the rest of the madeleines. These are pretty dusted
with icing sugar, but just as good plain.

Spiced Honey and Almond Madeleines

These are adapted from a recipe of Tamasin Day-Lewis's in *Simply the Best* (London: Weidenfeld & Nicolson, 2001), and they are particularly sticky and delicious. Of all the honey things I have made, these are my favourite. Day-Lewis is a lover of honey, and her father, the poet C. Day-Lewis, translated Virgil's *Georgics*, which seems fitting. I have changed the recipe by using black raisins in place of Day-Lewis's sultanas, and often use whole eggs instead of just egg whites. I have also doubled the quantities, because there are never enough.

> 2 ounces black raisins
> 1 generous ounce flour
> 5 ounces superfine sugar
> 1 generous ounce ground almonds
> a pinch each of ginger, cinnamon, cloves and mace
> 4 ounces unsalted butter
> 2 tablespoons honey
> 4 large egg whites or 2 whole eggs, beaten

Preheat the oven to 360°F. Soak the raisins in hot water for 20 minutes. Mix all the dry ingredients except the raisins together in a bowl. Melt the butter with the honey. Cool slightly, then add to the dry ingredients. Beat together in an electric mixer. Gradually add the beaten eggs until well mixed. Ideally chill the mixture for 30 minutes at this stage, though I have omitted this without major disaster. Chill a nine- or twelve-mould madeleine sheet. Brush the moulds with melted butter, dust with flour, shaking out any excess, and scatter the drained raisins over the bases. Spoon in half the mixture, and bake for 15–20 minutes, checking after 10 minutes, until golden and just firm to touch. Repeat with the other half of the mixture.

5

Life and Death

'O death, where is thy sting?'
St Paul, 1 Corinthians 15:55

IN A QUIET corner of a quiet church in a quiet county of
England lie some dead earls, sleeping in honey. Henry
Wriothesley, the third earl of Southampton, was one of
Shakespeare's most important patrons, the dedicatee of *The Rape
of Lucrece* and *Venus and Adonis*. It was in *Venus and Adonis* that
Shakespeare wrote, 'A thousand honey secrets shalt thou know.' It
later turned out that Wriothesley, a beautiful youth with long
auburn hair, had a honey secret of his own. Like Achilles in *The
Odyssey* and like Alexander the Great (if rumour were true), he
wanted his body to meet its end in liquid honey.[1]

The earls of Southampton were Renaissance men who established themselves in Titchfield, a sleepy part of Hampshire now
famous for its strawberries. How a gentleman was buried was very
important then, and as the Wriothesleys' stock rose at court, so too
did their expectations of how they should be commemorated.
They chose Titchfield parish church, St Peter's, for their final resting place, colonizing an entire chapel for their family mausoleum.
The requisite statuary was commissioned in 1581 by Henry's
father, the second earl. He demanded 'two faire monuments' to be
set up in the church, consisting of 'portraitures of white alabaster,
one for my lorde my father and my ladye my mother, the other
for mee'.[2] In the end, only one monument was made, but the vault

was large enough to house four generations of earls. The first earl's body was dug up and reinterred there. Then Henry died, in the Low Countries, in 1624, and finally Henry's son, in 1667. So, in the end, four earls joined each other in the mausoleum, all of them preserved in honey – a dynasty united in sweet death.

It all seems too exotic – too Egyptian – for Britain, especially for this most conventional part of the island. Walking through the cool grey space of St Peter's, with its mood of moderate Anglicanism, its prosaic noticeboards advertising toddler groups and local history societies, the thought of a honey tomb seems quite absurd. For many years, Titchfield residents spoke of the earls being buried in honey, without quite believing in it. It seemed like a local myth, no more plausible than the Loch Ness monster. Then, in the early 1900s, some renovation work was done on the mausoleum. The coffins were moved, and one of them cracked open ever so slightly. Out trickled a black, sticky liquid. Without even thinking, the workman reached out with a finger to taste it – and what he tasted was sweetness.

It is hard to find solid confirmation of this story. It is not mentioned in the standard biographies of Henry Wriothesley. St Peter's Church, however, describes the Wriothesleys as being 'preserved in honey' on a fact sheet about the building. And the world's leading expert on the history and archaeology of honey, Dr Eva Crane, has assured me she believes the story really is true.

Whether true or not, it makes us shudder slightly. It is the proximity of food and death which is hard to take. For us, to eat is to belong to the land of the living; and death is a place where no one eats. In our world, honey and corpses do not belong together. But in former ages honey was always a way of joining the living with the dead.

Honey Coffins

Honey is an effective embalming fluid because it is very good at killing bacteria. Honey is hygroscopic, meaning that it absorbs moisture, much as salt does. (Think of what happens when you pour table salt over spilled red wine – how the salt seems to suck up the liquid, turning pink.) Even bacteria need a little bit of liquid nourishment to stay alive, and honey sucks it out of the corpse, starving them of it. In addition, when honey comes into contact with animal tissue, hydrogen peroxide is produced, a chemical which helps to inhibit putrefaction. What this means it that, should you ever have a dead body on your hands which you want to prevent from rotting, it would not be a bad idea to coat it in honey.

Burial in honey goes back at least 4,000 years, if not longer. It was common practice among the Babylonians before the 1100s BC, and was later sometimes adopted by the Greeks, especially the Spartans. Honey provided an answer to what one should do when great leaders died in battle away from home. In the burning Greek sun, a noble corpse could easily turn to stinking meat long before it reached home. Hence, Xenophon tells us, when the king of Sparta died far away from his native soil in Asia in 371 BC, he was 'placed in honey' before he was 'carried home'.[3]

The Egyptians too set great store by the preservative powers of honey, and would sometimes use it in place of mummification, as is illustrated in a rather macabre story told by the great Egyptologist E. A. Wallis Budge. A modern Egyptian told Budge that:

> Once when he and several others were occupied in exploring the graves and seeking for treasure near the Pyramids, they came across a sealed jar, and having opened it and found that it contained honey, they began to eat it. Someone in the party remarked that a hair in the honey turned round one of the fingers of the man who was dipping his bread into it, and as they drew it out, the body of a small child appeared with all its limbs complete and in a good state of preservation; it was well dressed, and had upon it numerous ornaments.[4]

Herod I, king of Judea, was said to have had had his beautiful wife Mariamne executed, but kept her body for seven years preserved in honey, 'for he loved her even in death'.[5]

Not all these stories are necessarily true, but they show how important an ingredient honey was in the preservation of the dead, especially those dead who were thought to be worth preserving. This is confirmed by the most famous honey coffin of all, the one in which the body of Alexander the Great may or may not have been entombed. Alexander died in Babylon in 323 BC and was eventually taken back to Alexandria. Everything else about the death of this extraordinary man remains disputed, because the contemporary Greek histories on the subject are lost. The Roman geographer Strabo (born *c.* 64 BC) says that Alexander's body was placed, following his own order, in white honey in a golden coffin. Another source claims that Alexander was 'steeped in the nectar of Hybla', referring to the prized honey of Hybla. Yet another writer claims that Alexander commanded that he should be buried in a leaden coffin filled with honey, myrrh and oil of roses.[6] These are poetic details. Any of these honeyed caskets might be fitting for a hero of Alexander's stature – which does not mean that he actually ended up in one of them. The full story of what happened to Alexander's body after death will probably never be known, though it seems likely that the corpse, so far from resting in fine honey, was violently seized and partially cremated long before his remains returned to Alexandria. It doesn't really matter. Everyone was agreed that such a man ought to have been preserved in honey. Honey was what such a death demanded.

Honey and Death Rituals

In the death rituals of ancient times, honey is everywhere – not just preserving the body, but exorcising evil spirits and feeding good spirits, nourishing the mourners, sweetening the mood of the gods, and adorning the consecratory rites. In an ancient funeral hymn of the Rig Veda, priests are directed to pour out honey for the god of death.[7] In India, honey was a good funeral offering because it was a 'life substance'; to offer it to the gods was therefore fitting. 'It is bee's honey, they say; for bee's honey means the sacrifice,' intones the Satapatha Brahmana.[8] Sometimes ancient Greek tombs would be daubed with a mixture of honey, oil and meal. In all these rituals, it is hard to disentangle to what extent honey was being used as a food, to what extent as a preservative, and to what extent as a symbol. Honey was such a valuable funeral food because it symbolized both life and death; but it was such a powerful symbol only because it was such a valuable food.

It was assumed that honey was the food that the dead would want to take with them, wherever they were going. From ancient Egyptian times, jars of honey were buried alongside the dead to sustain them on their long journey to the other world.[9] In the *Iliad*, Achilles places honey and rich olive oil on the funeral pyre of his friend Patroclus, in the hope that he might enjoy the same foods in death that he had enjoyed in life.[10] Libations to the dead almost always included honey in some form, sometimes mixed with milk, sometimes with oil, sometimes with wine. In a writing of the Greek philosopher Lucian (born *c.* AD 120) we are told that, when someone dies, men dig a trench and pour in expensive wine and honey, believing 'that the dead are summoned up from below to the feast, and that they flutter round the smoke and drink the honey draught from the trench'.[11] For the same kind of reason, it was traditional at funerals in ancient Russia to set aside a portion of honey and cakes for the corpse, and to put it near an open window, so that the spirit of the dead one could come back and taste again the sweetness of life.

Up to a point, the use of honey in these rituals was arbitrary. The Greeks fed their dead with honey because honey was often to hand; this corpse food could just as well have been jam or date syrup, if these had been available and the dead person had happened to prefer them. And yet honey claimed a special place in funerary rites for reasons that went beyond taste, because it was not just jam or date syrup after all, but a sacred food. Only honey could really propitiate the spirits of the dead, because only honey came from sacred bees.

Many beekeepers still believe that bees must be 'told' in the event of a death in the family, otherwise the bees will bring misfortune, or even sting the dead spirit. The news is whispered into the apiary, or else conveyed by rapping three times on each hive. In Germany, the custom was for a senior member of the household to call on the bees, saying, 'Little bee, thy master is dead, leave me not in thy sorrow.'[12] Throughout Christian Europe, it was long thought that bees would grieve after a human death, ceasing to hum, or else humming mournfully. Pretty much anything the bees did – making more honey, or less, dying or not dying – could be interpreted as a sign that they were grieving. On occasion, hives would even be put in mourning, covered in black cloth or ribbons. These curiosities all have their roots in the pre-Christian belief that bees could make sense of death, because bees were human souls.

In the ruins of ancient tombs there have often been found tiny golden or bronze bees, as decoration for the stone casket. These glowing golden bees have been found in Crete, the Crimea, Etruria and Sardinia.[13] For the Greeks, they were not just pretty trinkets but symbols of the human soul. The bee was a *chthonian* animal, or one relating to the underworld – a creature which could somehow carry personality from the world of the living to the world of the dead.[14] The disembodied souls of men used the bodies of bees to move about the heavens.[15] The third-century Greek author Porphyry says that the soul comes down from the moon goddess Artemis in the form of bees, which are called *melissae*. The name of *melissa* – which now seems nothing more than a nice, everyday girl's name – was given to souls about to be born. It had overtones of reincarnation, fitting with the Greek belief in the transmigration of souls. Not just any soul could be a *melissa*. You had to be righteous. Bee souls, says Porphyry, were special spirits 'who live justly, and who, having performed such things as are acceptable to the gods, will return whence they came. For this insect loves to return to the place whence it came, and is eminently just and sober.'[16] Hence, the special power of honey to salve the passing from life to death.

What worked one way must work the other way too: from death to life as well as from life to death. It was often believed that anyone who drowned in honey would automatically revive, as in the legend of Glaucus, son of King Minos of Crete, who fell into a honey jar but came back to life again.[17] Honey was prized in death not least because it was considered to be such a giver and enhancer of life, beginning with birth itself. After all, we come into the world glazed and slick and sticky, so it is perhaps not surprising that that is how many should have wanted to leave it as well.

Honey, Birth and Infancy

The chances of small children drowning in jars of honey, allowing us to test its miraculous powers, are not what they were. Not only are the jars much smaller these days, but most now come with an alarming message on the label: 'Not suitable for infants under the age of 12 months'. The reason for the warning is the tiny risk that honey may contain botulism spores, which the infant gut is not yet developed enough to digest. There is no risk at all for grown-ups, and yet in a culture which constantly babies itself, pampering our skin with baby oil and our bellies with milky coffee, the thought of infant botulism has put many adults off honey for life. This is not how things used to be. In fact the risk of infant botulism in honey has only been known since the 1970s, but already it has completely overturned our perception of honey in infant feeding. 'No honey for your honeys!' as one parenting web site puts it. Yet for centuries honey was thought of as a food so pure you could give it to a newborn, before he or she had taken so much as a sip at the breast.

What are we now so afraid of? Probably the word 'botulism'. However, there are two kinds of botulism.[18] One is a classical form of acute food poisoning, first identified over 200 years ago and associated with badly preserved meat products. Symptoms occur

This cherub driving a chariot of bees is advertising the health-giving properties of honey

within a few hours of eating, and can lead to a horrible death (as lovingly described in Francis Iles's classic meat-paste melodrama *Malice Aforethought*, 1931). The other, infant botulism, though caused by the same bacterium – *Clostridium botulinum* – is very different in its effects, and by no means always fatal (the mortality rate is about 1.3 per cent – ten times lower than for the other kind of botulism). The symptoms develop only slowly. First the baby becomes constipated; then listless; he loses the ability to suck properly, and his cry is diminished; his facial expressions become flaccid, and his muscular reflexes stop working properly. In other words, the symptoms are the usual ones when small children get sick, and it was only in 1976 that infant botulism was first diagnosed in its own right. But the times being what they were, a study was immediately done in California to try to identify any foods which might have harboured the bacteria. The only food to be implicated was honey, though *C. botulinum* was present only in a minority of cases. Botulism spores are found everywhere in nature and are not harmful in themselves. Only in the absence of oxygen do they germinate and become potentially poisonous. It therefore seemed possible that the very qualities that made honey so effective at killing other bacteria could also make it a good home for botulism spores to grow.

The mere thought of infant botulism is so terrifying that paediatricians now advocate excluding honey from a baby's diet altogether, even though the number of cases of botulism in babies over six months is negligible, even though infant botulism is much more widespread in California than elsewhere (there have only ever been six cases in Britain), and even though honey is implicated in fewer than a fifth of all cases. Some of the babies in the overall statistics for infant botulism had been given honey smeared on a dummy, to quieten them when they cried. Some of these sticky dummies may have been dropped on the floor and picked up botulism spores in that way. Even in California only 10–13 per cent of the honey samples tested are contaminated. But no risk is now too small to ignore when it comes to babies and food. Giving honey to babies is almost the only factor in infant botulism that can be controlled; and so we must not do it.

In other words, we have gone slightly mad. After my baby daughter was weaned, I would sometimes see her looking curiously at the honey on the table and wish I could give her a spoonful on her porridge, or swirled into her apple puree, or just as it was, to soothe her frequent colds. Only extreme prudence – or cowardice – prevented me. In a baby world full of rusks thick with vegetable oil, yoghurts laced with sugar, infant paracetamol mixed with artificial sweeteners, it seems a little cruel to place this most natural and delicious of foodstuffs out of bounds. To our ancestors it would have been unthinkable.

'Behold, a virgin shall conceive, and bear a son, and shall call his name Immanuel. Butter and honey shall he eat, that he may know to refuse the evil, and choose the good.'[19] Baby Jesus was actually nothing special in this regard (unlike in the method of his conception). It was a traditional Jewish practice to give babies a taste of honey and butter before they suckled, and in fact one far from exclusive to Judaism. The practice of giving honey to newborns is more widespread and older than any other honey cult.[20] The Papyrus Elders in 1600 BC mention honey as an infant food. The custom goes on to this day, in places where the latest Californian research sometimes passes people by. 'Babies in the West Indies are given a mixture called "Luck", of honey, olive oil and spices; in Samoa, they are fed cane juice in the first week; in Upper Burma, muslin dipped in honey is given; while in Pakistan, a mother will put a mix of ghee, sugar and honey on her finger for the baby to suck.'[21] Among the Muslims of Punjab, the most senior member of the family feeds the infant with its first food, which is *ghutti* made from honey, to ward off evil spirits.

This warding-off of evil was a frequent reason given for feeding the baby with honey. It happened in Scotland and Finland; in Greece and the Caucasus; in India and Africa. Once honey had been smeared on the tiny lips, the child was officially alive; his or her life was now sacrosanct. According to the ancient laws of Friesland in Germany, a father was allowed to kill his own offspring until such time as they had tasted honey. This was even a theme in the story of Zeus, king of the Greek gods. In the myth, Zeus's father, Kronos, had killed his five previous children. When Zeus was born, his mother, Rhea, was desperate to save him from his father. She hid him in a cave in Mount Dicte, where he was fed milk by a mountain goat and, depending on which version of the myth you read, fed honey either by bees or by nymphs known as bee-maidens or *melissae*. This worked like a charm, and whenever hostile honey-hunters entered the cave their armour would fall off. Baby Zeus was saved by his honey diet.

Honey was also thought to offer babies protection of a more prosaic kind – protection for their health. The Roman medical writer Galen recommends honey mixed with butter for teething problems, as well as for diarrhoea and malnutrition. More recently, in the first half of the twentieth century, as children's sugar consumption showed its first signs of hurtling out of control, a number of doctors recommended honey for infant health. In particular a certain Dr Bodog F. Beck, a Hungarian doctor who emigrated to the United States after fighting on the losing side in the First World War, got a real bee in his bonnet about the superiority of honey over sugar. 'In infant feeding, after milk, honey ought to be considered first in importance', he wrote. In his opinion, children fed on too much sugar were 'badly-nourished, pasty-looking, irritable, restless, particularly at night, and frequently suffer from incontinence of urine during sleep; they have decayed teeth, are constipated at times, alternating with diarrhoea; they are subject to rheumatism, chorea, recurring bronchitis and sore throat'.

It was a great pity, he thought, that America had become the number one sugar-eating nation. Over the hundred years from the 1830s to the 1930s, US sugar consumption had risen twelvefold, from 45 calories' worth in a day to a whopping 550 calories.[22] And yet by today's terrifying standards that figure was still quite modest. Consumption of sugary soft drinks skyrocketed from the 1970s to the 1990s; by 1995 the average per-capita daily consumption of sugar in the USA amounted to 800 calories – almost enough calories to live on.[23] Beck wrote presciently in 1938 that Uncle Sam was in danger of losing 'his lanky figure' and acquiring 'the paunch of John Bull'. If only, Beck argued, all American families would learn to keep on their tables 'a handy drip-cut pitcherful of honey' they would not use sugar so indiscriminately. Parents, he said, should make up a mixture of honey butter, to spread on their children's bread; the honey stopped the butter going rancid, as well as making it taste lovely. Children fed on modest quantities of honey, according to Beck, were full of energy and goodness: 'Honey does not obtain any harmful chemicals and is entirely utilized by the digestive tract . . . While honey is nature's own sweet, untouched by human art, sugar is a concentrated, denatured and polluted substance, produced, as a rule, of sugar-cane . . . Industrial sugars are anti-physiological, dead, or, as a matter of fact, MURDERED sweets.'[24]

The language may be a bit over the top – and Beck didn't know about baby botulism – but he wasn't wrong. Apart from the fact that children love it – my son thought he had won the Lottery when I started work on this book and our house filled up with countless gooey jars and combs – honey is a good, rapidly assimilated food, easy on young stomachs. In 1931 a Finnish doctor called Sakari Lahdensuu published a 91-page study showing that babies who had a little honey added to their milk grew better and suffered from fewer digestive complaints. Unlike children fed sugar, they did not suffer from excess sugar in the urine (one of the first signs of diabetes).[25] Beck himself cites the value of honey in treating malnourished infants.[26] During the Depression, and for twenty-five years before that, Dr M. W. O'Gorman, the Director of Hygiene in the Department of Public Affairs in New Jersey, brought malnourished children back to health with the aid of honey – half a teaspoon at first, then a bit more and a bit more, so that their emaciated little bodies never got overloaded. It almost always worked.

Bodog Beck believed in the power of honey to feed children in part because he was a historian as well as a doctor. Beck knew that the ancients compared honey 'with molten gold'. He felt that there were still 'treasures buried in honey, yet undiscovered by science'. He saw that for thousands of years honey had provided a way of feeding children with love, rather than, as he put it, being a cajoling word that housewives used when they wanted 'a new fur coat, an automobile or jewelry'.[27] 'My son, eat thou honey, because it is good,' King Solomon had said,[28] and King Solomon usually knew what he was talking about.

Medicine from the Hive

Muhammad Ali, who was born Cassius Clay in the honey-rich state of Kentucky, boasted that he could 'float like a butterfly, sting like a bee'. In 1978, when he was thirty-six and many commentators were writing him off as past it, Ali used the products of honeybees to renew his sting. Just before the world heavyweight championship in September 1978, when he was due to meet the 25-year-old Leon Spinks in New Orleans, Ali swallowed a rejuvenating potion. The tonic was invented by a sprightly 70-year-old, Dr Alvenia Fulton, and consisted of bee pollen, vitamin E, magnesium, folic acid and lecithin, all mixed together with honey and orange juice. Apparently, it worked. Ali seemed to get stronger as the fight went on, and he won the championship for a record third time. When he returned home to Chicago, he praised the bee-rich concoction, saying with characteristic modesty, 'It was a great mixture and I danced and danced and tired Spinks out.'[29] The British newspapers reported his victory as a kind of voodoo: 'ALI'S MAGIC POTION' exclaimed the *Sunday Mirror*, attributing his success to this 'secret' mixture.[30] Yet there has never been any secret about the restorative powers of the products of the hive. Even Ali's namesake, the original Muhammad, knew about it, and he recommended honey in the Koran as 'a remedy for all diseases'.[31]

'In Ancient Egypt, honey was the most popular medicament of all; it is mentioned some 500 times in the 900 remedies that are known.'[32] Honey was 'the oldest panacea', and 'much older than the history of medicine itself'. Honey was often used to soften the bitterness of herbal cures – a spoonful of honey makes the medicine go down – and it was also believed to have considerable healing properties in its own right. In the opinion of Aristoxenus, a pupil of Aristotle's, anyone who ate honey, spring onions and bread for his breakfast every day would be free of all diseases throughout his lifetime, though it is unlikely that anyone has ever put this to the test.[33] In the fifth century BC the Greek doctor Hippocrates, who gave his name to the Hippocratic oath, recommended diluted honey as an expectorant, and also believed that 'it causes heat, cleans sores and ulcers of the lips, heals carbuncles and running sores'.[34] But Hippocrates noticed as well that honey was so widely used to treat the sick in his day that many people ended up disliking the taste of it, associating it with death; it was such a universal medicine that some developed the suspicion that honey actually made you ill. 'It has acquired a reputation for hastening death,' he said,[35] which is how some people still feel about doctors, despite the famous oath.

One of the main ancient uses for honey was to cure stomach disorders. In the first century AD Cornelius Celsus recommended it raw as a laxative and boiled as a cure for diarrhoea, because 'the acrimony is taken away by boyling'. Hindu doctors also used raw honey as a laxative. St Ambrose praised honey for 'inward Ulcers'. Pliny believed that honey would be an even more effective treatment for internal complaints if it were mixed with the bodies of the bees themselves: 'Powdered bees with milk, wine or honey will surely cure dropsy, dissolve gravel and stones, will open all passages of urine and cure the stopping of the bladder. Bees pounded with honey cure griping of the belly.'[36]

This belief in honey and bees as cures for stomach problems has persisted thoughout the centuries. In 1623 Charles Butler claimed that 'Hooni cleareth all the obstructions of the body, losseneth the belly, purgeth the foulness of the body and provoketh urine. It cutteth and casteth up Flegmatic matter and therefore sharpneth the stomachs of them, which by reason thereof have little appetite.' This rather smacks of the medical wishful thinking of the age, but it may nevertheless be true that honey has value in cases of gastrointestinal disorders. A few rare doctors in the twentieth century used honey to treat gastric and intestinal ulcerations, even claiming that in some cases eating honey in the right quantities could remove the need for operation.[37] More recently, Manuka honey from New Zealand has been shown to kill the bacterium (*H. pylori*) which causes ulcers.

Honey has also long been recognized as helpful in cases of coughs, catarrh and phlegm. In 1759 the honey merchant John Hill wrote 'Of the virtues of honey against a tough phlegm'. Hill noted that, as they got older, many people suffered from a 'tough phlegm' in the morning, 'a continual hawking and coughing' until they got out of bed. The cure, he argued, was some fine English spring honey, placed by the bedside. The sufferer should take a spoonful before sleeping and a spoonful on waking, and would soon be better. Hill cautioned that you should be careful to use the finest honey and not the adulterated kind, or else you might find yourself with a throat full of 'raw flour'. He went on to recommend the 'sweetness and balsamick quality' of honey for public speakers, opera singers, clergymen and asthmatics.[38] Current medical opinion would probably agree with him. Honey drinks are still recommended for ticklish throats, and honey is sold worldwide for use in commercial cough mixtures and cough sweets.[39]

Likewise, the folk remedy of taking local honey to cure hay fever is gathering ground by the year. The theory is that local honey – especially honeycomb with the cell cappings intact – will contain the same pollens which caused the symptoms in the first place. By eating it regularly, the sufferer is supposed to become immune to the pollen that is producing such itchy eyes and a sneezy nose. While there has been no definite confirmation of this remedy in conventional medicine, even the most conventional doctors will grudgingly admit that eating local honey will do hay fever sufferers no harm and maybe 'some good'.[40]

Unfortunately, many of the other claims made on behalf of hive products in the past were nothing but crazed quackery. Good sense and nonsense in medicine are never far apart. The same Charles Butler who recommended honey for the stomach also asserted that you could distil honey into a water called 'the Quintessence of Hooni' which could magically dissolve gold and render it drinkable. If anyone who was dying drank a dram or two of this mixture of gold and quintessence of honey, they would revive straight away. In the Middle Ages, great store was set by something called oxymel. This version of a Roman drink was nothing more than a mixture of honey, water and vinegar, but was credited with extraordinary virtues. 'It was an infallible cure for sciatica, gout and kindred ailments; and one writer also tells us that it was "good to gargarize with in a Squinancy"',[41] whatever that means. Much nonsense has also been written about the power of bees and honey to cure that godsend to quack medicine, male baldness. Galen insisted that powdered dead bees, mixed with honey, could be smeared on thinning or balding hair and it would grow back again.

EXTRACT OF
Honey and Flowers

Combines both the qualities of a Wash and Pomade; it gently stimulates the growth of the Hair, and imparts to it a soft and brilliant appearance.

Shake the Bottle before application.

. . PREPARED BY . .
F. M. PFOB,
2 Royal Arcade, Norwich.

A label from an old honey beauty treatment

This cure was quoted approvingly by Thomas Muffet (of Little Miss Muffet fame) in 1658.[42] Similarly dotty things were said about the power of bees and honey to bring back sight to the blind.

They were no more dotty, however, than the wild assertions that have been made over the past few decades on behalf of remedies from the hive. Now, as then, bees have been credited with an ill-defined and talismatic power to cure every human ailment. Royal jelly is a case in point. The *gelée royale* or brood food fed to the larva in the queen cell who would then turn into the queen had been identified in the 1700s, but it was not sold as a commercial product until the 1950s.[43] Beekeepers in France discovered that, by feeding bees with pollen and sugar syrup, they could produce royal jelly even in areas lacking enough flowers for honey production. Each colony would be given 40–45 larvae in queen cells. As soon as the worker bees had fed these cosseted larvae with the full amount of royal jelly, the jelly would be sucked off and the procedure would be repeated. The jelly would be frozen and put into capsules, then sold on to fools gullible enough to believe that they were experiencing something like Butler's Quintessence of Hooni. In the hive, royal jelly results in a 1,300-times increase in body weight in just six days, and extends the life expectancy of the individual bee from a matter of weeks to years. The idea behind royal jelly depends on a complete identification between bees and humans: royal jelly turns ordinary bees into queens, so just think what it would do for the human body . . . Well, nothing actually.[44] The health claims made on behalf of royal jelly have been described by doctors, in technical medical parlance, as 'rubbish' and 'a waste of money'. Royal jelly consists of 67 per cent water, 11 per cent proteins, 9 per cent sugars, 6 per cent ether extract, 1 per cent ash, and some vitamins, but no hidden magic – at least not for humans.[45] For all that, royal jelly is still bought in large quantities, especially by the Japanese, who set great store by its supposedly rejuvenating properties.

Much the same mentality has informed the use of honey and related products in beauty treatments over the ages. There is scarcely a famous beauty in history whose magical good looks have not been ascribed, at least in part, to honey: Cleopatra, with her baths of donkey's milk and honey; Madame du Barry, the infamous last mistress of Louis XV, who liked honey applications every morning; our own Catherine Zeta Jones, who has said that she rubs her body with honey and salt. Honey and wax do, in truth, have a legitimate place in cosmetics. Honey really is a natural humectant, or moisture-giving agent, so the chances are that applying it to human skin will make the skin more moisturized, as well as smelling very nice. Beeswax genuinely does have the ability to soothe chapped lips. The marketing of honey cosmetics, however, has always involved much more than mere moisturizing. Nothing less than complete rejuvenation will do. In 1972 Revlon brought out a balm made from Clover Honey ('nature's own moisturiser') and skimmed milk. Charles Revlon announced at the

L'Occitane honey soap, a product which cleverly borrows both
the architecture of the honeycomb and the supposed beautifying
properties of honey

time, 'I believe I have tapped a great new natural resource of beauty in 100% fat-free milk, rich with proteins . . . and moisturizing honey. Nothing I have seen gives skin such a look of vitality as these pure, natural organic ingredients.'[46] This did not reflect too well on the rest of the Revlon range. It was also complete nonsense. The Internet now offers a rich new resource for people trying to sell this kind of tosh. Search for the 'gift of life' and you are liable to find yourself directed to sites marketing expensive royal-jelly creams from New Zealand 'to protect against ageing'.[47]

Vastly inflated assertions have also been made for bee pollen, not infrequently by those with an interest in selling it. In 1979 health-food guru Maurice Hanssen, who later wrote the much better-known *E for Additives*, published a book praising the astonishing usefulness of pollen. Pollen, he wrote, was 'amazing', a 'mysterious nutriment'.[48] Pollen gave bees their protein and made them grow; for humans, it contained the secret of 'health and happiness'. Hanssen marketed several costly pollen concoctions under various made-up names: 'Melbrosia', 'Pollenflor', 'Pollen-B', 'Florapoll', 'Pollitabs'. It seemed that there was no human malaise that couldn't be treated with bee pollen. Got a cold? Take some pollen! Upset stomach? You need pollen! Period pains? I have just the thing for you – some more pollen! Tired? Diabetic? Nervous? Menopausal? Suicidal? Need I go on?

Hanssen hinted that pollen might actually hold the key to human potency itself; after all, the copiously eyelashed novelist Barbara Cartland was taking it (in the form of Melbrosia), and she was 'not only glamorous but also exceptionally hard working', having written twenty-four books in her seventy-sixth year alone. How could the British public resist? Hanssen published an eye-opening range of testimonials from various happy customers. Mr C. J. of Long Island wrote to say that his daughter had sent him some Pollen-B from England, which had given him 'increased virility', which was 'just what he wanted' (what a broad-minded girl she must have been). Dr J. B. of Scotland commended Melbrosia for Men, which had improved his 'troubled' sex life. Mrs R. T. of Perth told Hanssen he may have 'saved a marriage'. Her husband made her take Melbrosia PLD while she was going through 'The Change'. While at first she felt she was 'wasting rather a lot of money', she now felt 'truly happy'. Most remarkably of all, Miss R. N. O. of Enfield, a housekeeper in a stately home, wrote in to describe the 'acute embarrassment' she used to feel about her small breasts: 'I then tried a course of Melbrosia

PLD because of what I had read and the results have been wonderful. My breasts have gained two inches in size and altogether they are firmer and better shaped. Also I feel much better and more relaxed in myself.'[49] Who is to gainsay evidence such as this? It would be a cruel-hearted soul indeed who would wish Miss R. N. O. to feel less relaxed in herself. On the other hand, testimonials such as hers do little to win over conventional doctors to the medicine of the hive.

This is perhaps the most unfortunate aspect of apiarian quackery, with its crazy identification of bees and men: it has closed the eyes of many doctors to what bees really can do for us. One good example is the use of honey in wound dressings. Honey was used extensively in treating wounds in the ancient Egyptian world, and well into early modern times it was valued for its ability to 'knit together . . . disjoined flesh'.[50] But the practice was neglected by surgeons for centuries.[51] Only in the 1930s did doctors, mainly in Central Europe and Russia, begin to experiment with honey dressings again.[52] One Swiss surgeon treated a man whose finger was smashed in a grinding machine.[53] His finger had broken right off and hung on only by a skin flap. But when the finger was wrapped in place in honey it grew back together again, as if by magic. It seemed that the Egyptians knew what they were doing after all. It is now recognized that honey really does have the ability to 'ward off wound infections, reduce inflammation and promote healing'.[54] The reasons are the same ones that made honey such a good medium for embalming corpses: the fact that it is hygroscopic (absorbing moisture) and antimicrobial (generating hydrogen peroxide). Even now that this is known, however, the use of honey in wound dressing is still far from mainstream (though it is becoming more so, especially in Australia). Modern doctors are still reluctant to be seen to take seriously their ancestors' adoration of the bees.

Dr Bodog F. Beck lamented that the usual attitude of his colleagues to honey cures was one of derisive laughter. For this, he partly blamed vested interest:

The acceptance of honey by the medical profession as a protective and curative substance and their endorsement would create pandemonium not only in medical circles but among pharmaceutical chemists, wholesale and retail druggists, radio announcers, even undertakers, not to mention the sugar refining companies, the candy manufacturers and retailers, soda counters etc. It would be a veritable economic catastrophe. The sale of laxative remedies . . . digestive and headache powders, bicarbonate of soda, and rectal suppositories might entirely stop. To these we may add sedatives, various cough remedies, expectorants, throat lozenges, gargles etc.[55]

The modern rejection of honey-cures seems to be founded at least partly on the fear that honey is *too* natural. Whereas Hippocrates saw all foods as having medical properties, we now like to keep our food and our medicine apart – medicine is more often what we take to deal with the sickly food we have eaten. In so far as we are prepared to use 'natural' remedies such as honey, we want man to have put his pharmaceutical mark on them. Hence the unnatural appeal of Manuka honey from New Zealand, which comes packaged in dark glass like cod-liver oil, usually with a UMF rating. It is, as they say, 'reassuringly expensive' – as much as £13.99 for a 500 g jar in the UK (and $25 in the US). 'UMF' stands for 'Unique Manuka Factor', a classification first identified in the early 1990s by a Dr Peter Molan of the University of Waikato.[56] Dr Molan discovered that, while all honeys are antibacterial to some extent, some honeys are more so than others. Honey made by bees gathering nectar from the manuka bushes native to New Zealand (coincidentally, home of the University of Waikato) was especially potent – as much as 100 times more effective than other honeys. Active Manuka honey has since then proved valuable in the treatment of leg ulcers, stomach ulcers, psoriasis, eczema, acne, irritable bowel syndrome, fungal infections and sore eyes. All this has the backing of an official academic 'Honey Research Unit'. Manuka honey is undoubtedly an excellent thing – a particularly delicious, unctuous honey – but over the last decade its virtues have become so well accredited that you could almost forget its natural strengths and believe it to be a drug. Manuka honey prides itself on being 'lab-tested'. It is so well tested it seems as if it must be the work of men, not bees.

So what is honey then? Is it a preservative of the dead? A baby-killer? A life-saver? A cure-all? A pharmaceutical product? Or is it something else again – is it a more universal poison?

Poison Honey

In the autumn of 1790, the people of one particular neighbour-hood of Philadelphia, then the capital city of the USA, seemed to be dropping like flies. This was bad news for the city of brotherly love. The brand-new American government set up an investigation. It turned out that honey was to blame. All those falling sick and dying had eaten a special kind of honey, which had been obtained from the mountain laurel *Kalmia latifolia*, one of the rare plants whose nectar causes the bees to make honey unfit for human consumption.[57] Honey, it seemed, could be poisonous.

Ovid refers to 'hemlock honey'.[58] Other plants causing toxic honey include leather-leaf and rhododendrons. From ancient times it became clear that honey from the *Rhododendron ponticum* was not fit for human consumption. We know now that this is because it contains the poison andromedotoxin. All the ancients knew was that it made them very ill. The fullest account comes in Xenophon's *History of the Persian Expedition*, which describes what happened when Xenophon's army of 10,000 Greek soldiers stole some honey near Trebizond on the Black Sea:

> The Greeks ascended the mountain and camped in a number of vil-
> lages which were well stocked with food. There was nothing
> remarkable about them, except that there were great numbers of bee
> hives in these parts, and all the soldiers who ate the honey went off
> their heads and suffered from vomiting and diarrhoea and were
> unable to stand upright. Those who had only eaten a little behaved

as though they were drunk, and those who had eaten a lot were like mad people. Some actually died. So there were numbers of them lying on the ground, as though after a defeat, and there was a general state of despondency. However, they were all alive on the next day, and came to themselves at about the same hour as they had eaten the honey the day before. On the third and fourth days they were able to get up, and felt just as if they had been taking medicine.[59]

Most commentators now assume that this poisonous honey of Trebizond came from the rhododendron. Other honeys from the Trebizond region were also reported to be toxic. Honey from Colchis, further north, was known as 'maddening honey' on account of its power to make those who ate it slightly deranged, and honey from Heracleia Pontica, in north-east Asia Minor, sometimes made those who ate it roll around in pain. However, it is also possible that Xenophon's soldiers got an especially bad case of poisoning because the honey was unripe. Unripe honey is honey straight from the bees' honey sac which has not yet been sufficiently evaporated by the flapping of workers' wings. It has a high moisture content, ferments very easily, and is still known to cause dysentery on occasion. If honey can be shaken from a honeycomb when it is harvested, then some of the cells are filled with unripe honey, because the bees always seal the honey with wax when it is ripe. Xenophon's men's illness might just have been suitable punishment for stealing the honey from the hives before it was ready to eat.

Of all the ways of being poisoned, honey poisoning seems especially treacherous. The word 'sardonic' now means 'grimly mocking' or 'cynical'. Originally, however, it referred to the bitter expressions – like grotesque, spasmodic laughter – on the faces of Sardinians who had eaten local toxic honey. Lord Macaulay said that the melancholy of Dante resembled 'that noxious Sardinian soil of which the intense bitterness is said to be perceptible even in its honey'.[60] But he was wrong. It wasn't the soil of Sardinia that was bitter, but the nectar from a local variety of wild parsley, the source of honey which caused agonizing griping.

In many of the accounts of toxic honey, one gets the sense that it is all so unfair – how can something so good be so dangerous? 'My son, eat thou honey, for it is good' does not have such a ring if you add 'except when it makes you throw up'. On the other hand, toxic honey confirmed all of man's latent fears about bees as dangerous creatures – creatures who sting.

Stings

The sting has always been the main stumbling block for those who would see the bee as the most perfect creature in creation. 'Thou painful Bee, thou pretty creature / False . . . and impure,' wrote the Greek poet Pindar in the fifth century BC. It is so hard to reconcile the sweet honey-makers with their sting, that complex organ which combines a piercing instrument, barbed lancets and a venom sac containing a mixture of toxic peptides and enzymes. It evolved from the egg-laying devices of earlier insects, and eventually became a weapon.[61] For those of us who adore bees it is hard not to experience a sting as a betrayal. 'But no, I am your friend! I'm writing a book about you!' I thought, ridiculously, the first time my presence in the apiary angered a bee enough for it to sting me.

The bee's sting – this 'living stiletto' – casts doubt on the entire proposition that bees and men were made for each other. For one thing, stinging humans is extremely bad for bees. Whereas the bee is able to withdraw its sting from insect enemies, it cannot do the same when it stings human flesh, or that of other mammals with elastic skins: 'In its struggle to withdraw its sting from a mammal the entire sting apparatus is frequently torn from the bee, a mortal injury, but the penetrating movements of the lancets continue for up to a minute driving them further into the victim and increasing envenomation.'[62] When unleashed on human flesh, the bee's sting is a suicide bomb, only not a very effective one: a normal human reaction is a 'raised white bleb', followed by red and hot swelling, lasting one or two days, whereas a bee sting will kill or immobilize other insects. The best thing to do when a bee stings you is what Charles Butler recommended in 1623: 'Instantly wipe off the Bee, sting and all, and wash the place with your spittle.'[63]

The effects of a bee sting on a beekeeper from Oberlin, Ohio

On the other hand, in some terrible cases, bee stings can pose a fatal threat to human health. In the early sixteenth century, in the German city of Worms, just before the famous 'Diet' of 1521 at which Martin Luther defended his iconoclastic beliefs, some bees killed a child by stinging it. The Great Council of the City decided that the city must exact punishment on the bees, ordering that the hives and bees be burned in the public square, to set an example to other insects. But the bees have carried on stinging, and occasionally killing, regardless. Most human fatalities have resulted from stings to the face, ear, nose, eye, mouth, throat or neck. Stings to the throat are especially terrifying, because the soft tissues may swell, resulting in asphyxiation, but only gradually. In one dreadful case, a rich landowner drank a glass of cider containing a live bee. He scarcely even noticed he had been stung, and carried on eating a sumptuous dinner, during which time he might have been saved. By the time he realized his throat was beginning to swell it was too late.[64] Some deaths have been caused by multiple stings, especially to the face, but there have also been cases where grown healthy men have been killed by a single sting to the neck.

Since the beginning of the twentieth century, when the French physiologist Charles Richet began to develop the concepts of allergy and anaphylaxis, it has been known that some unfortunate humans can acquire hypersensitivity to bee stings, even when they don't occur on a sensitive part of the body.[65] Worryingly, the condition can strike at any time, and it can even affect beekeepers who have been safely stung many times before; this hovering threat of disaster has persuaded some to abandon their craft. In the unhappy victim, a bee sting is not just a 'local irritant' but a substance with a 'far-reaching constitutional effect'.[66] As with other allergies, the sufferer's body produces excess antibodies in response to the foreign substance, which then cause a severe reaction. Anaphylaxis brought on by a bee sting can result in faintness, vomiting, confusion, stupor, vertigo, dizziness, troubled sleep, sweating, pustules, dull throbbing, a sallow waxiness to the skin, stinging eye pain, frothy saliva, bad breath, swollen lips, poor hearing, stiffness, accelerated pulse, palpitation, loss of appetite or craving for milk, griping and diarrhoea, biliousness, renal pain, frequent urination, swollen testicles and long erection in men, ovarian pain, swelling breasts, violent menstrual pain and miscarriage in women, and, ultimately, death. Insect stings are responsible for forty to fifty deaths every year in the USA, and four or five in Britain. The list of symptoms of anaphylaxis is as long as the ancient lists of honey's benefits.

Fortunately, there is a long-term cure for anaphylaxis that comes yet again from the hive. Bees and hornets can be 'milked' of their venom on electrically charged grids which force them to sting again and again. (The colonies in question become very bad tempered.) As many as 210 colonies may have to be 'milked' to obtain a single gram of venom, which is then freeze-dried and marketed by pharmaceutical companies, being targeted at bee-keepers in particular. Immunotherapy for stings consists of very small doses of bee venom, injected at regular intervals in grad-ually increasing quantities, until the patient can tolerate the equiv-alent of two full stings. Once this is the case, the doctor may expose the patient to live bee stings, to allay their fears around bees.[67] Assuming there is still no reaction, they are then safe to resume beekeeping, should they wish. Such immunotherapy is now a professionally recognized practice, with backing from the Food and Drugs Administration.[68]

Bee venom, however, is used for more than just curing those sensitive to it. For centuries, bee-lovers have wondered whether bee venom might not be a therapeutic agent in its own right. The emperor Charlemagne was said to have been cured of his gout and arthritis by bee stings.[69] Bee-venom therapy really took off among a group of German and Austrian experimental doctors of the late nineteenth century. Dr Philip Terc, a particularly zealous Austrian, experimented with live bees on numerous patients in the 1870s and 1880s, in treatments which must have taken some selling. In 1879 a woman came to him complaining of terrible neuralgia and deafness. He decided to risk applying ninety live stings to her head, but had no luck. (What the patient must have been suffering is not reported.) He tried again, with another fifteen stings to her neck and shoulders. This caused the poor woman's face to swell up so much she was unable to open her eyes. Otherwise, however, she was 'jubilant, as all her pains were gone'. She told Terc that she had heard the sound of church bells.[70] Over the course of his career, Terc treated more than 500 patients in this way, using more than 39,000 stings.[71]

There are still those who swear that bee venom can cure severe arthritis and rheumatism. The trouble is that the claim has never been tested in proper clinical trials.[72] Though many beekeepers swear that frequent stings have enabled them to remain vigorous into old age, you will meet those who, despite being stung as often as thirty times a day at the height of summer, are still crippled by arthritis. Many of the cases of arthritis being cured by bee stings may be attributed to chance: remission just happened to occur around the same time as a sting. It is possible that stings sometimes have the effect of acupuncture as well. In any case, the intense desire of bee-venom advocates to argue for its benefits is yet another instance of the human love affair with bees. Bee-venom therapy is a way of rebelling against the disappointment of finding that bees are not always friends of humanity – a way of taking the sting out of stinging.

In more warlike and less neurotic times, the bee sting commanded more respect. 'He is not worthy of the honeycomb that shuns the hive because the bees have stings', as the old saying goes. It was understood that bees needed their stings, as all creatures need weapons, for protection. In 1767 the beekeeper John Mills argued, 'The sting is very necessary for the working bee, both as an offensive and as a defensive weapon; for their honey and wax excite the envy of many greedy and lazy insects.'[73] For Joseph Warder, in the same century, the sting was the bee's 'chief instrument of war'.[74] For our ancestors, the bee's sting did not alienate it from man. On the contrary, it showed that bees, like men, were born to fight.

Bees and War

It is often said that the feeling of standing in the middle of battle in an air thick with bullets is not unlike the sensation of being surrounded by whizzing bees in an apiary. 'The bullets sang like swarming bees and their sting was death,' remembered one soldier of the American Civil War.[75] The notion of bees being like an

Bees swarming out of a helmet: a symbol of victory in warfare, from a sixteenth-century book of emblems

army goes at least as far back as the Old Testament, where the Amorites pursued the Israelites 'as bees do'.[76] Bees themselves have also been turned into heat-seeking missiles in human battles on numerous occasions. Just as often they have been used as pre-emptive frighteners, fantastical weapons of mass destruction designed to scare people to death.

Beehives have been used for both attack and defence since ancient times. The Romans sometimes catapulted hives into the fortifications of their enemies to create panic and pain when they were trying to seize a settlement. The same trick could also be used in the opposite direction: if beehives could be thrown into a city, they just as effectively be thrown out of one, on to the heads of assailants. In AD 908, in Saxon England, invading Danes under Hingamund attacked the city walls of the town of Chester. The Danes seemed to be winning until the defending English, under Ethelfleda, hurled skeps full of bees on their attackers, confounding the assault and making the swollen Danes retreat. Military beehives also feature in several accounts of the crusades. During the First Crusade, the Christian armies laid siege to the stronghold of Marrah, near Antioch. They were repulsed by Muslims firing beehives at them. By the time of the Third Crusade the Westerners had adopted beehive missiles for themselves, if we are to believe the famous poem *Richard Cœur de Lion*, a panegyric to the wonderful military prowess of Richard the Lion Heart. The poem claims that King Richard of England set off on crusade with:

> Two hundred shippes well victualled
> With force hawbecks, swords and knives,
> Thirteen shippes lade with hives of bees . . .

According to the poet, Richard later successfully deployed these bees against the Saracens, who were so scared by the 'biting of his bees' that they ran off to hide in a deep cellar.[77]

Brave King Richard and his biting bees are a medieval example of military propaganda – or rather, since the poem was written 200 years after the event, of military myth-making. The story depends on the premiss that bees could be loyal, terrifying and deadly, like a crack troop of real soldiers. This was a familiar theme in medieval Christian mythology, the most famous example being that of the wonderfully named St Gobnat of Ballyvourney, from County Cork in Ireland, a beekeeper-nun who probably lived in the sixth century, and was later credited as a patron saint of bees. Various fairy tales survive linking Gobnat with bees and warfare.[78] In one of these, a powerful chief was on the point of waging war with another clan when he noticed that his troops were too feeble. He took himself to a neighbouring field, where there happened to stand a beehive, and prayed to St Gobnat for assistance. She obliged by turning the bees into disciplined warriors, who followed the leader into battle, where they were victorious. After the battle, the grateful chief returned to the field where Gobnat had granted his request, only to find that the hive itself had become transformed into a brass helmet. This hive-

helmet supposedly survived as a relic in the possession of the
O'Hierley family well into modern times, when a drop of water
drunk from it was still thought to bestow good luck in battle.

The Gobnat legend is obviously a fantasy, but not an unappeal-
ing one: that stings, the only aspects of bees that have always
troubled honey-lovers, are not destined to persecute all men, just
the wicked and the unrighteous. It embodies the dream that bee
stings can be enlisted on the side of virtue against evildoers, and
that bees sting not because they are hurt or afraid, but because they
are noble and patriotic friends of the righteous warrior.

By the twentieth century this dream had turned sour. Bees
would still get mixed up in human wars every so often, but the
stories told about military bees were no longer so golden, in the
context of other killing machines available that were ever more
sophisticated. The Battle of Antietam, which culminated on 17
September 1862 – the bloodiest day in American history, bloodier even than 11 September 2001 – offered one of the earliest and
nastiest glimpses of what modern warfare would become. The toll
of the battle was 7,753 dead and 18,440 wounded. It was made still
bloodier when Confederates shot into a beeyard on Roulette
Farm as Union soldiers advanced, leaving them in a state of welt-
ridden hysteria and unable to defend themselves. Seven hundred
soldiers were buried on that farm after the war. It would take a
skilful fabulist to find anything very wonderful in such a graveyard,
or to take much pleasure in the honey that was made there.

Men did not cease to fantasize about bees in warfare, but the
fantasies took on a new, darker, tone. Whereas medieval myth-
makers hoped that stinging honeybees could be enlisted on the
'right' side, modern storytellers began to treat bees as dangerous
creatures, not to be trusted. Bees were malevolent, not benevolent; not patriots, but potentially traitors to the cause.

The Battle of Tanga was the first major engagement of the First
World War to take place in German East Africa. It was fought in
November 1914, when some innocent souls were still hoping that
the war would be over by Christmas. The Battle of Tanga, named

after the port in Tanzania, is also known as the 'Battle of the Bees', because the defeat of the British was brought about partly by the presence of angry swarms of bees fighting (or so many people believed) for the Kaiser. Tanga, an ill-fated amphibious attack, was a particularly embarrassing setback for Britain. The British leader in the region, General Arthur Aitken, had been sent into battle with hopelessly ill-prepared troops. The result of his attack was 847 British dead or wounded, compared with only 148 German casualties. For several months the defeat at Tanga was concealed from the public at home. Long after the war, and after the next one too, on 16 January 1953, a letter in *The Times* tried to lessen the shame of losing Tanga by claiming that the Germans had snared the jungle pathways with tripwires fastened to hives in nearby trees. The British, wearing only tropical uniforms of shorts and shirts, would pull over the hives, enrage the bees, and be stung all over their pale, exposed skin. A devilish trick! How could the honest British troops ever have triumphed against such underhand tactics?

But another letter in *The Times* a week later suggested that the attacking bees were following their own agenda rather than one dictated by the Germans. Their stinging was probably set off not by tripwires but by machine-gun fire, and they attacked both sides indiscriminately, with no particular loyalty to the Germans. It was because the British were more poorly equipped that they suffered worse damage from the onslaught of stings. William Boyd imagines the terrible confusion of Tanga in his novel *An Ice Cream War* (1982). He pictures a British soldier surrounded by 'black dots and specks, whizzing erratically through the air', which he assumes, as a matter of course, must be bullets. He gets hit. 'Oh God, he thought, not in the neck. He stumbled, but ran on, clapping a hand to the wound to staunch the blood, bullets buzzing and darting past. But wait, he thought, they weren't bullets, they were bees! He stopped and turned round. His men were leaping about or writhing on the ground like epileptics as the swarming myriads of bees attacked.'[79]

When they are involved at all, bees simply add to the horror of modern warfare. We no longer have the crusading impulse to believe in the patriotic biting bees of Richard the Lion Heart. The stinging bees of the modern imagination are more vicious than noble. This is partly because of the increasing phenomenon of Africanized 'killer bees', which are spreading from South America to the USA. This particularly aggressive strain of bee resulted not in nature but from a mistake in human science: in the 1950s, Brazilian entomologists cross-bred European bees with more aggressive African bees, thinking that these would be suited to the hot Brazilian climate. By the time they discovered their mistake, it was too late: swarms of Africanized feral bees had overpowered the gentler honeybees and were multiplying and moving through South America and, by 1990, up into Texas. They have been described as 'the greatest danger in the US to American beekeeping'.[80] The reason is that Africanized bees are much more easily riled than their European counterparts. When one Africanized bee stings, it releases a pheromone smelling of bananas which can make the whole colony agitated and enraged for days. You can run away from an angry swarm, but don't try to hide under water: the swarm will wait for you to re-emerge and then attack.

Killer bees have infected our collective apian imagination, inspiring disaster movies and apocalyptic thrillers in which angry bees take over the world – notably *The Swarm* (1978), in which Michael Caine plays an entomologist who tries to persuade the US military not to open fire on rampaging bees. 'I never dreamed it would turn out to be the bees', he laments. 'They have always been our friend.' Even in Europe, where killer bees are not much of a menace, we have developed a kind of Winnie-the-Pooh attitude to the bees: they are dangerous, they are unpredictable, and they are usually acting to thwart us. Like Winnie-the-Pooh, we find all this a little unfair. Selfishly, we still want bees to see things from our point of view. This is a bit rich. Our hysteria about stinging obscures the fact that the harm caused by bees to men is as nothing compared to the harm caused by men to bees.

The Death of Bees

For much of human history, a beekeeper's life involved killing all his bees every year. This was not inevitable, as a farmer kills a pig for bacon, but because the beekeeper could not work out any consistent way of taking the honey while preserving the bees. A particular culprit in this regard was the homely straw skep, the hive that most of us still think of when we visualize a beehive – a design which seems to stand for all that is most comforting and good about bees. It wasn't good for the bee colony, however, since it meant annihilation. Though they came to symbolize the happiness of domesticity, skeps were in fact about as cuddly as a mausoleum soon to be stuffed with tiny corpses.

At the end of summer, around Bartholomew-tide, the skep beekeeper would decide which hives to keep and which to destroy for their honey. Any hive that was brimfull with honey would be taken, as would old hives. This is how one historian of beekeeping explains the process of harvesting honey by the skep method:

> A pit would be dug in the ground and towards evening sulphur burned in it. The skep was placed over a pit and the bees quickly poisoned by the fumes. When dead they were easily shaken from the combs and the honey drained into large earthenware containers. The honey was allowed to settle in the container and any wax debris that floated to the surface was removed. This honey was called virgin honey. The remaining honeycombs were pressed to yield what was called common honey. The combs that remained after pressing were soaked in water and made into mead.[81]

The theory behind sulphuring was partly that you would avoid getting stung, and partly a mistaken belief that the hives which remained would multiply much quicker with the old ones gone. Most skeppists do not seem to have cared much about the lives of the bees themselves. In 1634 the annual bee massacre received a shameless defence from John Levett. He argued that, of all the ways of harvesting honey, killing the bees was 'simply the best, and most profitable, both for the owner, and the increase of his bees'. If a beekeeper failed to kill bees after taking their honey, the hungry bees would only fall to robbing the surrounding hives. Levett was aware that some people said it was 'a pity to kill the bees that have so laboured for us', but he called this 'a foolish and fond conceit':

> Hath not God given all creatures unto us for our benefit, and to be used accordingly as may seem good unto us for our good? We see that many other creatures of greater account are daily killed in infinite numbers for our sustenance and often for our pleasure, and is it not lawful for us, to use these silly creatures in such sort as they may be most for our benefit, which I take to be the right use of them and the very end of their creation?[82]

Not all of Levett's contemporaries agreed, however. In 1655 Samuel Hartlib noted that 'The Ancients made a constant Revenue of their Bees without killing them at any time.'[83] This was true. The ancient Greeks and Romans had recommended various methods for sharing the honey with the bees. Columella advised scraping the honeycomb away in the early morning, before the bees became 'exasperated by the midday heat'.[84] Pliny recommended taking honeycomb only from the back of the hive, so that plenty would be left for the bees.[85]

Gradually, skeppists began to try ways of harvesting honey without killing the creatures who produced it. By the eighteenth century, outrage at killing bees had gathered ground. One bee expert, John Keys, wrote, 'Alas! Ill-fated bees! Doomed to be victims of your own industry!'[86] Thomas Wildman cast doubt on the proposition that killing off some hives would help the bees to 'increase': 'Were we to kill the hen for her egg, the cow for her milk or the sheep for her fleece it bears, every one would instantly see how much we should act contrary to our own interest; and yet this is practised every year, in our inhuman and impolitic slaughter of bees.'[87] The fate of the bees was even lamented in a well-known poem, *The Seasons*, by James Thomson (1700–1748):

Ah see where robbed and murdered, in that pit,
Lies the still heaving hive! At evening snatched,
Beneath the cloud of guilt-concealing night,
And fix'd o'er sulphur . . .

.　　.　　.　　.　　.　　.　　.

O man! Tyrannic lord! How long, how long
Shall prostrate nature groan beneath your rage
Awaiting renovation? When oblig'd
Must you destroy? Of their ambrosial food
Can not you borrow; and in just return,
Afford them shelter from the wintry winds.[88]

The trouble was, it was easier to lament the bee's fate than to do anything about it. Old countrymen practised techniques for 'driving' the bees out of skeps, mostly by using rhythmical beating on the side of the hive to hypnotize the bees, before driving them upwards into an empty skep.[89] Some villages held bee-driving competitions. But, as long as the claustrophobic skep was the hive of choice, bee driving was a hit-and-miss affair, and most of the bees still perished every harvest.

Salvation for bees could come only with a new design of hive. From the eighteenth century onward, scientifically minded beekeepers began to design what were called 'collateral' bee boxes, where individual combs could be lifted out on bars without damaging the entire colony. A particularly elegant variant was François Huber's leaf hive, which opened up like a book. In the 1830s the 'Never Kill A Bee' movement became popular in America.[90] In 1838 a self-styled 'conservative bee-keeper', W. C. Cotton, wrote *A Short and Simple Letter to Cottagers,* setting out the moral and practical arguments, and signing it simply 'A Bee Preserver'. Thomas Nutt's plea for the bees was more direct still: *Humanity to Honey Bees* was the name of his book of 1832.

But it was not until the work of an American clergyman called Lorenzo Lorraine Langstroth in the middle of the nineteenth century that these noble schemes became a practical reality. It was through Langstroth that the collateral or movable-frame beehive was perfected. The problem with existing collateral hives was that the combs would often get stuck together, either with more comb or with the sticky dark stuff called propolis. Langstroth's great discovery was bee space: the distance to leave between frames, large enough that bees would not start to build more combs, and small enough that they would not feel the need to glue it together with propolis. This magical figure was ⅚ inch (around 8 mm). Langstroth discovered that if all the frames in a hive were separated by exactly this space, they would be completely movable. It was a true 'Eureka' moment. (Langstroth later said that he had indeed felt like Archimedes when he made the discovery, and had wanted to run through the streets proclaiming it.) It has been said that every movable-frame hive built since 1851 is effectively a Langstroth hive, because all of them make use of bee space.[91] What they also now do is keep the bee brood separate from the honey, by means of queen excluders, which means that bee eggs do not have to be destroyed at harvesting time either. With this design of hive, wrote one admirer, the beekeeper suddenly had 'total control over his bees'.[92] The honeybees could be saved, if the beekeeper wished it.

But this 'total control' has been an ambivalent legacy for the bees. The efficiency offered by modern hives makes the power of life and death that men have over bees seem all the more stark. When the old skeppist killed his bees, he could tell himself that the decision was really out of his hands. Modern, rational beekeepers, by contrast, seem to have the ability to play God with their bees, and no one from the RSPCA will turn up to stop them. In Sylvia Plath's poem 'The Arrival of the Bee Box', written in 1962–3, she writes of the sensations of taking delivery of a fresh consignment of bees.

> They can be sent back.
> They can die, I need feed them nothing, I am the owner.[93]

These feelings are not uncommon. In a dark and depressing novel about a beekeeper, a modern Scandinavian writer called Lars

Gustaffson expresses the creepiness inherent in the beekeeper's powers:

> I know few things which give rise to a Napoleonic complex to the same extent as does beekeeping. One can have all the experiences of a Napoleon without being cruel to horses and without seeing one single human being die. Instead, one sees a whole bunch of bees die.[94]

For honeybees, the attractions of humanity rather depend on what kind of human beings they end up with.

Life and Death: Recipes

I cannot vouch for the efficaciousness of any of these potions, offering them more for interest's sake than for usefulness. If you are ill, please see your doctor!

Syrup of Capillaire

An eighteenth-century cough medicine from John Hill's *The Virtues of Honey* (1759):

> Pick from the stalks four ounces of fresh leaves of the true maiden-hair, while they are young, and without seeds. Pour upon these a quart of boiling water. Let it stand eighteen hours; then filter it through paper, add to this four pounds of pure Honey. Boil this a few minutes and then strain it through flannel.[95]

Of the Aristaean Confection

This also comes from John Hill, and is recommended for 'that flatulent cholick, to which hypochondriack people are peculiarly subject'. Aristaeus was the Roman god of beekeeping.

> Slice very thin four scruples of Assafoetida, grind it in a marble mortar, with four ounces of fine Honey. Put this into a pan, and set it in a vessel of water: put the whole over a gentle fire. And let it remain, frequently stirring it, till the Assafoetida is perfectly dissolved, then strain it through a coarse linen cloth. Then mix in a mortar one drachma of cinnamon in fine powder, two scruples of powder of ginger, one scruple of amomum cleaned from the husks

and rub'd also to fine powder, with the assistance of a quarter of an ounce of the finest sugar; when all are perfectly mix'd add them to the rest while it is yet warm, and mix them perfectly by long stirring. Then keep it carefully tied up for use.

Hill says that a dose is a teaspoonful, containing only two or three grains of assafoetida, yet equal to ten in its effects.[96]

Honey and Lemon for a Cold

Juice half a lemon into a mug. Add a large dessert spoonful of honey and some cloves, then fill with hot water. Drink, sniffling slightly. I was told about the cloves by a Polish lady: they are a good addition.

Toddy

Good for opera singers or anyone with a sore larynx. Mix two tablespoons whisky with one tablespoon honey, adding hot water to taste.

Honey Water to Cleanse the Skin

This is taken from Eva Crane's *A Book of Honey* (Oxford: Oxford University Press, 1980). Dissolve two tablespoons of the best honey in one litre warm water, then add three times as much warm water and wash the face and neck for five minutes. Rinse with warm water and pat dry.

Beeswax Lip Balm

> 2 tablespoons grated beeswax
> 4 teaspoons almond oil
> 2 teaspoons finest honey

Place all the ingredients into a double boiler over simmering water. When they have completely melted, remove from the heat, stir together, and pour into small containers. Wait for the mixture to cool before putting the lids on. You can add a few drops of essential oil if you like, after the mixture has come off the heat.

Milk and Honey Bath

This is adapted from Stephanie Rosenbaum's *Honey: From Flower to Table* (San Francisco: Chronicle Books, 2002). Rosenbaum says this is a 'modern version' of Cleopatra's milk bath.

> 3½ ounces powdered milk
> 4 tablespoons honey

Mix the milk and honey into a paste, then dissolve this in a warm bath as you run it.

Hair Treatment

Sarah, Duchess of Malborough, was praised after her death in 1744 for having 'the finest hair imaginable, the colour of which she had preserved unchanged by the constant use of honey water'.[97] Should you wish to emulate her, mix together a couple of spoonfuls of honey with some warm water and use to rinse your hair every time you wash it.

Honey and Salt Scrub

> 8 ounces coarse sea salt
> 5 tablespoons honey
> 1 or 2 tablespoons of olive oil

Mix all the ingredients together and use as a body scrub in the bath, especially on your elbows, knees and heels. Go easy if you have sensitive skin.

Victorian Hand Cream

Another recipe from Eva Crane's *A Book of Honey*. I include it not because I really recommend smearing lard on yourself, but to show that the transference of kitchen ingredients to beauty remedies was not invented by The Body Shop. This hand cream ends up smelling just like marzipan. As hand creams go, it is rather impractical: you'd have to use it up straight away, before the egg yolks went off.

    4 ounces lard
    2 egg yolks
    1 tablespoon honey
    1 tablespoon ground almonds
    ½ teaspoon almond essence

Mix all the ingredients into a stiff paste and smother on your hands.

6
The Beekeeper

'And live alone in the bee-loud glade'
W. B. Yeats, 'The Lake Isle of Innisfree' (1888)

M OST BEEKEEPERS THAT one meets nowadays are benign
amateurs – people who love what they do, but don't like to
make a song and dance about it. You see them at country shows,
wearing sandals and bearing home-grown potatoes. They are
nature enthusiasts, hobbyists for whom a few hives are a way of
staying in touch with the seasons, while producing some jars of
something sweet to please their dear ones (or not, as the case may
be – I know of people who will feign a diet just to escape eating
their friend's oilseed-rape honey). Amateur beekeepers are gentle,
even depressed, people for the most part; if they have a social sting,
then, like the queen, they hardly use it. They are used to keeping
their cool in the midst of an angry multitude. Almost by
definition, they are sensitive types – responsive to the delicate feelings of their little companions, always alert to the slightest changes
in the weather and the mood of the colony. They often see their
hobby as a sort of affliction, quoting the beekeeper R. O. B.
Manley – 'Bee fever: a form of insanity from which you never
really recover'. It sounds like an apology, but really it's a modest
kind of boast.

Beekeeping suits reserved types, people of a solitary disposition
who find their happiness among this most social of animals.
Inevitably, there are many beekeeping bores, who will drone on

about the superiority of their own special rosemary honey because they have nothing else to talk about. But there are other, shyer, souls who really find themselves in the apiary. However diffident they may be around other human beings, beekeepers have an aura of the superhuman about them. It's partly the costume, with its overtones of battle. In the eighteenth century bee costumes resembled fencing gear; now they look more like astronaut's suits. When the poet Sylvia Plath first turned up to a meeting of village beekeepers, she didn't realize she needed protective clothing, and found herself wearing a 'sleeveless summery dress', feeling 'nude as a chicken neck'. The villagers, meanwhile, were indistinguishable under their veils and 'ancient hats':

> Which is the rector now, is it that man in black?
> Which is the midwife, is that her blue coat?
> Everybody is nodding a square black head, they are knights
>   in visors,
> Breastplates of cheesecloth knotted under the armpits.[1]

I too turned up to my first meeting of the local beekeeper's association – on a hot June day with the smell of thunder in the air – absurdly dressed in flowery, feet-baring sandals and wide-legged trousers with plenty of room for insects to fly up. When I first entered the apiary, my heart juddering every time a bee skimmed my trouser-leg, I realized how little I had in common with the calm, white-hatted people surrounding me. Their strange disguises only added to the impression that they were the possessors of secret powers – an impression which was not altogether wrong. The bees were frantic that day, black bullets, sensing the storms to come. I was loaned a veil, but a bee got inside it, buzzing near my face until I thought I would scream. One of my companions reached in and removed it with his hand, as calmly as if he were picking a berry. His look told me it was me, not the bee, that was the irritant.

Beekeepers have the power to master fear, and even to love the thing they ought to fear. Some beekeepers claim they don't get stung as much as other people. Others claim they just don't mind it as much, weathering as many as thirty stings a day at the height of summer. Stings or not, beekeepers can walk among the bees more easily than among men. They understand the power of stillness. In human life, self-effacement makes you fade out of view; but, in the apiary, self-effacement makes you strong. (As Sylvia Plath put it, 'If I stand very still, they will think I am cowparsley.')[2] When you see the beekeepers later, with their disguises off, talking about brood and comparing honeycomb, they are ordinary again: from Superman to Clark Kent. But while they are in the eye of the swarm they seem curiously invulnerable. Beekeepers can seem more than human because they seem to have mastered the secret of the hive, and therefore the secret of nature itself.

These are the magicians who extract 'honey from the weed'.[3] They are weather-hardened farmers who have learned how to find happiness in modest circumstances. Peter Fonda exemplifies this idea in his 1997 film *Ulee's Gold*, where he plays a Florida beekeeper specializing in tupelo honey – the 'Gold' of the title. Fonda is a beekeeper himself, and acts the part with quiet authority, lifting supers and inspecting brood cells. 'The bees and I have an understanding,' Ulee says. 'I take care of them. They take care of me.' Ulee stands for the old ways of doing things. He learned from his father, who learned from his father. 'Young folks can't be bothered', not with the hard work of moving hives and heaving barrels of honey. To the young folks in the film – Ulee's criminal son, drug-addict daughter-in-law and rebellious teenage granddaughter – Ulee seems as redundant and ineffectual a figure as a drone. Yet, at the end, he triumphs over some nasty bad guys through a combination of hard work, stoic consistency and the same passive bravery that makes him such a good beekeeper. 'You've got to keep your calm around bees.' People who dedicate their lives to beekeeping may be a little strange, but they are also peculiarly self-possessed.

This last chapter looks at the three great archetypes of the beekeeper. Each of these archetypes depends on a certain relationship to nature, different from that of the ordinary beekeeper-as-hobbyist who simply uses bees as a way of enjoying nature and getting good honey. First there is the beekeeper as *scientist,* who studies the colony and uses the bees to *understand and know* nature. Then there is the beekeeper as *showman,* who parades his fearlessness and uses the bees to *control* nature, and earn the respect of other men. Finally there is the beekeeper as hermit or *sage,* the leader of the quiet life, who, through the bees, *submits* to nature, knowing, stoically, that humans cannot change anything.

But, before we look at these three types of beekeeper, we need see how beekeeping has developed over time.

The History of the Beekeeper

Many customs relating to beekeeping have remained more or less constant since hive beekeeping began, in Egypt, 4,000–4,500 years ago. To take just one example, beekeepers have always made sure that they do not smell offensive to bees when they visit the hive. This precaution dates as far back as the earliest written records. In 200 BC, Aristophanes of Byzantium noted that 'Bees sting and drive away those who approach them wearing perfumed oil, as if oil was an enemy. For this reason, indeed, people try to approach them unanointed, and in Egypt even with shaven heads, so that no moisture of oil remains.'[4] Countless ancient authors advise against visiting the bees smelling strongly of onions, sweat or wine, and beekeepers today still avoid eating garlic bread before examining a colony. There are good reasons for this continuity: foul odours can indeed act as a stimulus to stinging, and to bees in the wrong mood even a faint tang of human sweat under a watch strap can be foul enough to provoke them to sting en masse.

Another continuity is the use of smoke to calm the bees before the hive is examined, though the kind of smoke used has changed: the Romans and Egyptians burned dried cow dung in earthenware pots; the Victorians experimented with rotten rags and tobacco; and in 1877 T. F. Bingham, an American, invented the bellows smoker, which could blow out just enough smoke to calm the bees, but not so much that they became asphyxiated. Now most beekeepers use small metal smokers filled with woodchips or straw or leaves, but the principle remains the same. It is still not quite clear why smoke works – are the bees acting on some primal memory of forest fires which makes them panic and gorge on honey? Or does the smoke work because it masks the scent of alarm pheromones in the hive? The practical beekeeper probably does not need an answer to these questions, so long as the smoke continues to work, making the bees docile.

In contrast to the use of smoke, other aspects of beekeeping have changed to such an extent that its ancient practitioners would find it hard to recognize it as the same activity. In all ages and all countries there has been a respect for bees and a thirst for their honey, but the role of the people responsible for getting that honey has assumed multiple different forms. The hive itself has varied in form from cylinders of mud to cones to straw skeps to elaborate mahogany constructions, and these changes in the hive have been accompanied by huge modifications in the position of the hive manager.

Roman authors of the republic (509–27 BC) saw beekeeping as a noble pursuit, the occupation of an independent citizen-farmer, well-versed in poetry and botany. Virgil's ideal republican bee-keeper was a self-sufficient type, who knew how to revive his bees with roses and wine and to fumigate them with thyme, and who put great expertise into dressing the hive to the bees' liking. But this rugged kind of beekeeper was already in decline in the poet's lifetime (70–19 BC), which explains the elegiac tone of the *Georgics*: Virgil was celebrating a way of life he feared was ending. Under the Roman empire (27 BC–fifth century AD) the important person was no longer the person who looked after the bees but the person who owned them. The beekeeper was no longer independent, but a *mellarius* – a slave.[5] The bee-owner did not care

Beekeeping in Roman times, as depicted by Wenceslaus Hollar,
in his illustrations to Dryden's translation of the *Georgics*. These
beekeepers are trying to make a swarm settle in a hive by
'tanging', or making a loud noise

about sunny days and thyme and the wisdom of the bees: he cared only whether his *mellarius* was delivering enough honey. The *mellarius* was not credited with much intelligence. In feudal England people who looked after bees occupied a similarly lowly status. In the Domesday Book they were called bee-ceorls or bee-churls, 'churl' designating the lowliest of freemen. A bee-ceorl had much the same rank as a swineherd. In medieval Russia there were *bortniki* or 'bee-men', who collected honeycomb from trees in pails to give as tribute to princes.[6] As long as the status of beekeeper was debased, there was no incentive for knowledge about bees to grow. In the Middle Ages the art of beekeeping stagnated.[7]

During the Renaissance, however, the ancient respect for bee-keeping was revived, along with so many other forms of classical knowledge. Beekeeping was now seen as a branch of husbandry, of cottage agriculture, something analogous to tree-grafting or sugarcrafting, a practical and respectable occupation. Moreover, men now sought to make their mark on the beehive, to mould it to their liking. During the sixteenth and seventeenth centuries in England, bees were not *kept* so much as *ordered*. The first book in English entirely devoted to bees was Thomas Hyll's translation of a Continental work, *A Profitable Instruction of the Perfite Ordering of Bees* (1574); this was followed by Edmund Southerne's *Treatise Concerning the Right Use and Ordering of Bees* (1593) and John Levett's *The Ordering of Bees* (1634). Levett wrote, in an aggressively patriarchal style, of *driving* the bees, and of *using* them. Bees might be superior to all other insects, but they were still of a different estate from men. Levett had no compunction about killing them. After all, nature was man's playground, designed for 'our pleasure'. God gave bees to man 'for our benefit'.[8]

Over the course of the seventeenth century, however, a different conception of nature emerged – one in which man's privileged place in creation was questioned. Sceptics argued that men were 'morally no better than animals, possibly even worse'. Others – the so-called mortalists – challenged the Christian dualism of body and soul and argued that men and beasts were 'equally mortal'. Some writers even proposed that animals had their own reason. Suddenly it could be argued that bees had 'a kind of wisdom coming near unto the understanding of men', or even surpassing it.[9] The role of the beekeeper now had to be rethought. Man could no longer presume that he was either worthy or capable of 'ordering' the bees, as Levett had believed. At best he might grow to understand them enough to 'manage' them, as a gardener manages an orchard. This helped to turn beekeeping into a branch of 'husbandry', or rural economy. The beekeeper came to be seen as above all a practical figure – *The Practical Bee-Master* is the title of several eighteenth-century beekeeping manuals. More bee books were now directed at women. Bee books became analogous to cookbooks – practical guides full of recipes for getting more honey and keeping the bees happy, as they deserved.

By the nineteenth century, however, huge advances in the technology of beekeeping had led the status of the beekeeper to change yet again. Beekeeping could now claim to be a science as much as an art. The skep was replaced by the rational top-bar hive, from which frames of comb could be easily lifted out, along with many more Professor Branestawm-ish models, involving multiple cabinets and pivots. Beekeepers expressed their new-found scientific status by referring to themselves as 'apiarists' instead of 'bee-masters'. Everything became 'new' and 'improved' – there were new artificial wax foundations, new smokers, new breeds of bee. In Russia, this was the era of 'rational' beekeeping, of the hive as experimental laboratory, as the old peasant ways were cast off.[10] Model apiaries were founded; beekeeping schools were established; scholarly journals were set up. For the first time in history, beekeeping or apiary was a properly professional career. Beekeepers increasingly stood in relation to the bees as a biologist stands towards a dissected frog.

But during the same period, in part as a reaction against this new spirit of scientific detachment, beekeeping veered off in a number of divergent directions. One of these was charitable. There had long been a strong humanitarian tradition in bee writing, and this now found new expression.[11] Loving bees could be a way of loving one's fellow man. During the nineteenth century there emerged a strong paternalistic desire to help the poor learn self-sufficiency by encouraging them to keep bees and giving

The Globe Bee Veil, as worn by a very insouciant nineteenth-century beekeeper

them the knowledge to do so. This attitude to beekeeping still prevails in charities such as Beekeeping for Development, which advises people in the Third World on keeping bees and understanding the honey they get from them. There is a kind of enduring zeal to these people, with their good works. They try gently to enlighten Africans against the evils of honey-hunting and encourage them in the ways of hive beekeeping. Like the Victorians, they think bees might be able to civilize the uncivilized – though they would never use such language.

The nineteenth century was also the era when beekeeping became newly commercialized. The Great Exhibition of 1851, which had itself been compared to a giant beehive, gave fresh impetus to commercial bee farming. The beekeeper as entrepreneur

knew that honey meant money, which entirely went against the old
bee-master's superstition that the products of the hive should never
be sold, only bartered. This attitude now seemed quaintly old-
fashioned.

A female beekeeper at work in her apiary in Lismore, Ireland,
1890. She is collecting honey with a bowl and spoon

At the same time, beekeeping also took a completely different
tack. Just as beekeeping was becoming properly scientific and pro-
fessionalized, it also became truly amateurish for the first time.
Some of the middle classes now enjoyed a novel thing called leisure, and looking after bees seemed one of the best ways to fill it.
Children's books on bees proliferated, in both England and
America, with whimsical titles such as *The Wonderful World of the
Busy Bee*. Beekeeper's associations were founded, giving rise to
gentle honey competitions. Bee books now became chatty and
personal – like W. C. Cotton's *My Bee Book* (1842) or Amos Ives
Root's *ABC and XYZ of Bee Culture* (1877).

As factories belched out smoke, and sugar consumption proliferated, the beekeeper began to seem a folksy, reassuring kind of
figure, a link with the old ways, rugged and self-sufficient. He
might take account of progressive developments, but his real
wisdom lay deep in the hive and was as old as time. In 1898 a clergyman called Tickner Edwardes published a book which would
become a huge bestseller, *The Bee-Master of Warrilow*. This fictional
bee-master epitomizes much of the myth that had accumulated
around the image of the beekeeper. 'Long, lithe and sinewy, with
three score years of sunburn on his keen, gnarled face, and the sure
stride of a mountain goat, the Bee-Master of Warrilow struck you
at once as a notable figure in any company.' The bee-master of
Warrilow speaks in a 'tangy Sussex dialect', but, like Virgil's beekeeper, he is part botanist, part poet. Just by tasting, he can tell the
source of honey, discriminating between white clover and sain-
foin, and easily detecting when 'the detestable honey-dew had
entered into its composition'. He uses his hives to predict the
weather: 'His bees were his weather-glass and thermometer in
one'. He is part of 'another and a kindlier century', and seems to
be in touch with the secrets of the universe. '"There's many a
thing about bees," he said, "that no man 'ull come to the rights
of, until all airthly things is made clear in the Day o' Days."'[12]

Even now, beekeepers retain this feeling of mystery before their
bees, this mixture of arrogance and humility. The best beekeepers
are still 'notable' figures in any company. They still seem to belong
to an older, kindlier world, and can still read the weather through
their bees. The difference, however, is that even the most amateurish of local beekeepers now understands more about the workings
of the hive than the rugged old bee-master of Warrilow ever did.
This is because of the extraordinary developments in bee science
that took place over the twentieth century, and above all thanks to
the work of Karl von Frisch, the man who discovered that bees
can talk.

Karl von Frisch
The Beekeeper as Scientist

Bees were not the first love of Karl von Frisch. This great biologist first gave his heart, aged eight, to a large green parakeet, with which he developed a 'close and lasting friendship'. Born in 1886 in Vienna, the youngest of four sons, Karl had always liked animals,

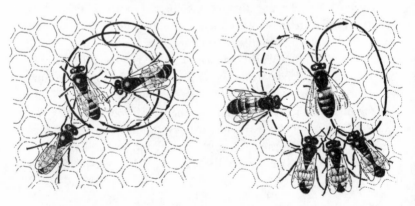

Karl von Frisch and his diagram of the famous 'waggle dance'

filling his parent's home with all manner of peculiar friends. His father and uncles were scientists, and Karl, being a good, dutiful boy, naturally followed in their footsteps. The Frischs were a close, musical Austrian family, not unlike the von Trapps. Karl's father was a urologist. His mother, whom he worshipped, indulged Karl by buying him blue tits, which he would set free each year as a way of learning respect for other creatures. She was a pious and joyful woman, who taught him that nature was a 'great garden of wonders'. Before he was born, she had longed for a girl, after three boys, and, as if in response to her desire, Karl's personality became soft and feminine. At his family's holiday home in Brunnwinkl, in upper Austria, on the shore of the Wolfgangsee, Karl kept a 'museum' of butterflies, moths, and beetles, which grew and grew. While other boys might have been out playing with bows and arrows, Karl was busy observing living beings: 'I simply enjoyed watching the manifestations of their biological functions and mental stirrings in all the variety related to the different stages of animal development.' This aged eight! When he grew up, and became a professional scientist in Munich, he chose to observe fish, trying to find out why minnows changed colour in different lights. Only in 1912, aged twenty-six, did Frisch discover bees. But once he had 'fallen under their spell', they patterned the whole of his subsequent career, and won him the Nobel Prize for Physiology in 1973.[13] Ever dutiful, he was always grateful to the family of bees for what they had done for him.

It was colour that first excited Frisch's interest in the hive. His graduate work was on the colour vision of fish, and this was what made him notice the dubious theory of a certain Professor C. von Hess. This Hess was an arrogant and rude ophthalmologist at the Munich Eye Clinic, who in 1910 had asserted the theory that bees were definitely colour-blind, on the basis of some observations done in very bright light. To Frisch, even though he had never studied bees in any detail, Hess's theory seemed highly unlikely. If bees were colour-blind, what on earth was the point of flowers being so brightly coloured?

An unbiased observer was much more inclined to believe the theories of the flower biologists who thought that the bright colours of petals served to make the inflorescences conspicuous to bees and other pollinating insects; that they were, in fact, colourful inn signs announcing where nectar was to be had, the guests paying for their meal by the service of pollination. Was it credible that this relationship was falsely regarded as the perfect example of mutual adaptation, and that the glory of the flowers should be nothing but a meaningless display before the eyes of colour-blind insects?'[14]

Frisch decided to risk the wrath of Professor Hess and set out to prove that the bees had colour vision. To do so, he invented an experiment of elegant simplicity.[15] The crucial thing was to demonstrate that bees could distinguish colours from each other *as colours* and not merely as different shades of grey. Frisch began his experiment by training bees to feed on sugar water set on a blue coloured card. Next he set the blue card in the middle of a table covered with various grey cards. If bees were colour-blind, they would not be able to distinguish the blue card from a grey card of equal brightness. But, to Frisch's delight, the bees could indeed tell the blue card from the others, seeking it out even when he moved it to a different place on the table and even when the sugar water was removed. He had proved that bees had a colour sense. Professor Hess was furious, and engaged in a 'heated and acrimonious feud' with Frisch, flatly denying the truth of his findings and more or less accusing him of being a fake.[16] As Frisch later recalled, 'readers of our papers frequently were at a loss whom to believe'.[17] In the German academic system, with its heavy emphasis on deference and hierarchy, the hostility of a senior figure could be enough to finish your career before it had even started. Frisch was himself deeply deferential, and it was painful for him to clash with Hess in this way.

His desire for truth, however, was stronger than his fear of offending authority. He was 'furious' at Hess's attempts to discredit him, and boldly continued his research, now extending the experiment to other colours: orange, yellow, green and purple. All achieved good results. The bees could distinguish all these colours from grey. But when he did the experiment with a red card, the bees seemed suddenly confused: they could not tell the difference between red and black. This led Frisch to another great discovery:

> Bees are red-blind. That is very interesting. We understand why scarlet red bee-blossoms are so rarely found. There are very many red flowers in America, for instance, but only in bird-blossoms. Bird's eyes are very sensitive to red. In Europe there are some plants with red flowers, but their pollination is – with few exceptions – effected by certain butterflies. These butterflies are the only insects which are not red-blind. There is an exception to the rule – the poppy, the flowers of which are visited by bees although they are scarlet red. But these flowers reflect many ultra-violet rays. Bees are able to perceive ultra-violet rays. Ultra-violet is a special colour for them, distinguishable from blue and all other colours. It is evident that the colours of flowers have been developed as an adaptation to the colour-sense of their visitors.[18]

This was a colossal breakthrough, because it confirmed that the colour of flowers *did* have a biological meaning. Frisch's career as a scientist was now well on its way, and the horrid Professor Hess had been seen off.

Having answered the question of colour, Frisch moved on to other aspects of the bees' senses. Taste, for example. Frisch demonstrated that the well-known liking of bees for sweetness is very 'fastidious' indeed. If the bees were offered a solution containing only 5 per cent saccharose, they would taste it and refuse it. At 10 per cent saccharose some bees would drink it, but other, fussier, individuals would reject it. At 20 per cent, all the workers would drink it, though not with as much enthusiasm as their customary nectar, which has a sugar content of 40 per cent. Through similar experiments, he found out that bees have a stronger sensitivity to salt than human beings, but are far less sensitive to bitterness: 'They seem to enjoy a mixture of quinine and sugar which is so disgusting to the human sense of taste that anyone would spit it out at once.'[19]

Frisch's work was founded on a profound sympathy with bees, which brought him nearer and nearer to an understanding of what it would be like actually *to be* a honeybee. He achieved this sympathy through summer after summer of long, hard and methodical research at his Brunnwinkl hives, but, as he himself admitted, much of what he discovered was no more than a confirmation of what any beekeeper would guess for himself through common sense. To take the most striking example, Frisch wrote that 'any attentive beekeeper' would see that bees must have a way of communicating among themselves. This ordinary, 'attentive beekeeper' might notice that a jar of honey could stand for days unnoticed by the bees in the open air, but that as soon as a single bee had discovered it, 'after the shortest time dozens and hundreds of bees from the same hive are on the spot, to rob the supply. They must have talked about it at home!' But as for how the bees could talk to one another about the best nectar sources, the ordinary beekeeper must draw a blank. It was here that the beekeeper-scientist came into his own. What Frisch, with his painstaking observation, discovered, was the so-called 'dance of the bees', a 'performance so charming to watch that one despairs of describing it in bare words'.[20] There is something bizarre and touching about the spectacle of this punctilious biologist spellbound at the sight of dancing insects.

Frisch knew that two things would be necessary if he was to find out how the bees talked to one another. The first and most important was an observation hive, built so that the wax combs were alongside each other instead of behind one another, to give a full view of the business of the colony. Transparent hives had been built for centuries by scientist-beekeepers, possibly as early as Roman times, when they were made from a transparent mineral or horn. In his diary, Samuel Pepys described dining with John Evelyn and admiring his glass hive in which 'you may see the Bees making their honey and combs mighty pleasantly'.[21] The trouble with many of these early observation hives was that they were often more decorative than useful, emulating the architectural beauty of honeycomb. Frisch's design, though very ugly, took the observation hive to new levels of scientific utility. He developed a hive which could be tilted, to study the bees more precisely, and he used his knowledge of the bees' eyesight to include a polarizing glass panel that allowed consistent illumination. Such a hive would have been of no interest to the old-fashioned skeppist, who cared little what went on inside his straw hives, so long as he got plenty of honey by the end of the summer. But the scientist-beekeeper is completely unlike other beekeepers in not really caring about honey. He wants the bees for themselves, rather than for what they produce. What Frisch cared about was making the bee colony easier to observe than ever before.

The second thing he needed, apart from the observation hive, was some kind of tracking device for the bees. Frisch learned how to paint the bees in combinations of different colours in such a way that 599 workers could be identified. Now, at last, it was possible to spot the bee who discovered a new source of nectar.

Frisch and his team noticed that, after first depositing her honey with other bees in the hive, this forager bee performed a strange and complicated dance: 'On the same spot [the bee] turns round and round in a circle with quick, tripping little steps, once to the right, once to the left, very vigorously, often half a minute or a full minute on the same spot. The dance is then often repeated on another spot.'[22] The more Frisch studied this bee dance, the more subtle a language he discovered it to be.

If the bee was trying to tell her fellow workers about a source of nectar very near the hive, she would do a simple circular dance, in the thick of the hive. The bees near to the dancer would become 'greatly excited', trooping close behind her as she whirled round and round, and trying to touch her abdomen with their feelers. Frisch became not a little excited himself at the 'striking and attractive' movements of the dance.[23] This round dance is a compelling sight, almost like watching ravers on Ecstasy engaging in a crazed love-in, with accumulating numbers of bees joining the whirligig in the dark of the hive, before peeling off one by one and leaving the hive in search of nectar. After watching this scene of enthusiasm countless times, Frisch worked out that the circular dance must contain the message 'Go out and look for nectar in the vicinity of the hive.' Frisch deduced that the reason that the other bees seem so eager to touch the body of the dancer is that they are trying to smell the flower scent on her, so that they will know which kind of flower to plunder for food. He proved this hunch by putting sugar solution near to cyclamen flowers. After the first forager had found this food and performed her dance, all the bees came out in search of cyclamen, ignoring any other flowers nearby.

Frisch's greatest revelation of all – one which came close to the wildest myths about the intelligence of the hive: that bees could mourn or fight or build churches or pray using rosaries – was that bees could use more elaborate 'waggle dances' (*Schwänzeltänze*) with very precise angles and tempos to tell the rest of the hive about food sources much further away. The 'waggle dance' turned Frisch into an international celebrity.

> In these dances the bee runs along a narrow semi-circle, makes a sharp turn, and then runs back in a straight line to her starting point. Next, she describes another semi-circle, this time in the opposite direction, thus completing a full circle, once more returning to her starting point in a straight line. She does this for several minutes, remaining on the same spot all the time: semi-circle to the left, straight back, then semi-circle to the right, straight back, and so on indefinitely. The characteristic feature which distinguishes this 'wagging dance' from the 'round dance' is the very striking, rapid wagging of the bee's abdomen performed only during her straight run.[24]

Over the decades, Frisch constantly refined his understanding of the language, uncovering more and more about the extraordinary accuracy of the information that bees could convey to each other with this waggling. A dance straight up the comb would tell them to fly towards the sun; straight down would mean away from the sun. A slow dance meant the honey was far away; a faster one meant it was nearer. If the food was within a short distance of the hive, the dancing bee would finish the waggle dance very quickly. But the further away the nectar was, the longer the dance went on, and the more slowly the waggling part of it was performed. Using a stopwatch, Frisch was able to determine that in 15 seconds there would be 9–10 repetitions of the waggle part of the dance if the distance between hive and feeding place was 100 metres, 6 repetitions if it was 500 metres, 4–5 repetitions for 1,000 metres, 'and barely more than once at a distance of ten thousand metres'. Moreover, the consistency of these measurements across different colonies was 'simply amazing'. The bees, wrote Frisch, must have 'a very acute sense of time, enabling the dancer to move in the rhythm appropriate to the occasion', which was 'all the more remarkable as the bees do not carry watches'.[25] This, one imagines, is a joke, but with Frisch and the bees you can never quite be sure.

Having set out with the limited goal of proving that bees are not colour-blind, Frisch unearthed more than he could have ever imagined about the mechanisms governing the hive – that 'mental heritage' that gives bees the ability to build hexagonal cells, to fill pollen baskets, 'to advertise a worthwhile crop by means of dances, and to kill off the drones in [the] hive at the appropriate time'.[26]

It might be supposed that unravelling the mysteries of the hive would have made Frisch less enchanted by bees. But the opposite seems to have been true. The more he studied the bee language, the less he felt he really understood it, or the creatures themselves. At times he adopted a lofty attitude towards the hive, as if to show the bees who was boss, remarking 'we cannot form a very high opinion of the bee's mental capacity' because of its narrow range.[27] But from almost all his other writings it is clear that he esteemed the mind of the bees very highly indeed. At one point in his researches the outcome of his experiments seemed so 'fantastic' to him, that he wondered if his own bees in the observation hive had perhaps turned into some kind of 'scientific bee', distinct from ordinary bees.[28] It is as if he had spent so long watching the bees that he had begun to wonder if it was actually they who were watching him. Further research, unsurprisingly, showed that even the 'ordinary' bee was just as special, and just as adept at communicating.

Like earlier, less well-informed, observers of the hive, Frisch couldn't help noticing the contrast between the solidarity of the bees and the discordance of so many human relationships. In his preface to the English edition of *The Dancing Bees*, which came out in 1954, Frisch thanked his translator in these terms:

> Suppose German and English bees were living together in the same hive, and one of the Germans found a lot of nectar; its English companions would easily understand what it had to say about the distance and direction of the find. Human language is not so perfect. So I am indebted to Dr Dora Isle for translating my book . . . for English readers.[29]

Frisch, who had been horrified by all aspects of the Second World War, was all too aware that it was not only language that separated the Germans (and Austrians) from the English; all too aware that the notion of German bees sharing nectar with English bees would have seemed not just wishful but abhorrent to much of his English-speaking audience. Frisch deplored the human 'maelstrom' of 1939–45 (a period during which the bees suffered too, for the years 1940–42 saw a calamitous epidemic from a parasite called *Nosema apis*).[30] Compared to warring humans, the bees were serene and purposeful. If only, he lamented, men could emulate them – 'If only human beings would be intelligent enough to keep all harm and ill away from future generations voluntarily, and if only a generation of noble beings could arise, who would help one another, and share honestly in the fruits of the earth.'[31] What it is about bees that provokes such big 'if onlies'? The career of Karl von Frisch suggests that a lifetime spent studying the hive makes it hard to turn back to human society without a pang of regret.

Since Frisch, there have been other great beekeeper-scientists:

Dorothy Hodges (1898–1979), who did pioneering work on the pollen loads of bees; Colin Butler (1913–), who in 1961 discovered how pheromones in the hive govern the relationship between queen and workers, noticing that a certain pheromone will prevent workers from rearing another queen; and Francis Ratnieks, whose ongoing work at the University of Sheffield has uncovered much new information on how the bee community polices itself. For all of them, studying the bee colony is, among other things, a lesson in humility before the works of nature. As Frisch himself expressed it, 'Nature has unlimited time in which to travel along tortuous paths to an unknown destination. The mind of man is too feeble to discern whence or whither the path runs and has to be content if it can discern only portions of the track, however small.'[32]

But this humility before nature has not been the attitude of all beekeepers. On the contrary, the wonder of the hive has taken many of them in the opposite direction. Some beekeepers have focused less on knowing and more on doing, using the hive to show not the smallness of man's understanding but the largeness of his power. These beekeepers have been not scientists, but entrepreneurial showmen.

The Wildmans: The Beekeeper as Showman

Of all the beekeepers who have ever lived, perhaps none was a greater showman than Thomas Wildman, who liked to parade before an adoring public with various parts of his body covered in bees: his arms, his chest, his eyes, his head, and particularly his chin. Wildman, who came to fame in the 1760s, was an extrovert through and through, a social climber and an exhibitionist. He used his complete 'mastery' over the hive to make himself seem like a magus, a controller of nature. Wildman treated the bees much as a circus tamer treats his lions – to the astonishment of the English aristocracy, among whom he made beekeeping a fashionable pursuit.

Wildman presented himself as a nature-lover, but he was really a beekeeping wideboy, 'willing to use the ballyhoo of a market trader', to promote himself and his act in any way he could.[33] Like any exhibitionist, Wildman stirred things up. His antics made many people furious, and to this day many beekeepers still get rather sniffy if you mention his name.

Not much is known of Thomas Wildman's early life, except that he was born in Devon and later lived in Plymouth. All that is certain is that he always wanted to make his mark and escape his humble origins. Luckily for him, he had the kind of highly advanced dexterity coupled with personal charm that could turn ambition into fame. It was in Plymouth that Wildman perfected the art of moving swarms of bees around at will. The trick was really very simple, and had been known at least since the time of Jan Swammerdam, who a hundred years earlier had found that if you could capture the queen, by tying silk thread round one of her legs, then you could move the rest of the bees from place to place: wherever the queen went, the other bees would obediently go too.[34] The way Wildman did it was to gather the queen up in his hands, and then play on the bees' attraction to the scent of the queen's body to get the colony to follow him.[35] Few people in eighteenth-century Britain had read Swammerdam, and, to the laypeople who saw it, Wildman's control over the bees seemed more or less magical. He seemed to be exerting a 'secret influence' over the colony, speaking the language of the bees and befriending these dangerous animals. His secret was artificial swarming.

A natural swarm happens when some of the bees in the colony, by some unfathomable instinct, decide to leave their habitation to a new queen, and go off with their old queen in search of a new place to live. This usually happens in spring. All the bees move as one, in a seething mass, flowing like water, buzzing at a higher pitch than usual, in what Maeterlinck called 'this riotous bewildering spectacle'.[36] Bees in a swarm are usually contented, because they have gorged themselves on honey before they set off, to give them energy for the expedition. In wild colonies swarms are very important, because they are the means by which honeybee communities multiply and stay healthy; but they are also unpredictable. Tickner Edwardes calls the swarm 'one short hour of joyousness and madcap frolic' after a lifetime of 'order, commendable toil, chill, maidenly propriety'.[37] Nowadays beekeepers will do everything they can to prevent swarming – removing the queen cells a colony builds before it swarms, or clipping the queen's wings to stop her leaving. In previous years, by contrast, the art of beekeeping lay not so much in preventing swarms as in catching them in a hive when they happened. Before the advent of mail-order bee packages, all beekeeping started with hiving a swarm in spring. The ancient Columella recommended rubbing hives with herbs such as balm and wild parsley, to make them more attractive for the swarm. For much of history, it was believed you could encourage a swarm to settle by 'tanging', or banging two metal things together to make a loud noise.[38] Then, once it had settled on a tree, you might cut the branch and hope to maneouvre it to an empty hive without being badly stung. You might endeavour to trap the bees in a honey-pot, or else in a piece of moss soaked in human urine.[39] You could also encourage a hive's bees to swarm by smoking them out, by burning puffball to make them drowsy, and hope they settled where you wanted them, rather than on your head (as sometimes happened). In any case, it was all an uncertain and risky business; the swarm has always been the point at which bees seem most beyond human control.

How magical and effortless it must have seemed to do as Thomas Wildman did and move a swarm without any apparent trouble, and not even at swarming time. What Wildman did was to mimic the conditions of a natural swarm: he made the bees gorge on sugar syrup and then removed their queen. This kept the workers tranquil, and made them follow the queen and her pheromones – not that Wildman knew about these – wherever she might go. Wildman had as cool a head as any good beekeeper, but he played on the anxiety of his audience about being stung, working them up into a frenzy of apprehension before his act began.

Like a magician, he surely knew how to divert attention, using patter. He did not reveal the secret of what he was doing, but encouraged his audiences to believe he could train the bees through sheer force of personality. Instead of a rabbit in a hat, he produced a perfectly 'tame' swarm of bees. In the early days, this act was very simple: he would just move the bees from one hive to another, without any of them stinging him or his audience.[40] But then Wildman discovered that he could also hold the queen in his hand for a while, and that the bees would settle 'in such numbers as to hang in a cluster from his hand'. And if bees would hang from a hand, why not try to attach them to other body parts?

As Wildman's fame spread, so his performances became more elaborate. The time was ripe for him. He and his bees flourished during the era of Capability Brown and Humphrey Repton, when the English aristocracy thrilled to the spectacle of nature domesticated in 'the picturesque'. Garden designers were putting all their efforts into making scenery look effortless. It was a time when nobles enjoyed romping with tame bears, and there was an admiration for 'exuberant natural forms', such as giant conch shells and weird crystal specimens.[41] The spectacle of hypnotized bees fitted well with this mood.

In 1766 Wildman put on a show for Lord and Countess Spencer at Wimbledon in Surrey. The audience was composed of fashionable nobility, who watched as Wildman strutted before them with bees all over his hat. 'Then he returned into the room, and came out again with them hanging on his chin, with a very venerable beard.' Next he made the bees swarm among all the fancily dressed ladies, who were doubtless giddy with alarm; but no one was stung. As if this were not amazing enough, Wildman then managed to make the bees go on to the table 'and took them up by handfuls, and tossed them up and down like so many peas'. For his pièce de résistance – you can imagine the gasps – Wildman, having withdrawn from the room, returned carpeted in bees all over his head, face and eyes. He then mounted a horse and made the bees swarm all over his chest as well, so that half his body was covered.

At the end, he calmly dismounted and 'at his word of command' the bees retired to their hive. We are told that 'the performance surprised and gratified the Earl and Countess and all the spectators who had assembled to witness the great bee-master's extraordinary exhibition', which sounds like an understatement.[42] To an audience unacquainted with Wildman's methods, his act must have seemed thrilling and terrifying beyond measure – like fireworks combined with Russian roulette.

Wildman, a canny businessman, knew that his management of bees also gave him great sway among men. 'Spectators wonder at my attaching the bees to different parts of my body, and wish much to be possessed of the secret means by which I do it,' he observed.[43] In a book, he reluctantly revealed the secret of his 'command over bees', but noted that few other men would have the skill to do what he did. He was probably right. It is one thing to know how to control the hive, another altogether to let bees swarm over your face without flinching. On the strength of Wildman's reputation as bee sorcerer, nearly 500 people paid for his *A Treatise on the Management of Bees* (1768) before it was even published – among them dukes and earls, fellows of the Royal Society, professors and architects. He also made a pretty penny as a professional beekeeper to the aristocracy.

However, Wildman knew enough about the traditional expectations of a beekeeper's personality to deny that his interest in the hive was wholly mercenary. On the contrary, he protested, he was motivated by love. Perhaps he even believed his own lies. He was more of a genuine charlatan – a showman who believed his own patter – than a cold-hearted mountebank or swindler. It was 'tender regard' for the 'precious life of the queen', he insisted, that had spurred him on to perfect his technique of artifical swarming.[44] Wildman's admirers agreed. A poem in the *Mirror* praised Wildman as the man who 'with uncommon art and matchless skill / Commands those insects who obey his will':

With bees others cruel means employ,
They take the honey and the bees destroy;
Wildman humanely, with ingenious ease,
He takes the honey, but preserves the bees.[45]

But not all bee experts saw it this way. To John Keys, a less famous contemporary, Wildman was a disgraceful trickster whose exploits showed exactly the wrong attitude towards bees. Keys, a quiet countryman who described himself as a 'practical bee-master', seems to have resented Wildman's glittering courtly life. For him, Wildman's exploits were a way of misleading the public and showed scant respect for the hive. 'This gentleman's extraordinary performances with Bees', wrote Keys, 'attracted the notice of the curious few, as well as of the public; but however advantageous they may have been to himself, I fear they will be found of little utility to the world.' Despite Wildman's 'expectations' that his techniques would revolutionize beekeeping, Keys argued loftily that there was little in Wildman's book that could be used by other beekeepers. (In fact the book is still sometimes used by beekeepers today.) As for the business with the bee beards on horseback, 'Mr. Wildman has no secret power over the Bees to cause them to come out of their Hives at the word of command, as many people have erroneously imagined.'[46]

It was not just the deception that Keys objected to. It was also the way that Wildman reduced beekeeping to a spectacle. Keys admitted that there was something compelling about bee beards – that it was 'very wonderful that such wild, ferocious and revengeful creatures' should 'become so tame as to suffer themselves to be taken up in the hand'. But just because it was possible to attach bees to the human body did not mean that it was right to do so, he argued. The activities of Wildman were 'merely tricks, that tend more to destroy than improve Bees'. Besides, the sight of bee beards was 'so very distressful a scene, that no true lover of these very useful insects can practise it without regret'.[47] Keys hated bee beards for the same reason that so many people now are unsettled or offended by the sight of horses being made to stand like humans in a circus: bee beards seemed *unnatural* – a way of depriving the creatures of their dignity.

If Thomas Wildman irritated people, they were even more annoyed by his nephew, Daniel Wildman, who continued his uncle's bee act in a still more boastful manner. At least Thomas Wildman had paid his dues as a beekeeper. He was highly skilled in the apiary, and was one of the first to offer his services as a professional beekeeper to others. He contributed articles to the *Encyclopaedia Britannica* on insects, and his book on beekeeping was a serious and valuable work, crammed with charming observation as well as careful précises of the views of other beekeepers. Daniel Wildman's book, on the other hand, was a flimsy 48-page brochure which seemed primarily designed to advertise his London shop at 326 Holborn, where he sold all kinds of bee-related products: stocks of bees, virgin honey, and de-luxe and newfangled hives: the modest 'flat-topped straw hive with slides', the pricier mahogany hive with glasses, and the 'curious and elegant' mahogany model with partitions as well as glass.[48] All these could be bought direct from Wildman junior. The braggadocio somehow worked. Despite being slight and often inaccurate, Wildman's book was a best-seller, running to many editions, which goes to show that brazenness in advertising was just as effective then as it is now.

Thomas Wildman invented his performance with bees in part because he loved working with them: 'The bees are a pacific people that labour for our good and in return we interest ourselves for them.'[49] Daniel Wildman, on the other hand, seems to have interested himself in bees primarily as a way of enriching himself. He took his uncle's bee beard act to new levels of bravado, often boasting that when armed with bees he could face the fiercest of mastiffs without fear. He claimed that he was once set upon by three dogs, at which he made one of the bees sting an attacker on the nose, which saw them off. While his uncle entertained the aristocracy in private homes, Wildman junior put on popular performances for money, mainly in Islington. Here is the advertisement for one of his shows, on 20 June 1772:

At the Jubilee gardens, late Dobney's, this evening and every evening until further notice (wet evenings excepted), the celebrated
Mr. Daniel Wildman will exhibit several new and amazing experiments, never attempted by any man in this or any other kingdom
before. He rides standing upright, one foot on the saddle and the
other on the horse's neck, with a curious mask of bees on his head
and face. He also rides standing upright on the saddle with the
bridle in his mouth, and, by firing a pistol, makes one part of the
bees march over a table, and the other part swarm in the air and
return to their proper hive again . . . The doors open at six, begins
at quarter past seven. Admittance on the boxes and gallery is Two
Shillings, other seats One Shilling.

On several occasions he also appeared before George III, 'with a
swarm of bees hanging in festoons from his chin'. One can only
wonder what mad King George made of this spectacle.[50]

Today, there are still beekeepers, of the Wildman type, who
enjoy covering their bodies in bees. At country fairs in the USA
where honey is sold, you will often find the odd beekeeper prepared
to drum up a little business by making himself hirsute with bees.
Sometimes there are even beauty queens – honey princesses – who
can be persuaded to do the same. Beekeepers in general are still
undecided on the merits of bee beards. Some find them to be harmless fun. Others, like John Keys, dislike the contrivance of them.
The Illustrated Encyclopedia of Beekeeping (1985) cautiously calls bee
beards 'a form of exhibitionism and/or entertainment'.[51]

But there is another perspective. Bonnie Pierson is a beekeeper
of ten years' standing from North Ridgeville, Ohio – and one of
an increasing band of female bee-beardists. She tells me that she
began wearing bee beards at the Lorain County Fair 'for the nov-
elty of it and for recognition of my bravery'. But things soon got
more serious:

> Now, after being a beekeeper for ten years, I find I am in love with
> my bees! I like to wear a beard to get as close as I can to my beloved
> bees, to experience respect, trust, honesty and the intimacy of the
> colony. To me, it is now a very moving experience. There is the

Rob Green, an American beekeeper, displaying a fine bee beard

tactile experience of thousands of tiny pinchers gently attached to my face, weight gradually added. There is the sound of their flying and other audio communications. The pheromone mixture of smells adds another dimension. But, the most profound feelings that I get are harder to describe. I am overwhelmed with this feeling of letting go of everything else but just loving the bees. I am totally at peace and joined with the consciousness of the colony. I feel their beginning confusion, then the excitement of connecting with the queen, then their peace as they settle in. I don't like it to end.[52]

For those who feel an unbearable itch at the mere thought of 'tiny pinchers' near the face, this is certainly odd, to put it mildly.

Modern exponents of this astonishing art say that bee beards and bee gloves – where two bee-lovers shake hands carpeted in a swarm – are great PR for bees, because they are showing that bees are benevolent and manageable animals. What they do not say – what the Wildmans never forgot – is that the show succeeds in impressing an audience only if onlookers believe the opposite – if those watching fear that at any moment the bee-beardist could be horribly stung. Bee-beardists claim that they want to allay exaggerated fears of bees; but what they do is itself an exaggeration. Bee beards do not convert the unconverted to beekeeping, any more than watching a fire-eater converts you to pyromania. The Wildmans knew that they were putting on a freak show. Daniel Wildman has been praised as the ultimate 'Crazy Bee Man' by some modern bee experts who like to think of themselves as a little zany. But Wildman wasn't crazy, except for money and fame. He was an exhibitionist, which is different from being insane. The tendency of modern bee-beardists, on the other hand, is to deny that they are simply making a spectacle of themselves. For the rest of us, this only makes their attitude all the weirder.

One of the greatest beekeepers of the twentieth century was a master of the bee beard who took it all very seriously. As well as running a family honey business, Champlain Valley Apiaries, in Vermont, Charles Mraz (who died in 1999) was a world expert on bee-venom therapy, and believed in the power of bee stings to treat arthritis and multiple sclerosis. He therefore had particular reason to respect bees. But he also enjoyed covering himself with the honey-makers from time to time. He did so not as exhibitionism, but as a way of expressing the intimate union he felt with bees. In Mraz's view, it was the traditional beekeepers, decked out in veils and thick protective gear, who were artificial. To cowards like myself, even the sensation of bees crawling over a trouser-leg is a little uncomfortable. But Mraz would strip down to the waist and wander happily among his hives, confident that he would probably not be stung – for what could be more natural than to tend the bees wearing just his skin, to show them he felt no fear? – and sure that, even if he were, it would do him more good than harm. Sometimes he would also make the bees swarm over his face, enjoying the sensation, like a horserider who goes bareback. Only by going nearly naked into the hive could he demonstrate the closeness of bees and men, as two species united by the same nature.

It is perhaps rather an ostentatious way to make the point. A single sting to one of Mraz's eyeballs could have damaged his sight for life; a single sting to his throat could have constricted his windpipe and killed him.[53] Ordinary beekeepers do not need to get quite so physical to prove that they love their bees. 'Always wear a veil' is the first rule of amateur beekeeping. For many beekeepers, the real art is in withdrawing from the life of the hive as much as possible, and letting nature take its course without interference. Does strutting naked in an apiary show a love of bees or of oneself? Beekeeping does not have to be showy activity; it can be the opposite. The aim, as Maeterlinck saw it, is still to 'become the master of the bees' – but 'furtively, and without their knowledge; directing all things without giving an order, receiving obedience but not recognition'.[54] Veiled and heavily disguised, some beekeepers find the activity to be a good way of disappearing altogether.

The Beekeeper as Sage

When Sir Arthur Conan Doyle finally liberated his creation Sherlock Holmes from solving crime in Baker Street, he retired him to a quiet life of 'study and bee-farming on the Sussex Downs'. We first hear about this in the story 'The Second Stain' (1904), where Watson makes it clear that Holmes – never a sociable man – has now become a near-recluse, except for the company of his bees. 'Notoriety has become hateful to him.'[55] For Watson, the fact that Holmes has chosen this beekeeper's life is a sign he has given up on worldly affairs.

Watson is incredulous, then, when in the late story 'His Last Bow' (1917) Holmes emerges from his retreat for one last time to defeat the evil German spy von Bork. 'But you had retired, Holmes,' he exclaims, with typical literal-mindedness. 'We heard of you as living the life of the hermit among your bees and your books in a small farm upon the South Downs.' Holmes's reply is characteristically lofty:

'Exactly, Watson. Here is the fruit of my leisured ease, the *magnum opus* of my latter years!' He picked up the volume from the table and read out the whole title, *Practical Handbook of Bee Culture, with some Observations upon the Segregation of the Queen.* 'Alone I did it. Behold the fruit of pensive nights and laborious days, when I watched the little working gangs as once I watched the criminal world of London.'[56]

Watson thinks that Holmes had turned his back on life, not realizing that Holmes's existence among the 'little working gangs' has contained as much incident as any day in Baker Street. *Practical Handbook of Bee Culture* sounds like one of the finest works of the great detective, along with his monograph on tobacco ash. Moreover, true to its title, the volume has a very practical application indeed. Holmes uses this 'irrelevant' book to distract the wicked von Bork, before chloroforming him and handing him over to the authorities.

Like everything else about Holmes's life, his elderly vocation as beekeeper has attracted keen debate among those Conan Doyle enthusiasts who like to call themselves Sherlockians – endearing souls who seem far from sure that Homes was actually fictional. Where in the Sussex Downs did Holmes base his apiary? When was he there? Could he have joined forces with a young female apprentice to fight crime in the area?

Such questions need not detain us here. What is interesting about Holmes's retirement as a beekeeper – a characteristically deft touch from Conan Doyle – is how it adds to the detective's mystique. It does so because of all the expectations of the beekeeper as wise hermit that have accumulated through the ages. Retiring to the life of the bees has again and again been seen as a way of attaining true wisdom by turning away from men and towards the 'little working gangs'. The reclusive beekeeper, like Sherlock Holmes, is a strange mixture of the worldly and the unworldly.

Until the twentieth century, many of the great beekeepers – and of the not so great ones – were either monks or clergymen. Bees seemed a natural accompaniment to a life of contempla-

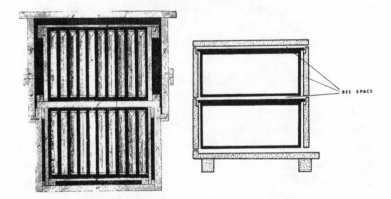

L. L. Langstroth and his tiered hive, which made use of his
discovery of bee space

tion – and often of melancholy. Lorenzo Lorraine Langstroth, the
man who more or less single-handedly created the modern bee
industry in America, by discovering the principle of bee space (as
discussed in Chapter 5), was primarily a conscientious and troubled church minister, who suffered from chronic depression or
what he called 'head trouble'.[57]

There was sadness, too, in the life of Brother Adam of Buckfast

Abbey, the most celebrated beekeeper-monk of all time.[58] Adam (who was born Karl Kehrle) arrived at his monastery in England from Germany in 1910, when he was only twelve, and remained there for the rest of his life, during which time he was often miserable and homesick. But once he discovered Buckfast Abbey's apiary his life had a purpose. He could at last express his 'love of nature'. Brother Adam's bees provided him with a way of escaping from human experiences yet also of furthering the cause of truth. He suffered several breakdowns, but always yearned to get back to his bees as quickly as possible.

With Adam in charge of the bees, the abbey became famous for its thick heather honey. Perhaps strangely for a celibate monk, Brother Adam spent almost all his time engaged in breeding, refining the genes of his bees, mating queens in a search for the perfect bee. 'Nature never breeds an ideal or perfect bee,' he wrote. 'The realization of this ideal has been left to the progressive, purposeful bee breeder of today' – in other words, to himself.[59] The Buckfast bee that he produced is said to be unusually clean and tidy and rather gentle, combining the hardiness of the British black bee with the disease-resistance of the Italian bee. Brother Adam had travelled all over the world – as far as the Sahara – searching for the purest strains of queen, which he brought home to cross-breed with drones from different strains. It is not known whether Adam saw any contradiction in encouraging all this insect copulation, while remaining chaste himself. This is not the kind of question he ever touched upon in his highly technical writings. He was so busy beavering away, absorbed in his beekeeping and mead-making, that he barely noticed the twentieth century unfolding, except in so far as it affected his hives. During the Second World War he suffered xenophobic abuse from anti-German locals, who accused him of arranging hives on the moor in patterns to send messages to attacking Luftwaffe aircraft.[60] He lost both his brothers in the war, and his mother died soon after. But Adam and his bees lived on, apparently impervious.

It is this apparent imperviousness that makes non-beekeepers feel that apiarists are either more or less than human. This is the theme of a wonderful children's story called *The Bee-Man of Orn*. It was written by Frank Stockton, and first published in 1887, though the version I grew up with came out much later and was illustrated by Maurice Sendak, author of *Where the Wild Things Are*. Here is how *The Bee-Man of Orn* begins:

In the ancient country of Orn, there lived an old man who was called the Bee-man, because his whole time was spent in the company of bees. He lived in a small hut, which was nothing more than an immense bee-hive, for these little creatures had built their honey-combs in every corner of the one room it contained, on the shelves, under the little table, all about the rough bench on which the old man sat, and even about the head-board, and along the sides of his low bed. All day the air of the room was thick with buzzing insects, but this did not interfere in any way with the old Bee-man, who walked in among them, ate his meals and went to sleep, without the slightest fear of being stung. He had lived with the bees so long, they had become so accustomed to him, and his skin was so tough and hard, that the bees no more thought of stinging him than they would of stinging a tree or a stone. A swarm of bees had made their hive in a pocket of his old leathern doublet; and when he put on this coat to take one of his long walks in the forest in search of wild bee's nests, he was very glad to have this hive with him, for if he did not find any wild honey, he would put his hand in his pocket and take out a piece of comb for his luncheon. The bees in his pocket worked very industriously, and he was always certain of having something to eat with him wherever he went. He lived principally upon honey; and when he needed bread or meat, he carried some fine combs to a village not far away and bartered them for other food. He was ugly, untidy, shrivelled, and brown. He was poor, and the bees seemed to be his only friends. But for all that, he was happy and contented; he had all the honey he wanted, and his bees, whom he considered the best company in the world, were as friendly and sociable as they could be, and seemed to increase in number every day.[61]

The rest of the story concerns the bee-man's encounter with a jargon-ridden 'Junior Sorceror', a student of necromancy, who becomes convinced that the bee-man cannot have been destined for such a rough, dirty life: he must have been transformed from something else. The bee-man sets out in search of his 'original form'. Will he turn out to be 'a giant or a powerful prince', or else 'a fiery dragon or a horrid snake'? After a series of odd encounters, he finally meet a baby, and becomes convinced that this was his original form. The Junior Sorceror turns him back into a baby and feels glad that the bee-man will have a 'fresh start in life and a chance to become something better than a miserable old man living in a wretched hut with no friends or companions but buzzing bees'. But many years later the Junior Sorceror, now an old man, passes by the same spot again. What should he see, but 'an old man in a leathern doublet, sitting at a table, eating honey'. "'Upon my word!" exclaimed the Sorceror, "He has grown into the same thing again!"'[62] The moral of *The Bee-Man of Orn* is that meddling will never alter anything about man's destiny. The only thing to do, therefore, is submit to the laws of nature.

Something about their slow, apparently unchanging buzzing seems to have made bees inspire this thought in men more often than other animals. As Tickner Edwardes's bee-master of Warrilow gnomically says, 'The bees have their definite plan of life, perfected through countless ages, and nothing you can do will ever turn them from it . . . You can delay their work or you can even thwart it altogether, but no one has ever succeeded in changing a single principle in bee-life. And so the best bee-master is always the one who most exactly obeys the orders from the hive . . .'[63]

This was something that the great Russian novelist Leo Tolstoy could have concurred with. In his view it was futile of men to struggle against nature, even though this struggle is precisely what makes us human. Tolstoy himself was perhaps the ultimate beekeeper-sage, communing with his hives on his estate at Yasnaya Polyana after he had become a long-bearded spiritual thinker.

Tolstoy in his peasant smock at Yasnaya Polyana, the estate where he kept bees

Yasnaya Polyana – which means 'Clear Glade' in Russian – belonged to Tolstoy's mother's family. (His mother was a princess, a title which was commoner in Russia than elsewhere, but still undeniably grand.) The estate was situated among silver birch trees about 200 km from Moscow. It was there that Tolstoy was born, in 1828, and it was there that he felt most at home throughout his life, eventually inheriting it – and its 233 serfs – in 1847. Like most estates of the Russian nobility, it was virtually self-sufficient, providing everything the owner's family needed in the way of hogs, chickens, game, sweet cream, butter and breads, with boletus mushrooms to gather and pickle in the autumn and strawberries and honey in the summer.[64] The honey would be harvested by tough old bee-men working from upright log hives,[65] like the swollen-eyed bee-man in *Anna Karenina* (1875–7). The Russians were always great honey-lovers and mead-drinkers. The summers that Tolstoy and his large family spent at Yasnaya Polyana were sweet with the sensations of buzzing bees, sticky jam and honey.[66]

During Tolstoy's youth, beekeeping was just one estate activity among many, and he himself was wedded more to the manly pursuit of hunting than to the slow ways of the bee-men. But, as time went on and he became more and more attached to the peasant ways, his hives came to have a special place in his life. The character of Levin in *Anna Karenina*, who is a rather idealized portrait of Tolstoy himself, spends much time among his bees. Visiting his apiaries is a chance for Levin to 'recover from the influence of ordinary, actual life'. On one occasion, when he is feeling particularly emotional, he settles his guests near the apiary in the cool shade of some aspen trees, before going to the peasant's hut near the hives to get them some bread, cucumbers and fresh honey.

> Trying to make his movements as deliberate as possible, and listening to the bees that buzzed more and more frequently past him, he walked along the little path to the hut. In the very entry one bee hummed angrily, caught in his beard, but he carefully extricated it. Going into the shady outer room, he took down from the wall his veil, that hung on a peg, and putting it on, and thrusting his

hands into his pockets, he went into the fenced-in bee garden, where there stood in the midst of a closely mown space in regular rows, fastened with bast [a kind of bark] on posts, all the hives he knew so well, the old stocks, each with its own history, and along the fences the younger swarms hived that year. In front of the openings of the hives, it made his eyes giddy to watch the bees and drones whirling round and round about the same spot, while among them the worker bees flew in and out with spoils, or in search of them, always in the same direction, into the wood, to the flowering linden trees, and back to the hives.[67]

The life of the bees distracts him from his spiritual worries, and consoles him about them. It is a relief for Levin/Tolstoy to see that man's life is not the only one in God's creation – to see that his concerns are petty in the great scheme of things. He takes from this the message that all life is trivial compared to the life of the spirit.

As time went on, Tolstoy became increasingly ascetic, abandoning tea, coffee, meat, private property, the Orthodox Church, smoking and the government, and, to his poor wife's horror, even treating the marital bed as a kind of sin.[68] He rejected urban society as hypocritical and immoral, and rejected capitalism too, famously remarking that socialism was nothing more than a kind of 'unconscious Christianity'.[69] At this time the bees gave him a model of wisdom that he couldn't find elsewhere. In a little-known short story, 'Two Different Versions of the History of a Hive with a Bast Roof' (1889), Tolstoy used the hive to show the evils of being parasitical like the drones – like the ruling aristocracy.[70] At the end of the summer, the workers attack and overcome the drones. Tolstoy, who was now dressing in a peasant's smock and ignoring his own aristocratic birth, hoped that 'the people' would do the same in Russia.

He accumulated followers – the Tolstoyans – many of whom kept bees.[71] Tolstoy also turned to the bees of Yasnaya Polyana, both for honey and for wisdom. Hunting was now out of the question for him – it was too violent – whereas beekeeping seemed more natural. In his main religious work, *The Kingdom of God is Within You* (1893), Tolstoy used the bees to attempt to bring men to God. Men in their current state, he claimed, were 'like a swarm of bees hanging in a cluster to a branch'. But this was only a temporary state: men, like the bees, must find a new place to live – the place of God. The bees are able to escape their position on the branch because each of them is 'a living, separate creature, endowed with wings of its own'. Similarly, men should be able to escape their current toils because each is 'a living being endowed with the faculty of entering into the Christian conception of life'. Bees can show men the way:

> Only let one bee spread her wings, start off, and fly away, and after her another, and another, and the clinging, inert cluster would become a freely flying swarm of bees. Just in the same way, only let one man look at life as Christianity teaches him to look at it, and after him let another and another do the same, and the enchanted circle of existence in the state conception of life, from which there seemed no escape, will be broken through.[72]

In other words, Tolstoy, like countless others before him, believed that the bees have a message for us, if only we can grasp it – the message of Christianity. To which we might reply, But what about all the other messages of the hive? The message to work? To love? To live? To die? To govern? To eat? To dance?

While Tolstoy as religious thinker imposed his rather crude spiritual metaphors on the beehive, Tolstoy as novelist knew that bee colonies were infinitely too intricate and subtle to be pinned down to a single human idea. In the epilogue of *War and Peace* he used the beehive to illustrate the limits of human knowledge before nature:

> Just as the sun and each atom of ether is a sphere complete in itself, and at the same time is only a part of a whole inconceivable to man through its vastness, so every individuality bears within it its own ends, and yet bears them so as to serve general ends unfathomable by man.

A bee settling on a flower has stung a child. And the child dreads bees, and says the object of the bee is to sting people. A poet admires the bee, sipping honey from the cup of the flower, and says the object of the bee is to sip the nectar of the flower. A beekeeper, noticing that the bee gathers pollen and brings it to the hive, says that the object of the bee is to gather honey. Another beekeeper, who has studied the life of the swarm more closely, says the bee gathers honey to feed the young ones, and to rear a queen, that the object of the bee is the perpetuation of its race. The botanist observes that the bee flying with the pollen fertilises the pistil, and in this he sees the object of the bee. Another, watching the hybrid-isation of plants, sees that the bee contributes to that end also, and he may say that the bee's object is that. But the final aim of the bee is not exhausted by one or another, or a third aim, which the human intellect is capable of discovering. The higher the human intellect rises in the discovery of such aims, the more obvious it becomes that the final aim is beyond its reach.

All that is within the reach of man is the observation of the analogy of the life of the bee with other manifestations of life.[73]

However much human beings have projected themselves on to the hive, identifying themselves with drones, workers and the queen, and idealizing the morals of the waxen community, there will always remain mysteries about the life of the bees which men can never discover. And it is for this very reason that humans will continue to search for truths about themselves in the gold of the honeycomb.

Notes

Full details of the works cited in short-title form can be found in the bibliography.

Introduction

1. Crane, *A Book of Honey*, p. 133.
2. Fife, 'The sacredness of bees, honey and wax', p. 121.
3. Pliny, trans. Healy, *Natural History*, p. 141.
4. Ransome, *The Sacred Bee*, p. 22.

Who's Who in the Beehive

1. An exception: about 1 per cent of worker bees also have ovaries sufficiently developed to lay drone eggs parthenogenetically. But when they do so, as Professor Francis Ratnieks has shown, the other workers usually destroy the eggs, to maintain the social unity of life under a single mother.
2. Root, *The ABC and XYZ of Bee Culture*, p. 430.

Chapter 1: Work

1. *Daily Telegraph*, 3 July 2003, p. 5.
2. For more on the waggle dance, see Chapter 6, 'The Beekeeper'. For a counterview, the suggestion that Aristotle might have identified the waggle dance, see Davies & Kathirithamby, *Greek Insects*, p. 55.
3. Proverbs 6:6–9.
4. Purchas, *A Theatre of Politicall Flying-Insects*, p. 13.
5. Crane, *A Book of Honey*, p. 14.
6. Levett, *The Ordering of Bees*, p. 60.
7. Xenophon, *Oeconomicus*, VII.17–38, quoted in Fife, 'The sacredness of bees, honey and wax', p. 126.

8. Cowper, 'The Bee and the Pineapple', ll. 13–24, *Complete Poetical Works*, p. 296.

9. Crane, *A Book of Honey*, p. 149.

10. Ibid., p. 141.

11. T. H. White, *The Book of Beasts*, p. 245.

12. Ratnieks, 'Are you being served?', pp. 26–7.

13. T. H. White, *The Book of Beasts*, p. 156.

14. Klingender, *Animals in Art and Thought*, p. 256.

15. Shakespeare, *Henry V*, I.ii.187–204.

16. Fife, 'The sacredness of bees, honey and wax', p. 127.

17. Tarrant, 'Bees in Plato's Republic', p. 33.

18. Taillardat, *Les Images d'Aristophane*.

19. Fife, 'The sacredness of bees, honey and wax', p. 127.

20. Crane, *The World History of Beekeeping*, pp. 565, 587.

21. Fife, 'The sacredness of bees, honey and wax', p. 402; a variant has the devil creating wasps.

22. Frisch, *Bees*, p. 15.

23. Burton, *The Anatomy of Melancholy*, vol. 2, p. 70.

24. Shelley, *Complete Poetical Works*, p. 572 ('Song to the Men of England').

25. Dickens, *Bleak House*, p. 93 (ch. VIII).

26. On the history of beekeeping in the United States, see Beck, *Honey and Health*, and Crane, *The World History of Beekeeping*.

27. Tocqueville, *Democracy in America*, vol. 2, p. 152.

28. Withington, 'Republican bees', p. 57.

29. Baker, *The Revolt of the Bees*, p. 83.

30. Rodda, *'Go Ye and Study the Beehive'*, epigraph.

31. Knoop, *The Early Masonic Catechisms*.

32. Worrel, 'The symbolism of the beehive and the bee'.

33. T. H. White, *The Book of Beasts*, p. 156.

34. *Geoponica*, XV.3, 10.

35. Maeterlinck, *The Life of the Bee*, p. 160.

36. Fife, 'The sacredness of bees, honey and wax', p. 128.

37. Purchas, *A Theatre of Politicall Flying-Insects*, p. 2.

38. Marx, *Capital*, vol. 1, III, ch. 7.

39. Mills, *An Essay on the Management of Bees*, p. 13.

40. Crane, *The World History of Beekeeping*, ch. 49.

41. Hillier, *A History of Wax Dolls*, p. 19.

42. More, *The Bee Book*, p. 126.

43. Ibid., p. 131.

44. Fife, 'The sacredness of bees, honey and wax', p. 244.

45. Luke 2:32.

46. More, *The Bee Book*, p. 132.
47. Fife, 'The sacredness of bees, honey and wax', p. 220.
48. Crane, *The World History of Beekeeping*, p. 408.
49. My discussion here owes a very heavy debt to *The Beehive Metaphor* by Juan Antonio Ramírez, the only person to my knowledge to have written a book on the beehive metaphor in architecture.
50. Le Corbusier, *Towards a New Architecture*, p. 10.
51. Ramírez, *The Beehive Metaphor*, p. 154.
52. This point is made in Ramírez, *The Beehive Metaphor*.
53. Morse, 'The beekeeping industry'.
54. Crane, *The World History of Beekeeping*, p. 490.
55. Cohn, 'Bees and the law', p. 289.
56. Frier, 'Bees and lawyers', p. 106.
57. Ibid., p. 109.

Chapter 2: Sex

1. Barnfield, 'The Affectionate Shepherd', l. 96, in *Complete Poems*, p. 82.
2. Maeterlinck, *The Life of the Bee*, p. 42.
3. Beck, *Honey and Health*, p. 213.
4. Ransome, *The Sacred Bee*, p. 45.
5. Anacreon, *The Odes*, Ode 70.
6. Ibid., Ode 35.
7. Newbolt, *The Book of Cupid*, pp. 52, 50.
8. Barnfield, 'The Affectionate Shepherd', II. 97–8, 99–102, in *Complete Poems*, p. 82.
9. Proverbs 3:4.
10. Shakespeare, *Hamlet*, III.iv.82–3.
11. Beck, *Honey and Health*, p. 212 (Idyll of Moschus).
12. Ballad 'Rob Roy', at http://www.worldwideschool.org/library/books/lit/poetry/ACollectionofBallads/chap22.html, accessed 7 March 2004.
13. Beck, *Honey and Health*, p. 224.
14. Ibid., pp. 220–35
15. Aristotle, *De Generatione Animalium*, III.10, pp. 758–60.
16. Aristotle, *Historia Animalium*, V.21, p. 553.
17. Aristotle, *De Generatione Animalium*, III.10, pp. 758–60.
18. Ibid.
19. Crane, *The World History of Beekeeping*, p. 571.
20. Merrick, 'Royal bees', p. 23.
21. Debraw, 'Discoveries on the sex of bees'.
22. Fife, 'The sacredness of bees, honey and wax', p. 396.

23. Ransome, *The Sacred Bee*, p. 33.
24. Ovid, *Fasti*, I.376–80, p. 14 (I have adapted the translation).
25. Ransome, *The Sacred Bee*, p. 114.
26. Osten-Sacken, *On the Oxen-born Bees of the Ancients*, p. 23.
27. Ransome, *The Sacred Bee*, pp. 112–18.
28. Ibid., p. 117.
29. See Cook, 'The bee in Greek mythology', pp. 9–10.
30. Virgil, *Georgics*, IV.302, 312.
31. Ransome, *The Sacred Bee*, p. 114.
32. Hartlib, *The Reformed Common-Wealth of Bees*, pp. 2–3.
33. Dr Arnold Boate in Hartlib, *The Reformed Common-Wealth of Bees*, p. 2.
34. Shakespeare, *2 Henry IV*, IV.iii.79.
35. Jonson, *The Alchemist*, II.iii.
36. Osten-Sacken, *On the Oxen-born Bees of the Ancients*, p. 25.
37. Redi, *Experiments on the Generation of Insects*, p. 38
38. Osten-Sacken, *On the Oxen-born Bees of the Ancients*, p. 4.
39. B. G. Whitfield, 'Virgil and the bees'; Fraser, *History of Beekeeping in Britain*.
40. Osten-Sacken, *Additional Notes*, p. 40.
41. Virgil, *Georgics*, IV.453, 556, 553.
42. Michelet, *L'Insecte*, pp. 305–11.
43. Porter, 'Let's Do It', from *Paris 1928*.
44. Virgil, *Georgics*, IV.197–202.
45. Fife, 'The sacredness of bees, honey and wax', p. 276.
46. Crane, *A Book of Honey*, p. 139.
47. Ibid., p. 138.
48. Ibid.
49. Fife, 'The sacredness of bees, honey and wax', pp. 125, 281, 125.
50. Butler, *The Feminine Monarchy*, sect. 1.35.
51. Steiner, *Bees*, p. 3.
52. Ibid., pp. 3–5.
53. Ingrams, *Arabia and the Isles*, p. 165.
54. Ibid., pp. 163–4, 165.
55. Shakespeare, *Henry V*, I.ii.190.
56. See Davies & Kathirithamby, *Greek Insects*, p. 62; Hudson-Williams, 'King bees and queen bees'.
57. Davies & Kathirithamby, *Greek Insects*, p. 62.
58. Galton, *Survey of Beekeeping in Russia*, pp. 10ff.
59. Crane, *The World History of Beekeeping*, p. 591.
60. Thomas, *Man and the Natural World*, p. 62.
61. Merrick, 'Royal bees', p. 15.
62. Lawson, *A New Orchard and Garden*, *passim*; Levett, *The Ordering of Bees*, pp. 68ff.

63. Crane, *The World History of Beekeeping*, p. 591.
64. Ibid., p. 569.
65. Butler, *The Feminine Monarchy*; see also Fraser, *History of Beekeeping in Britain*, ch. 4.
66. Butler, *The Feminine Monarchy*, sects. 4.6, 4.5, 4.11.
67. Ibid., sects. 4.6–4.23.
68. Edwardes, *The Lore of the Honey-Bee*, p. 165.
69. Remnant, *A Discourse or Historie of Bees*, pp. 9, 31–3.
70. Merrick, 'Royal bees', p. 22.
71. Simon, *Le Gouvernement admirable*, pp. xix, 4–14.
72. Merrick, 'Royal bees', p. 24.
73. Vanière, *The Bees*, pp. 19, 22, 12, 20.
74. Boerhaave, 'The life of John Swammerdam', pp. viii–ix.
75. Ibid., pp. xiv, ii.
76. Ibid., pp. 14, ix.
77. Swammerdam, *The Book of Nature*, pp. 169, 197, 222.
78. Ibid., p. 221.
79. Mace, *Bee Matters and Bee Masters*, p. 13.
80. Dodd, *Beemasters of the Past*, p. 43.
81. Huber, *Nouvelles observations sur les abeilles*, vol. 1, pp. 6ff.
82. Mace, *Bee Matters and Bee Masters*, pp. 11–18.
83. Huber, *Nouvelles observations sur les abeilles*, vol. 1, pp. 58–94.
84. Ibid., p. 63.
85. Maeterlinck, *The Life of the Bee*, p. 137.
86. Crane, *The World History of Beekeeping*, p. 572.

Chapter 3: Politics

1. Virgil, *Georgics*, IV.2–5.
2. Fourier, *Le Nouveau Monde industriel et sociétaire*, pp. 528, 288.
3. Frisch, *The Dancing Bees*, p. 1.
4. Hobbes, *Leviathan*, p. 119.
5. Rousseau, *Political Writings*, 'Part I of the Constitutional Project for Corsica'.
6. Darby, Ghalioungui & Grivetti, *Food*, vol. 1, p. 430.
7. Ransome, *The Sacred Bee*, p. 24.
8. Ibid., p. 24.
9. Crane, *The World History of Beekeeping*, p. 604.
10. Varro, *On Farming*, p. 325.
11. Plato, *Republic*, 520b.
12. T. H. White, *The Book of Beasts*, p. 154.
13. Fife, 'The sacredness of bees, honey and wax', p. 271.
14. Butler, *The Feminine Monarchy*, sect. 1.2.
15. T. H. White, *The Book of Beasts*, p. 154.
16. Klingender, *Animals in Art and Thought*, p. 356.
17. Purchas, *A Theatre of Politicall Flying-Insects*, p. 18.

18. Seneca, *Moral and Political Essays*, p. 150.
19. Erasmus, *The Education of a Christian Prince*, p. 29.
20. Rusden, *A Further Discovery of Bees*, pp. 16–17.
21. Butler, *The Feminine Monarchy*, sect. 1.6.
22. Merriman, *A History of Modern Europe*, p. 234.
23. Crane, *The World History of Beekeeping*, p. 592.
24. Butler, *The Feminine Monarchy*, sect. 1.6.
25. Ibid., sect. 1.10.
26. Levett, *The Ordering of Bees*, p. 68.
27. Fraser, *History of Beekeeping in Britain*, p. 36.
28. Purchas, *A Theatre of Politicall Flying-Insects*, pp. 16–20.
29. Rusden, *A Further Discovery of Bees*, Epistle Dedicatory and pp. 2, 16–21.
30. Warder, *The True Amazons*, preface.
31. Ibid., pp. 116, vi, 42, viii, xii.
32. Ibid., p. 7.
33. Simon, *Le Gouvernement admirable*.
34. Bazin, *The Natural History of Bees*, p. 21.
35. Ramírez, *The Beehive Metaphor*, ch. 1.
36. Ibid.
37. By Crabb Robinson in his diary. See Mandeville, *The Fable of the Bees*, vol. 1, p. vi.
38. Mandeville, *The Fable of the Bees*, vol. 1, p. 17.
39. Ibid., pp. 17–37.
40. Ibid., p. 18.
41. Withington, 'Republican bees', pp. 45, 69.
42. Crane, *A Book of Honey*, p. 140.
43. Kelly, *The Oxford Dictionary of Popes*, p. 280.
44. Merrick, 'Royal bees', p. 9.
45. Connolly, 'The star and bee as Napoleonic emblems', p. 140.
46. Edwardes, *The Lore of the Honey-Bee*, pp. 74–5.
47. Maeterlinck, *The Life of the Bee*, p. 27.
48. Edwardes, *The Lore of the Honey-Bee*, pp. 98, 118.
49. Ratnieks, 'Conflict in the bee hive'.
50. J. Whitfield, 'The police state', p. 782.
51. Ratnieks, 'Prisons in the bee hive'.
52. J. Whitfield, 'The police state'.
53. Ibid.

Chapter 4: Food and Drink

1. *Petits propos culinaires*, 6 (1980), p. 58.
2. Ransome, *The Sacred Bee*, p. 136.
3. Crane, *A Book of Honey*, p. 18.

4. Fife, 'The sacredness of bees, honey and wax', p. 35; see also Pliny, trans. Healy, *Natural History*, p. 153.

5. Butler, *The Feminine Monarchy*, sects. 6.40, 6.41.

6. Galen, *Galen on Food and Diet*, p. 186.

7. Toussaint-Samat, *History of Food*, p. 25.

8. Crane, *The World History of Beekeeping*, p. 598.

9. Ibid., p. 576.

10. The Honey Regulations 2003, D4, April 2003.

11. On sweeteners before sugar, see Galloway, *The Sugarcane Industry*, pp. 1–2; Davidson, *The Oxford Companion to Food*, entry on 'Honey'; Mintz, *Sweetness and Power*, ch. 3.

12. Darby, Ghalioungui & Grivetti, *Food*, vol. 1, p. 440.

13. Ransome, *The Sacred Bee*, p. 82.

14. Grainger, 'Cato's Roman cheesecakes', p. 171.

15. Exodus 3:8; Job 20:17; 2 Samuel 17:29.

16. Dalby, *Empire of Pleasures*, pp. 66, 141.

17. Apicius, *Cookery and Dining in Imperial Rome*, pp. 224, 169, 48.

18. Alcock, *Food in Roman Britain*, p. 76.

19. On tempering, see Scully in Adamson, *Food in the Middle Ages*, pp. 4ff.

20. Toussaint-Samat, *History of Food*, p. 32.

21. Exodus 16:31.

22. Toussaint-Samat, *History of Food*, p. 33.

23. Ibid.

24. Austin, *Two Fifteenth-Century Cookery Books*, p. 35. I have modernized the English of the recipe somewhat.

25. http://www.godecookery. com, accessed October 2003.

26. Riley, 'Learning by mouth', p. 194.

27. Chaucer, *The Prioresses Tale . . .*, p. 24 (my own rendering).

28. Lévi-Strauss, *From Honey to Ashes*.

29. Pliny, trans. Rackham, *Natural History*, vol. 4, bk 14, p. 261.

30. Digby, *The Closet of Sir Kenelm Digby Opened*, p. xxx (introduction by Stevenson & Davidson, who point out that this description of Digby is actually unfair, since he probably did not poison his wife deliberately).

31. Ibid., p. 26.

32. Ibid., pp. 59, 18, 7.

33. Toussaint-Samat, *History of Food*, p. 19.

34. Crane, *The World History of Beekeeping*, p. 494.

35. Galloway, *The Sugarcane Industry*, ch. 3.

36. Henisch, *Fast and Feast*, p. 124.
37. Mintz, *Sweetness and Power*, p. 83.
38. Mason, *Sugar-Plums and Sherbert*, pp. 42–3. I must also thank Laura Mason for expanding this point in conversation.
39. Crane, *A Book of Honey*, p. 144.
40. Cf. Richardson, *Sweets*: 'A sweet has to be made by a human hand' (p. 67).
41. Galloway, *The Sugarcane Industry*, p. 10.
42. Cobbett, *Rural Rides*, p. 283.
43. Sociologists have a technical way of putting this: liking sucrose is 'sweet-general'. See Mintz, *Sweetness and Power*, ch. 3.
44. Southerne, *The Right Use and Ordering of Bees*. Cf. Worlidge, *Apiarium*, ch. 1.
45. Southerne, *The Right Use and Ordering of Bees*.
46. Crane, *The World History of Beekeeping*, p. 493.
47. Mintz, *Sweetness and Power*, p. 101.
48. Ibid., *passim*.
49. http://www1.agric.gov.ab.ca, accessed November 2003.
50. Crane, *The World History of Beekeeping*, p. 494.
51. Gonnet & Vache, *The Taste of Honey*.
52. Butler, *The Feminine Monarchy*, sect. 10.13.
53. Hill, *The Virtues of Honey*, p. 40.
54. Crane, *The World History of Beekeeping*, p. 503
55. Garnsey, *Food and Society in Classical Antiquity*.
56. Crane, *The World History of Beekeeping*, p. 503.
57. Hill, *The Virtues of Honey*, pp. 12–16, 40.
58. Calder, *Oilseed Rape and Bees*.

Chapter 5: Life and Death

1. Homer, *Odyssey*, XXIV.68; Crane, *A Book of Honey*, p. 133.
2. Akrigg, *Shakespeare and the Earl of Southampton*, pp. 16–17.
3. Xenophon, *Hellenica*, V.3.
4. More, *The Bee Book*, p. 77; Crane, *The World History of Beekeeping*, p. 510.
5. Beck, *Honey and Health*, p. 232.
6. Crane, *The World History of Beekeeping*, p. 510.
7. Ransome, *The Sacred Bee*, p. 51.
8. Fife, 'The sacredness of bees, honey and wax', p. 42.
9. Darby, Ghalioungui & Grivetti, *Food*, vol. 1, p. 431.
10. Homer, *Iliad*, XXIII.170.

11. Ransome, *The Sacred Bee*, p. 121.
12. Fife, 'The sacredness of bees, honey and wax', pp. 430–53.
13. Davies & Kathirithamby, *Greek Insects*, pp. 64–5; Fife, 'The sacredness of bees, honey and wax', p. 61.
14. Cook, 'The bee in Greek mythology', p. 21.
15. Fife, 'The sacredness of bees, honey and wax', p. 98.
16. Ransome, *The Sacred Bee*, pp. 106–7.
17. Beck, *Honey and Health*, pp. 234–5.
18. Riches, *Medical Aspects of Beekeeping*, pp. 61ff.
19. Isaiah 7:14–15.
20. Fife, 'The sacredness of bees, honey and wax', p. 48.
21. Richardson, *Sweets*, p. 50.
22. Beck, *Honey and Health*, pp. 49, 136.
23. This statistic comes from http://www.ohsu.edu, accessed October 2003. In 1995 US per-capita annual sugar consumption was 170 lb (77 kg), compared with 108 lb (49 kg) in 1938 and just 7.5 lb (3.4 kg) in 1830.
24. Beck, *Honey and Health*, pp. 136, 135, 43.
25. Crane, *A Book of Honey*, p. 95.
26. Beck, *Honey and Health*, p. 213.
27. Ibid., pp. 134, 99.
28. Proverbs 24:13.
29. Hanssen, *The Healing Power of Pollen*, pp. 59–60.
30. *Sunday Mirror*, 24 September 1978, p. 1.
31. Koran XVI.77, p. 229.
32. Crane, *A Book of Honey*, p. 96.
33. Beck, *Honey and Health*, pp. 83, 89.
34. See Precope, *Hippocrates on Diet and Hygiene*, p. 62.
35. Hippocrates, *The Medical Works*, p. 143.
36. Beck, *Honey and Health*, p. 88.
37. Ibid., pp. 90, 97.
38. Hill, *The Virtues of Honey*, ch. 4.
39. Crane, *A Book of Honey*, p. 98.
40. Riches, *Medical Aspects of Beekeeping*, p. 70.
41. Edwardes, *The Lore of the Honey-Bee*, p. 444.
42. Beck, *Honey and Health*, p. 88.
43. Crane, *The World History of Beekeeping*, sect. 51.3.
44. Riches, *Medical Aspects of Beekeeping*, pp. 74–5.
45. Crane, *The World History of Beekeeping*, sect. 51.3.
46. Crane, *A Book of Honey*, p. 99.
47. http://www.manukahoney.co.uk, accessed 2003.
48. Hanssen, *The Healing Power of Pollen*, pp. 7–9.

49. Ibid., pp. 34, 87.
50. Butler, *The Feminine Monarchy*.
51. Bishop, *An Early History of Surgery*, p. 32.
52. Riches, *Medical Aspects of Beekeeping*, p. 67.
53. Beck, *Honey and Health*, p. 120.
54. Briffa, 'Tell 'em about the honey'.
55. Beck, *Honey and Health*, pp. 139–40.
56. http://www.manukahoney.co.uk, accessed 2003.
57. Beck, *Honey and Health*, p. 144.
58. Ibid., p. 143.
59. Xenophon, *The Persian Expedition*, p. 169. This passage was cited by T. Wildman, *The Management of Bees*, p. 52, among others.
60. Croft, *Curiosities of Beekeeping*, p. 62.
61. Morse & Hooper, *The Illustrated Encyclopedia of Beekeeping*, p. 362.
62. Riches, *Medical Aspects of Beekeeping*, p. 7.
63. Butler, *The Feminine Monarchy*, sect. 1.3.
64. Beck, *Bee Venom*, p. 82.
65. Riches, *Medical Aspects of Beekeeping*, p. 33.
66. Beck, *Bee Venom*, p. 65.
67. Riches, *Medical Aspects of Beekeeping*, p. 37.
68. Morse & Hooper, *The Illustrated Encyclopedia of Beekeeping*, p. 362.
69. Riches, *Medical Aspects of Beekeeping*, p. 75.
70. Beck, *Bee Venom*, p. 9.
71. Croft, *Honey and Health*, p. 45.
72. Riches, *Medical Aspects of Beekeeping*, p. 77.
73. Mills, *An Essay on the Management of Bees*, pp. 8–9.
74. Warder, *The True Amazons*, p. 3.
75. Miller, 'Historical natural history'.
76. Deuteronomy 1:44. See Fife, 'The sacredness of bees, honey and wax', p. 161.
77. Croft, *Curiosities of Beekeeping*, pp. 24, 25.
78. Ransome, *The Sacred Bee*, p. 213; Fife, 'The sacredness of bees, honey and wax', pp. 382ff.
79. Boyd, *An Ice Cream War*, p. 173.
80. http://www.desertusa.com, accessed 2003.
81. Croft, *Curiosities of Beekeeping*, p. 10.
82. Levett, *The Ordering of Bees*, pp. 40–41.
83. Hartlib, *The Reformed Common-Wealth of Bees*, p. 3.
84. Columella, *On Agriculture*, vol. 2, p. 497.
85. Pliny, trans. Healy, *Natural History*, p. 153.

86. Keys, *The Practical Bee-Master*, p. 269.
87. T. Wildman, *The Management of Bees*, pp. 93ff.
88. Thomson, *The Seasons*: 'Autumn', ll. 1083–1105, in *Poetical Works*, pp. 129–30.
89. Croft, *Curiosities of Beekeeping*, p. 18.
90. Crane, *A Book of Honey*, p. 121.
91. R. Brown, *Great Masters of Beekeeping*, p. 43.
92. T. W. Cowan, 1895, quoted in Crane, *A Book of Honey*, p. 122.
93. Plath, 'The Arrival of the Bee Box', in *Ariel*, p. 63.
94. Gustaffson, *The Death of a Beekeeper*, pp. 50–51.
95. Hill, *The Virtues of Honey*, ch. 13.
96. Ibid., ch. 14.
97. Crane, *A Book of Honey*, pp. 101–2.

Chapter 6: The Beekeeper

1. Plath, 'The Bee Meeting', in *Ariel*, p. 60.
2. Ibid., p. 61.
3. Shakespeare, *Henry V*, IV.i.11.
4. Ransome, *The Sacred Bee*, p. 81.
5. Fraser, *Beekeeping in Antiquity*, p. 43.
6. Galton, *Survey of Beekeeping in Russia*, p. 20.
7. Fraser, *History of Beekeeping in Britain*, p. 23.
8. Levett, *The Ordering of Bees*, p. 41.
9. Thomas, *Man and the Natural World*, pp. 122–3, 126.
10. Galton, *Survey of Beekeeping in Russia*, p. 37.
11. Lawes, *The Bee-Book Book*, p. 80.
12. Edwardes, *The Bee-Master of Warrilow*, pp. 17, 47, 194.
13. Frisch, *A Biologist Remembers*, pp. 21, 18–19, 22, 71.
14. Ibid., p. 55.
15. See Frisch, *Bees*, pp. 1–25.
16. Frisch, *A Biologist Remembers*, pp. 48, 49, 57, 84.
17. Frisch, *You and Life*, p. 57.
18. Frisch, *Bees*, p. 10.
19. Ibid., pp. 25–53.
20. Frisch, *You and Life*, pp. 157, 161.
21. Crane, *The World History of Beekeeping*, p. 380.
22. Frisch, *Bees*, pp. 55–6.
23. Frisch, *The Dancing Bees*, pp. 101, 103.
24. Ibid., p. 117.
25. Ibid., p. 119.
26. Ibid., p. 151.
27. Ibid., p. 149.
28. Frisch, *Bees*, pp. 53–97.
29. Frisch, *The Dancing Bees*, p. v.
30. Frisch, *A Biologist Remembers*, p. 128.
31. Frisch, *You and Life*, p. 264.

32. Frisch, *The Dancing Bees*, p. 179.

33. Dodd, *Beemasters of the Past*, p. 36.

34. Mills, *An Essay on the Management of Bees*, p. 5

35. T. Wildman, *The Management of Bees*, p. 108.

36. Maeterlinck, *The Life of the Bee*, ch. 2.

37. Edwardes, *The Lore of the Honey-Bee*, p. 123.

38. Crane, *The World History of Beekeeping*, p. 239.

39. Galton, *Survey of Beekeeping in Russia*, p. 24.

40. Mills, *An Essay on the Management of Bees*, p. 4.

41. R. J. White, *The Age of George III*, pp. 283–7.

42. Hone, *The Every-Day Book*, vol. 2, p. 662.

43. T. Wildman, *The Management of Bees*, preface.

44. Fraser, *History of Beekeeping in Britain*, ch. 5.

45. *Mirror*, vol. 34, 1772.

46. Keys, *The Practical Bee-Master*, pp. 146ff.

47. Ibid., p. 154.

48. D. Wildman, *A Complete Guide for the Management of Bees*, frontispiece.

49. T. Wildman, *The Management of Bees*, p. 1.

50. Croft, *Curiosities of Beekeeping*, pp. 26–7.

51. Morse & Hooper, *The Illustrated Encyclopedia of Beekeeping*, p. 38.

52. Bonnie Pierson, email to author, 2002.

53. Riches, *Medical Aspects of Beekeeping*, p. 83.

54. Maeterlinck, *The Life of the Bee*, p. 20.

55. Doyle, *The Complete Sherlock Holmes*, p. 650.

56. Ibid., p. 978.

57. Naile, *Life of Langstroth*.

58. On Brother Adam, see Bill, *For the Love of Bees*.

59. Adam, *Breeding the Honeybee*, Introduction, 'Nature as a Breeder'.

60. Bill, *For the Love of Bees*, p. 61.

61. Stockton, *The Bee-man of Orn*, pp. 1–2.

62. Ibid., p. 16.

63. Edwardes, *The Bee-Master of Warrilow*, p. 35.

64. A. Tolstoy, *Tolstoy*, p. 1.

65. On traditional Russian beekeeping, see Crane, *The World History of Beekeeping*, pp. 232–3, and Galton, *Survey of Beekeeping in Russia*.

66. I. Tolstoy, *Tolstoy, My Father*, pp. 21–2; A. Tolstoy, *Tolstoy*, passim.

67. L. Tolstoy, *Anna Karenina*, pt 8, ch. 14, p. 771.

68. A. Tolstoy, *Tolstoy*, p. 286.

69. Simmons, *Tolstoy*, p. 105.

70. Galton, *Survey of Beekeeping in Russia*, p. 41.

71. Jones, *New Essays on Tolstoy*, pp. 203–4.

72. L. Tolstoy, *The Kingdom of God is Within You*, ch. 4.

73. L. Tolstoy, *War and Peace*, epilogue, pt 1, ch. 4, p. 1229.

Bibliography

Adam, Brother, *Breeding the Honeybee* (Hebden Bridge: Northern Bee Books, 1987)

Adamson, Melitta Weiss, *Food in the Middle Ages: A Book of Essays* (New York: Garland, 1995)

Akrigg, G. P. V., *Shakespeare and the Earl of Southampton* (London: Hamish Hamilton, 1968)

Alcock, Joan P., *Food in Roman Britain* (Stroud: Tempus, 2001)

Alston, Frank, *Hives and Honeybees in Signs and Symbols* (Hebden Bridge: Northern Bee Books, 1998)

Anacreon, *The Odes of Anacreon*, trans. Thomas Moore (Fyrie, Scotland: New Concept Publishing, 1996)

Apicius, *Cookery and Dining in Imperial Rome: A Bibliography, Critical Review and Translation of the Ancient Book known as Apicius De Re Coquinaria*, by Joseph Dommers Vehling (New York: Dover, 1977)

Aristotle, *De Generatione Animalium*, trans. Arthur Platt (Oxford: Clarendon Press, 1910)

——, *Historia Animalium,* The Works of Aristotle, ed. J. A. Smith, vol. 4 (Oxford: Clarendon Press, 1910)

Austin, Thomas, ed., *Two Fifteenth-Century Cookery Books* (London: The Early English Text Society, 1888)

Bachofen, Johann Jacob, *Myth, Religion and Mother Right* (Princeton: Princeton University Press, 1967)

Baker, George M., *The Revolt of the Bees: An Allegory* (Boston: Lee & Shepard, *c.* 1872)

Barnfield, Richard, *The Complete Poems* (London and Toronto: Associated University Presses, 1990)

Bazin, Gilles Augustin, *The Natural History of Bees*, trans. from the original French (London: J. & P. Knapton, 1744)

Beck, Bodog F., *Bee Venom: Its Nature and Its Effect on Arthritic and Rheumatoid Conditions* (London: D. Appleton, 1935)

——, *Honey and Health: A Nutrimental, Medicinal and Historical Commentary* (New York: Robert McBride & Co., 1938)

Bevan, Edward, *The Honey-Bee: Its Natural History, Physiology and Management* (London: Van Voorst, 1838)

Bianciotto, Gabriel, ed., *Bestiaires du moyen âge* (Paris: Stock, 1980)

Bill, Lesley, *For the Love of Bees: The Story of Brother Adam of Buckfast Abbey* (Newton Abbot: David & Charles, 1989)

Bishop, W. J., *An Early History of Surgery* (London: Robert Hale, 1960)

Boerhaave, Herman, 'The life of John Swammerdam', in Jan Swammerdam, *The Book of Nature or the History of Insects*, trans. Thomas Flloyd (London: C. G. Seyffert, 1758)

Boyd, William, *An Ice Cream War* (London: Penguin, 1982)

Briffa, John, 'Tell 'em about the honey', *Observer*, 'Life' section, 26 January 2003, p. 90

Brown, Herbert, *A Bee Melody* (London: Andrew Melrose, 1923)

Brown, Ron, *Great Masters of Beekeeping* (Burrowbridge: Bee Books Old and New, 1994)

Burton, Robert, *The Anatomy of Melancholy* (London: J. M. Dent & Sons, 3 vols., 1932)

Butler, Charles, *The Feminine Monarchy or the History of the Bees* (1623, facsimile reprint Hebden Bridge: Northern Bee Books, 1985)

Calder, Allen, *Oilseed Rape and Bees* (Hebden Bridge: Northern Bee Books, 1986)

Campion, Alan, *Bees at the Bottom of the Garden* (London: Black, 1984)

Cantimpre, Thomas de, *Exemples du 'Livre des Abeilles'*, ed. Henri Platelle (Paris: Brepols, 1997)

Carroll, William Meredith, *Animal Conventions in English Renaissance Non-Religious Prose, 1550–1600* (New York: Bookman Associates, 1954)

Castiglione, Baldesar, *The Book of the Courtier*, trans. and intro. George Bull (Harmondsworth: Penguin 1967)

Chamberlain, Lesley, *The Food and Cooking of Russia* (London: Allen Lane, 1982)

Chaucer, Geoffrey, *The Prioresses Tale, Sir Thopas, the Monkes Tale, the Clerkes Tale, the Squires Tale*, ed. Walter W. Skeat (9th edn, Oxford: Clarendon Press, 1925)

Chauvin, Rémy, *Animal Societies from the Bee to the Gorilla*, trans. George Ordish (London: Victor Gollancz, 1968)

Child, Julia, & Beck, Simone, *Mastering the Art of French Cooking*, vol. 2 (New York: Alfred Knopf, 1970)

Cobbett, William, *Rural Rides* (London: Penguin 2001)

Cohn, E. J., 'Bees and the law', *Law Quarterly Review*, 218 (1939), 289–94

Columella, Lucius Julius Moderatus, *On Agriculture*, trans. E. S. Foster and Edward H. Heffner (London: William Heinemann, 3 vols., rev. edn, 1968)

Connelly, Owen, ed., *Historical Dictionary of Napoleonic France, 1799–1815* (Westport, Conn.: Greenwood Press, 1985)

Connolly, John L., 'The origin of the star and bee as Napoleonic emblems and a reflection on the Oedipus of J. A.-D. Ingres', in Harold T. Parker and William H. Reddy, eds., *Proceedings of the 1984 Consortium on Revolutionary Europe, 1750–1850* (Athens, Ga.: University of Georgia Press, 1986)

Cook, A. B. 'The bee in Greek mythology', *Journal of Hellenic Studies*, 15 (1895), 24ff.

Cotton, William, *A Short and Simple Letter to Cottagers from a Conservative Bee-Keeper* (2nd edn, Oxford: S. Collingwood, 1838)

Cowper, William, *The Complete Poetical Works of William Cowper* (Oxford: Oxford University Press, 1907)

Cox, Nadine, & Hinkle, Randy, 'Infant botulism', *American Family Physician*, 1 April 2002

Crane, Eva, *The Archaeology of Beekeeping* (London: Duckworth 1983)

——, *A Book of Honey* (Oxford: Oxford University Press, 1980)

——, ed., *Dictionary of Beekeeping Terms with Allied Scientific Terms* (London: Bee Research Association, 1951)

——, *The World History of Beekeeping and Honey Hunting* (London: Duckworth 1999)

Croft, L. R., *Curiosities of Beekeeping* (Hebden Bridge: Northern Bee Books, 1990)

——, *Honey and Health* (Wellingborough: Thorsons, 1987)

Dalby, Andrew, *Empire of Pleasures* (London: Routledge, 2000)

——, *Food in the Ancient World from A to Z* (London:Routledge, 2003)

Davidson, Alan, *The Oxford Companion to Food* (Oxford: Oxford University Press, 1999)

Davies, Malcolm, & Kathirithamby, Jeyaraney, *Greek Insects* (Oxford: Oxford University Press, 1986)

Darby, William J., Ghalioungui, Paul, & Grivetti, Paul, *Food: The Gift of Osiris* (London and San Francisco: Academic Press, 2 vols., 1977)

Debraw, John, 'Discoveries on the sex of bees', *Philosophical Transactions of the Royal Society of London*, 1776, 125–6

Deonna, W., 'L'abeille et le roi', *Revue Belge d'Archéologie et d'Histoire d'Art*, 25 (1956), 105–131

Dickens, Charles, *Bleak House* (London: Everyman's Library, 1991)

Digby, Kenelm, *The Closet of Sir Kenelm Digby Opened* (1669, reprinted Totnes: Prospect Books, 1997)

Dodd, Victor, *Beemasters of the Past* (Hebden Bridge: Northern Bee Books 1983)

Doyle, Arthur Conan, *The Complete Sherlock Holmes*, with a preface by Julian Symons (London: Secker & Warburg, 1981)

Dugat, M., *The Skyscraper Hive*, trans. Norman C. Reeves (London: Faber & Faber, 1948)

Edwardes, Tickner, *The Bee-Master of Warrilow* (London: Methuen 1920; facsimile reprint Bath: Ashgrove, 1983)

——, *The Lore of the Honey-Bee* (London: Methuen, 1908)

Elderkin, G. W., 'The bees of Artemis', *American Journal of Philology*, 60 (1939), 203–12

Erasmus, *The Education of a Christian Prince*, trans. Neil M. Cheshire and Michael J. Heath (Cambridge: Cambridge University Press, 1997)

Fife, A. E., 'The concept of the sacredness of bees, honey and wax in Christian popular tradition', unpublished Ph.D. thesis, Stanford University, 1939

Fourier, Charles, *Le Nouveau Monde industriel et sociétaire* (Paris: Flammarion, 1973)

——, *The Theory of the Four Movements*, trans. Ian Patterson, intro. Gareth Stedman Jones (Cambridge: Cambridge University Press, 1996)

Françon, Julien, *The Mind of the Bees* (London: Methuen, 1947)

Fraser, H. M., *Beekeeping in Antiquity* (London: University of London Press, 1931)

——, *History of Beekeeping in Britain* (London: Bee Research Association, 1958)

Free, John B., *Bees and Mankind* (London: George, Allen & Unwin, 1982)

——, *The Social Organisation of Honeybees* (Hebden Bridge: Northern Bee Books, 1977)

Frier, Bruce, 'Bees and lawyers', *Classical Journal*, 78 (1982), 105–14

Frisch, Karl von, *Bees, Their Vision, Chemical Senses and Language* (Ithaca: Cornell University Press, 1950)

——, *A Biologist Remembers*, trans. Lisbeth Gombrich (Oxford and New York: Pergamon Press, 1967)

——, *The Dancing Bees*, trans. Dora Ilse (London: Methuen, 1954)

——, *You and Life*, trans. Ernest Fellner (London: J Gifford, 1940)

Galen, *Galen on Food and Diet*, trans. and ed. Mark Grant (London: Routledge, 2000)

Galloway, J. H., *The Sugarcane Industry: An Historical Geography from its Origins to 1914* (Cambridge: Cambridge University Press, 1989)

Galton, Dorothy, *The Bee-Hive: An Enquiry into its Origins and History* (Sheringham: Dorothy Galton, 1982)

——, *Survey of a Thousand Years of Beekeeping in Russia* (London: Bee Research Association, 1971)

Garnsey, Peter, *Food and Society in Classical Antiquity* (Cambridge: Cambridge University Press, 1999)

George, Sara, *The Beekeeper's Pupil* (London: Headline, 2003)

Gonnet, Michel, & Vache,Gabriel, *The Taste of Honey: The Sensorial Analysis and Different Applications of an Evaluation Method of the Qualities of Honeys* (Paris: UNAL Publishing, n.d.)

Grainger, Sally, 'Cato's Roman cheesecakes: the baking techniques', in *Milk: Beyond the Dairy*, ed. Harlan Walker (Totnes: Prospect Books, 2000)

Gustaffson, Lars, *The Death of a Beekeeper*, trans. Janet K. Swaffor and Guntram H. Weber (London: Collins Harvill, 1990)

Hanssen, Maurice, *The Healing Power of Pollen and Other Products from the Beehive* (Wellingborough: Thorsons, 1979)

Hartlib, Samuel, *The Reformed Common-Wealth of Bees* (London: S. Calvert, 1655)

Henisch, Bridget Ann, *Fast and Feast: Food in Medieval Society* (University Park: Pennsylvania State University Press, 1976)

Hesiod, *Hesiod's Works and Days: A Translation and Commentary for the Social Sciences*, David W. Tandy and Walter C. Neale (Berkeley: University of California Press, 1996)

Hieatt, Constance B. *An Ordinance of Pottage: An Edition of the Fifteenth-*

century Culinary Recipes in Yale University's MS Beinecke 163 (London: Prospect Books, 1988)

Hieatt, Constance B., & Butler, Sharon, *Pleyn Delit: Medieval Cookery for Modern Cooks* (Toronto: University of Toronto Press, 1978)

Hill, John, *The Virtues of Honey* (London: J. Davis, 1759)

Hillier, Mary, *A History of Wax Dolls* (London: Souvenir Press, 1985)

Hippocrates, *The Medical Works of Hippocrates: A New Translation* by John Chadwick and W. N. Mann (Oxford: Blackwell, 1950)

Hobbes, Thomas, *Leviathan,* ed. Richard Tuck (Cambridge: Cambridge University Press, 1996)

Hone, William, *The Every-Day Book; or Everlasting Calendar of Popular Amusement etc.* (London: Hunt & Clarke, 2 vols., 1826)

Huber, François, *Nouvelles observations sur les abeilles* (Paris: J. J. Paschoud, 1814)

Hudson-Williams, C., 'King bees and queen bees', *Classical Review*, 49 (1935), 2–5

Iambichus, *On the Pythagorean Way of Life*, trans. John Dillon Jackson Herschbell (Atlanta: Scholars Press, 1992)

Ingrams, Harold, *Arabia and the Isles* (1942, reprinted London: John Murray, 1952)

Johnson, Paul, 'And another thing', *The Spectator*, 6 July 2002

Jones, Malcolm, *New Essays on Tolstoy* (Cambridge: Cambridge University Press, 1978)

Kelly, J. N. D., *The Oxford Dictionary of Popes* (Oxford: Oxford University Press, 1986)

Keys, John, *The Practical Bee-Master* (London, 1780)

Klingender, Francis, *Animals in Art and Thought to the End of the Middle Ages* (London: Routledge, 1971)

Knoop, Douglas, *The Early Masonic Catechisms* (Manchester: Manchester University Press, 1943)

The Koran, trans. E. H. Palmer (London: H. Milford, 1951)

Lawes, Geoffrey, *The Bee-Book Book: A Manual for Collectors* (Hebden Bridge: Northern Bee Books, 1991)

Lawson, William, *A New Orchard and Garden* (London: B. Alsop, 1618)

Le Corbusier, *Towards a New Architecture*, trans. Frederick Etchells (1927; reprinted London: Architectural Press, 1970)

Levett, John, *The Ordering of Bees* (1634; reprinted New York: Da Capo, 1971)

Lévi-Strauss, Claude, *From Honey to Ashes*, trans. John and Doreen Weightman (London: Jonathan Cape, 1973)

Mace, Herbert, *Bee Matters and Bee Masters* (Harlow: The Beekeeping Annual Office, 1933)

Maeterlinck, Maurice, *The Life of the Bee*, trans. from the French of 1901 by Alfred Sutro (London: The Folio Society, 1995)

Mandeville, Bernard de, *The Fable of the Bees,* ed. F. B. Kaye (Indianapolis: Liberty Fund, 2 vols., 1988)

Marx, Karl, *Capital: a critical analysis of capitalist production*, trans. from the 3rd German edition by Samuel Moore and Edward Aveling, ed. Frederick Engels (London: Swan Sonnenschein, 1887)

Mason, Laura, *Sugar-Plums and Sherbert: The Prehistory of Sweets* (Totnes: Prospect Books, 1998)

Mazzolini, Renaldo, & Roe, Shirley A., 'Science against the unbelievers: the correspondence of Bonnet and Needham, 1760–1780', *Studies on Voltaire and the Eighteenth Century*, 243 (1986), p. 243

Merrick, Jeffrey, 'Royal bees: the gender politics of the beehive in early modern Europe', *Studies in Eighteenth-Century Culture*, 18 (1988), 7–37

Merriman, John, *A History of Modern Europe from the Renaissance to the Present* (New Haven and London: Yale University Press, 1996)

Michelet, Jules, *L'Insecte* (1858; reprinted Paris: Calman-Levy, 1903)

Miller, Garry L., 'Historical natural history: insects and the Civil War', *American Entomologist*, 43 (1997), 227–45

Mills, John, *An Essay on the Management of Bees, Wherein is Shewn the Method of Rearing those Useful Insects* (London: J. Johnson & B. Davenport, 1766)

Mintz, Sidney W., *Sweetness and Power: The Place of Sugar in Modern History* (New York: Viking Penguin, 1985)

Moffett, Thomas, 'Theatre of Insects', in Edward Topsell, *The History of Four-Footed Beasts and Serpents and Insects* (London, 1658)

More, Daphne, *The Bee Book: The History and Natural History of the Honeybee* (New York: Universe Books, 1976)

Morse, Roger A., 'The beekeeping industry' (n.d.), http://www.bee-source.com/news/article/morse.htm, accessed February 2004

Morse, Roger A., & Hooper, Ted, eds., *The Illustrated Encyclopedia of Beekeeping* (Poole: Blandford Press, 1985)

Moulin, Daniel de, *A History of Surgery* (Dordrecht: Martinus Nijhoff, 1988)

Naile, Florence, *Life of Langstroth* (Ithaca and New York: Cornell University Press, 1942)

Nais, Hélène, *Les Animaux dans la poésie française de la Renaissance* (Paris: Didier, 1961)

Neumann, Erich, *The Great Mother* (New York: Pantheon, 1955)

Newbolt, H., ed., *The Book of Cupid: Being an Anthology from the English Poets* (London: Constable, 1909)

Nutt, Thomas, *Humanity to Honey Bees* (Wisbech: H. & J. Leach, 1832)

Osten-Sacken, C. R., *Additional Notes in Explanation of the Bugonia-Lore of the Ancients* (Heidelberg: J. Hoerning, 1895)

——, *On the Oxen-born Bees of the Ancients* (Heidelberg: J. Hoerning, 1894)

Ovid, *Fasti,* trans. A. J. Boyle and R. D. Woodward (London: Penguin, 2000)

Plath, Sylvia, *Ariel* (London: Faber & Faber, 1965)

Pliny the Elder, *Natural History*, trans. H. Rackham (London: William Heinemann, 10 vols, rev. edn, 1968)

——, *Natural History: A Selection*, trans. and ed. John F. Healy (London: Penguin, 1991)

Precope, John, *Hippocrates on Diet and Hygiene* (London: Zeno, 1952)

Purchas, Samuel, *A Theatre of Politicall Flying-Insects* (London: R. J., for T. Parkhurst, 1657)

Ramírez, Juan Antonio, *The Beehive Metaphor: From Gaudí to Corbusier* (London: Reaktion Books, 2000)

Ransome, Hilda M., *The Sacred Bee in Ancient Times and Folklore* (1937; reprinted Burrowbridge: Bee Books Old and New, 1986)

Ratnieks, F. L. W., 'Are you being served? Supermarkets and bee hives', *Beekeepers Quarterly*, 67 (2001), 26–7

——'Conflict in the bee hive: worker reproduction and worker policing', *Beekeepers Quarterly*, 70 (2002), 16–17

——, 'Prisons in the bee hive', *Beekeepers Quarterly*, 66 (2001), 15–16

Redi, Francesco, *Experiments on the Generation of Insects*, trans. from the Italian of 1688 by Mab Bigelow (Chicago: Open Court, 1909)

Remnant, Richard, *A Discourse or Historie of Bees, Shewing their Nature and Usage and the Great Profit of Them* (1637, reprinted London: International Bee Research Association, 1982)

Richardson, Tim, *Sweets: A History of Temptation* (London: Bantam Press, 2002)

Riches, Harry, *Medical Aspects of Beekeeping* (Northwood: HR Books, 2000)

Riley, Gillian, 'Learning by mouth: edible aids to literacy', *Food and Memory: Proceedings of the Oxford Food Symposium on Food and Cookery 2000* (Totnes: Prospect Books, 2001)

Ripa, Cesare, *Iconologia* (New York: Dover, 1971)

Rodda, Jeanette, *'Go Ye and Study the Beehive': The Making of a Western Working Class* (New York: Garland Publishing, 2000)

Root, A. I., *The ABC and XYZ of Bee Culture* (40th edn, Medina, Ohio: A. I. Root Co., 1990)

Rosenbaum, Stephanie, *Honey: From Flower to Table* (San Francisco: Chronicle Books, 2002)

Rousseau, Jean-Jacques, *Political Writings*, trans. and ed. Frederick Watkins (Edinburgh: Nelson, 1953)

Royds, T. F., *The Beasts, Birds and Bees of Virgil* (Oxford: Blackwell, 1914)

Rusden, Moses, *A Further Discovery of Bees* (London, 1679)

Seeley, Thomas D., *The Wisdom of the Hive: The Social Physiology of Honey Bee Colonies* (Harvard: Harvard University Press, 1995)

Seneca, *Moral and Political Essays*, trans. and ed. John M. Cooper and J. F. Procopé (Cambridge: Cambridge University Press, 1995)

Shelley, Percy B., *Complete Poetical Works*, ed. Thomas Hutchinson (Oxford: Oxford University Press, 1971)

Steiner, Rudolf, *Bees: Lectures*, trans. Thomas Braatz (Hudson, NY: Anthroposophic Press, 1998)

Simmons, Ernest, *Tolstoy* (London: Routledge, 1973)

Simon, Jean-Baptiste, *Le Gouvernement admirable, ou la république des abeilles* (La Haye, 1740)

Southerne, Edmunde, *A Treatise Concerning the Right Use and Ordering of Bees* (London: Thomas Orwin, 1593)

Stockton, Frank R., *The Bee-man of Orn and Other Fanciful Tales* (New York: C. Scribner, 1887)

Swammerdam, Jan, *The Book of Nature or the History of Insects*, trans. Thomas Flloyd (London: C. G. Seyffert, 1758)

Taillardat, Jean, *Les Images d'Aristophane* (Paris: Les Belles Lettres, 1962)

Tanzi, Maria G., 'Honey consumption and infant botulism in the United States', *Pharmocotherapy*, 22, 11 (2002), 1479–83

Tarrant, D., 'Bees in Plato's Republic', *Classical Quarterly*, 40 (1946), 33ff.

Thomas, Keith, *Man and the Natural World: A History of the Modern Sensibility* (London: Penguin, 1983)

Thomson, James, *The Poetical Works of James Thomson* (Dublin: J. Exshaw, 1751)

Thorley, John, *The Female Monarchy, Being an Inquiry into the Nature, Order and Government of the Bees* (London, 1744)

Tocqueville, Alexis de, *Democracy in America*, ed. Alan Ryan (London: Everyman, 1994)

Tolstoy, Alexandra, *Tolstoy: A Life of my Father*, trans. Elizabeth Reynolds Hapgood (New York, Harper, 1953)

Tolstoy, Ilya, *Tolstoy, My Father*, trans. Ann Dunnigan (London: Peter Owen, 1972)

Tolstoy, Leo, *Anna Karenin*, trans. Constance Garnett (1901; reprinted London: Heinemann, 1972)

——, *The Kingdom of God is Within You: Christianity Not as a Mystic Religion but as a New Way of Life*, trans. Constance Garnett (London: Heinemann, 1894)

——, *War and Peace*, trans. Constance Garnett (1904; reprinted London: Heinemann, 1971)

Toussaint-Samat, Maguelonne, *History of Food*, trans. Anthea Bell (Oxford: Blackwell, 1992)

Vangelova, Lubina, 'Botulinum toxin: a poison that can heal', *FDA Consumer Magazine*, December 1995

Vanière, Jacques, *The Bees: A Poem from the Fourteenth Book of Vanière's Praedium Rusticum*, trans. Arthur Murphy (London, 1799)

Virgil, *The Georgics of Virgil*, trans. C. Day-Lewis (London: Jonathan Cape, 1940)

Varro, M. T., *On Farming*, trans. and ed. Lloyd Storr-Best (London: G. Bell & Sons, 1912)

Warder, Joseph, *The True Amazons or The Monarchy of Bees, Being a New Discovery and Improvement of Those Wonderful Creatures* (1712; 4th edn, London: John Pemberton, 1720)

White, Joyce, *Honey in the Kitchen* (Charleston, Cornwall: Bee Books Old and New, 2000)

——, *More Honey in the Kitchen* (Charleston, Cornwall: Bee Books Old and New, 2001)

White, Stephen, *Collateral Bee-Boxes* (London: Davis & Reymers, 1764)

White, R. J., *The Age of George III* (London: Heinemann, 1968)

White, T. H., *The Book of Beasts, Being a Translation from a Latin Bestiary* (London: Jonathan Cape, 1954)

Whitfield, B. G., 'Virgil and the bees', *Greece and Rome*, 3 (1956), 99–117

Whitfield, John, 'The police state', *Nature*, 416 (April 2002), 782–4

Wildman, Daniel, *A Complete Guide for the Management of Bees throughout the Year* (London: the author, 1801)

Wildman, Thomas, *A Treatise on the Management of Bees* (London: T. Cadell, 1768)

Withington, Ann Fairfax, 'Republican bees: the political economy of the beehive in eighteenth-century America', *Studies in Eighteenth-Century Culture*, 18 (1988), 39–75

Worlidge, John, *Apiarium, or A Discourse of Bees* (London: Thomas Dring, 1676)

Worrel, Thomas D., 'The symbolism of the beehive and the bee' (2000), http://freemasonry.biz/mill-valley/worrel/beehive.htm, accessed 29 February 2004

Xenophon, *The Persian Expedition*, trans. Rex Warner (Harmondsworth: Penguin, 1949)

Picture Credits

The author and publishers would like to thank the following for permission to reproduce illustrations: p. 3, Capilano Honey Ltd; pp. 11, 28, 43, 72, 76, 101, 113, 155 and 236, the Syndics of Cambridge University Library; pp. 17 and 35, Northern Bee Books on behalf of the late Frank Alston; p. 62, © Christie's Images Ltd, 2004; p. 74, Tate & Lyle; p. 116, Northern Bee Books; p. 132, Château de Versailles, France/Bridgeman Art Library, London; p. 136, Queen Bee™ & © DC Comics. All rights Reserved. Used with Permission; pp. 140, 141, 196 and 204, The Robert Opie Collection; p. 206, L'Occitane Ltd; p. 239, L. R. Croft; p. 240, Heritage Image Partnership/www.topfoto.co.uk; p. 259, Rob Green, photograph Catharine Green; p. 267, Hulton Archive.

The illustrations on pp. 5, 111, 119, 130 and 150 are taken from Hilda Ransome, *The Sacred Bee in Ancient Times and Folklore*, 1937.

Index

Numerals in italics denote illustrations.